MW00809530

An Ancient Dream Manual

An Ancient Dream Manual

Artemidorus' The Interpretation of Dreams

PETER THONEMANN

OXFORD
UNIVERSITY PRESS

OXFORD
UNIVERSITY PRESS

Great Clarendon Street, Oxford, OX2 6DP,
United Kingdom

Oxford University Press is a department of the University of Oxford.
It furthers the University's objective of excellence in research, scholarship,
and education by publishing worldwide. Oxford is a registered trade mark of
Oxford University Press in the UK and in certain other countries

Published in the United States of America by Oxford University Press
198 Madison Avenue, New York, NY 10016, United States of America

British Library Cataloguing in Publication Data
Data available

Library of Congress Control Number: 2019953208

ISBN 978-0-19-884382-5

Printed and bound by
CPI Group (UK) Ltd, Croydon, CR0 4YY

Preface

Artemidorus of Daldis is the author of the only dream-book to have been preserved from Classical antiquity. His *Oneirocritica* ('The Interpretation of Dreams'), composed around AD 200, is a treatise and manual on dreams, their classification, and the various analytical tools which should be applied to their interpretation. He travelled widely through Greece, Asia Minor, and Italy to collect people's dreams and record their outcomes, in the process casting a bright and sometimes unexpected light on social mores and religious beliefs in the Severan age.

The present volume is conceived as a companion to the splendid new translation of the *Oneirocritica* for the Oxford World's Classics series by Martin Hammond, and I very much hope that it will encourage a few adventurous readers to explore this vast, complex, and endlessly fascinating text for themselves. Artemidorus himself is quoted from the new Oxford World's Classics edition. Except where otherwise stated, all other translations from ancient texts are my own.

Contents

List of Illustrations

The publisher and the author apologise for any errors or omissions in the above list. If contacted they will be pleased to rectify these at the earliest opportunity.

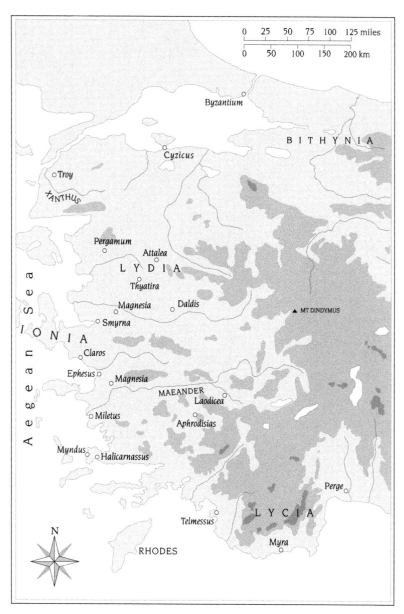

Map 1. Western Asia Minor

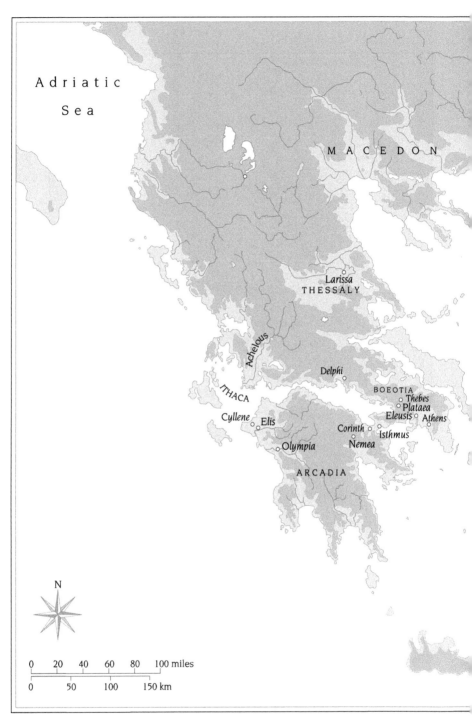

Map 2. The Aegean

THRACE

Troy

EGEAN

SEA

Daldis LYDIA

IONIA

Ephesus

DELOS

PAROS

CARIA

LYCIA

RHODES

CRETE

Map 3. The Eastern Mediterranean

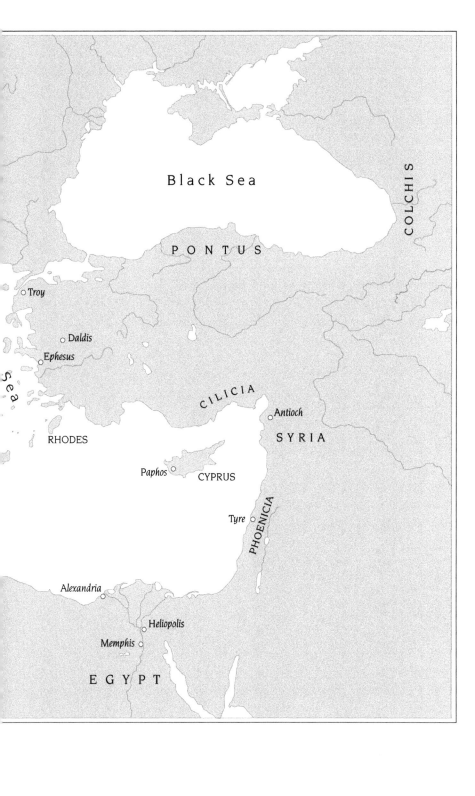

1

The Snake and the Whale

It is shortly before dawn. Two slaves, Sosias and Xanthias, are guarding a house, and both of them keep drifting off to sleep. In their moments of slumber, both men see curious dreams, sent—or so they claim to believe—by the god Sabazius. They start describing their dreams to one another. Xanthias goes first.

XANTHIAS: I seemed to see a huge eagle swooping down to the market-place, snatching up an *aspis* in its claws—a bronze-plated one—and carrying it up into the heavens; and then the *aspis* was dropped by... Cleonymus.

SOSIAS: Ah yes—Cleonymus makes a perfect riddle.

XANTHIAS: How so?

SOSIAS: It's the kind of riddle someone might pose for his drinking-companions: 'One and the same creature has thrown away its *aspis* on land, in the heavens, and at sea.'

XANTHIAS: Oh no—what evils do I have in store for me, now that I've seen a dream like that?

In his dream, Xanthias sees an eagle flying down and seizing a snake in its claws—specifically, an *aspis*, the kind of snake known to us as a cobra. Although eagles do catch snakes in real life, this image would immediately have evoked a world of terrifying omens for an ancient Greek dreamer. In the twelfth book of Homer's *Iliad*, the Trojan army are horrified at the sight of an eagle flying before them from right to left, carrying a monstrous blood-red snake in its talons, which they take to be an omen from Zeus (*Iliad* 12.200–29). Eagles clutching snakes in their talons are a common symbolic motif in Greek art, usually representing conflict and combat; the scene could even be used as visual shorthand for the profession of a seer (*mantis*), as on the fourth-century BC tombstone of the seer Cleobulus of Acharnae (Fig. 1.1). It is not hard to see why Xanthias instantly took this dream to foretell 'evils in store' for him.

In fact, the dream immediately veers off into parody and wordplay. (As I should perhaps have indicated at the outset, this is in fact the opening scene of Aristophanes' *Wasps*, a comedy first performed at the Athenian Lenaea festival of 422 BC.) The Greek word *aspis* ('cobra') also means 'shield', and this *aspis* is, says Xanthias, 'a bronze-plated one'. After being carried high up into the heavens, the cobra/shield is dropped by, not the eagle, but Cleonymus, a well-known Athenian politician of the 420s. Cleonymus allegedly once threw his shield away in battle (a stereotypical mark of cowardice), and this becomes a standard running joke in Aristophanes' comedies of the 420s and 410s. One can almost hear the audience groan.

Next it is Sosias' turn to recount his dream.

SOSIAS: During my first spell of sleep, I seemed to see a flock of sheep sitting together in assembly on the Pnyx [the meeting-place of the Athenian assembly], complete with their walking-sticks and worn cardigans. Then I saw a voracious whale haranguing these sheep with the voice of a blazing sow.

XANTHIAS: Ugh!

SOSIAS: What is it?

XANTHIAS: Stop, stop, don't go on: this dream reeks horribly of rancid hides.

SOSIAS: Then the disgusting whale was holding a balance and weighing out beef-fat (*dēmós*).

XANTHIAS: Woe is me! He's planning to dismember the citizen-body (*dḗmos*).

SOSIAS: And I seemed to see Theorus sitting on the ground next to him, but he had the head of a crow (*korax*). Then Alcibiades lisped in my ear: 'Look, there's Theolus with the head of a sycophant (*kolax*).'

XANTHIAS: Well, Alcibiades certainly lisped that one correctly.

SOSIAS: You don't find that dream inauspicious, Theorus turning into a crow?

XANTHIAS: Not at all, it's very good indeed.

SOSIAS: How so?

Fig. 1.1. Funerary stele of the seer Cleobulus of Acharnae (*c.*375–350 BC). Athens, NM 4473.

National Archaeological Museum, Athens (photographer W. von Eickstedt); © Hellenic Ministry of Culture and Sports/Archaeological Receipts Fund.

XANTHIAS: Well: a man who suddenly turned into a crow—surely the obvious interpretation is that he's about to leave us and go 'to the crows' [i.e. 'to hell']?

SOSIAS: Evidently I ought to be hiring you at a two-obol fee, since you're so smart at dream-interpretation.

Sosias' dream begins with a vision of the sheep-like old men of the Athenian assembly, listening in a stupor to a vile sea-monster spouting angry demagogic drivel at maximum volume. Xanthias instantly identifies the whale as the arch-demagogue Cleon, often mocked by Aristophanes for his background in the tanning industry (hence the smell of 'rancid hides'). This is followed by two bizarre images, both of which are 'translated' into political jokes by Xanthias by means of some nifty word-magic. Sosias dreams that the whale/Cleon is weighing out some beef-fat (*dēmós*), which signifies, according to Xanthias, a malign outcome: Cleon is going to 'divide against itself' the body of Athenian citizens (*dē̂mos*). The Greek words for 'fat' and 'people' are spelled the same (*dēmos*), but pronounced differently (like the English *sewer*, 'someone who sews' vs. 'a waste-pipe').

Finally, Cleon's sycophantic henchman Theorus appears with a crow's head on his shoulders. This is auspicious, says Xanthias, since it signifies he'll 'go to hell' (in Greek, 'go to the crows'). Aristophanes throws in a further bit of wordplay based on the similarity of the Greek words for 'crow' (*korax*) and 'flatterer' (*kolax*). Since the aristocratic politician Alcibiades was famously unable to pronounce the letter 'r', his attempt to describe Theorus as '*korax*-headed' serendipitously nails him as a *kolax*—the truth in a lisp, as it were.

At the risk of stating the obvious, neither of these dreams are real. They serve as warm-up jokes in the opening scene of a comedy: Aristophanes is trying to get his audience laughing (and I do apologize for killing the humour with my laboured explanations). But if we want to get at 'typical' ancient views on the nature and significance of dreams, comedy is perhaps not a bad place to take some preliminary soundings. The scene would simply not be funny if the assumptions underlying it were not instantly recognizable to the play's audience. So here are five simple propositions about the attitude towards dreams that seems to be assumed in the opening scene of *Wasps*.

(1) *Dreams—or at least some dreams—come from the gods.* That (some) dreams are sent by the gods is a standard assumption of Greek and Roman literary authors from Homer onwards: 'dreams too come from Zeus' (*Iliad* 1.63). In the opening scene of *Wasps*, the deity concerned is the obscure Anatolian god Sabazius, perhaps because fifth-century Athenians saw him as a typically 'slavish' deity (Sabazius comes from Phrygia, a major source of Athenian slaves in the fifth century BC). There were, it is true, a few sceptics. In the view of the philosopher Aristotle, the very fact that low-lifes such as Sosias and Xanthias get to see interesting dreams shows that dreams are unlikely to have a divine origin: 'Apart from its general irrationality, the idea that it is a god who sends dreams, and yet he sends them not to the best and most intelligent, but to random people, is absurd' (*On Divination in Sleep*, 462b21–3). We will come back to the divine origin of dreams in Chapters 3 and 9.

(2) *Dreams—or at least some dreams—are predictive.* When correctly interpreted, dreams can provide precognition of things that are going to happen in the future, which may be auspicious (Theorus will go to hell) or malign (Cleon will divide the people against itself). Today, I hope it is fair to say, not many of us believe that dreams offer encoded predictions of future events; in antiquity, even thinkers at the outermost sceptical and rationalist end of the intellectual spectrum (Aristotle again) were not prepared to rule this out altogether, as we shall see in Chapter 3.

(3) *Predictive dreams deal in symbols, not narratives.* In English, we tend to speak of dreaming 'that' something occurred ('Last night I dreamt I went to Manderley again'). That is to say, we are accustomed to think of our dreams as *narratives*, whose meaning (if they have one) is determined by the particular sequence of events or experiences presented to us. By contrast, Greek and Roman authors do not speak of 'having a dream' or 'dreaming that *x* happened', but rather of 'seeing a dream', where the dream is objectified or personified as a thing or person that appears to the dreamer in his or her sleep. The archetypal Greek or Roman dream is therefore not an *experience* ('having tea with the

Queen'), but a kind of *apparition*, like the ghost of Jacob Marley. In their dreams, Sosias and Xanthias 'see' a sequence of discrete and isolated dream-elements (an eagle, a flock of sheep, a whale), each of which is then individually decoded as a symbolic representation of a person or thing in their waking world. (As it happens, almost all of these static symbols consist of animals or parts of animals: an eagle, a snake, a flock of sheep, a whale, a sow, beef-fat, the head of a crow—see Chapter 6)

(4) *Predictive dreams are a bit like riddles.* The two slaves in *Wasps* 'decode' the meanings of their dream-objects in a variety of ways: by the intrinsic character of the thing concerned (sheep are subservient, like assembly-voters; a whale is big and horrible, like Cleon); by pseudo-etymology and wordplay on the thing's name (*dēmós*, 'beef-fat', sounds like *dêmos*, 'citizen body'); or by an associated myth or proverb (a crow signifies going 'to the crows'). Sosias is quite right to compare the 'decoding' of Xanthias' eagle-dream to the 'decoding' of a riddle at a drinking-party (what creature throws away its shield on land, in the heavens, and at sea?). Much of the ancient science of dream-interpretation, as we will see, is dedicated to formulating rules or guidelines for solving these riddle-like problems.

(5) *Accurate dream-interpretation calls for a professional dream-interpreter.* In Athens, in 422 BC, a slave with money to burn could go and consult a professional dream-monger, to have his dream interpreted at two obols a pop (cheap, but not that cheap: a third of a day's wage for a skilled craftsman at this period). And this is where we come in. Today, thanks to the vagaries of literary survival, this entire Graeco-Roman tradition of specialized, 'scientific' dream-interpretation is known to us essentially through a single book: the magnificent, credulous, labyrinthine, pedantic, and endlessly fascinating *Oneirocritica* of Artemidorus of Daldis.

2

Artemidorus and the *Oneirocritica*

The Man

Artemidorus is a curiously difficult man to place. Aside from what little he tells us about himself in the *Oneirocritica*, we really know almost nothing about him at all. Was he a Roman citizen—C. Iulius Artemidorus (say), or just plain Artemidorus? Was he writing under Antoninus Pius (AD 138–161), Caracalla (AD 211–217), or somewhere in the middle? How widely travelled was he? For whom was he writing? Elite litterateurs, or practising dream-interpreters? How widely was he in fact read? The mere fact that his book survives should not delude us into thinking that Artemidorus was in any sense a 'major author' in his own day; everything suggests that he was not. A high proportion of the Greek and Latin texts that survived the end of antiquity were already acknowledged classics in the ancient world, but the *Oneirocritica* is most emphatically not one of them.

Artemidorus' clearest statement about his background comes in the final lines of Book 3 of the *Oneirocritica* (3.66.7):

> As for the way I style myself as the author, do not be surprised that I have styled myself 'Artemidorus of Daldis' and not 'Artemidorus of Ephesus', as I often did in the books I have before now written on other subjects. Ephesus has come to be renowned in its own right and to be fortunate in the many distinguished men who can broadcast its name, whereas Daldis is a small and not very notable town in Lydia, which has remained in obscurity up to our time. So I am attributing this work to my native town on my mother's side as a thank-offering for my nurture.

Daldis, Artemidorus' home-town 'on his mother's side', was an obscure place in the remote hill-country north of Lydian Sardis, two days' journey inland from the western coast of Asia Minor. Ephesus, by contrast, was one of the largest cities of the eastern Mediterranean, and the capital of the Roman province of Asia. In order to have been able to choose between describing himself as *Daldianos* or *Ephesios*, Artemidorus must certainly have been a citizen of both cities, since these so-called 'ethnics' could only be used by members of the citizen body. This strongly implies that he was a man of relatively high social standing: dual *polis*-citizenship was not uncommon in the Greek world of the Roman imperial period, but only for members of the civic elite (one did not obtain dual citizenship simply by having an Ephesian father and a Daldian mother). Artemidorus seems normally to have presented himself as a citizen of Ephesus, and indeed a Byzantine dialogue of uncertain date refers to him simply as 'Artemidorus of Ephesus' (pseudo-Lucian, *Philopatris* 22). It was, he says, the chief local deity of Daldis, Apollo Mystes, who urged him to undertake the composition of the *Oneirocritica* (2.70.13), and his choice to self-identify in the *Oneirocritica* as 'Artemidorus of Daldis' should be seen (as he says) as an act of modest local boosterism.

As he tells us in these same lines from the end of Book 3, the *Oneirocritica* was not Artemidorus' first published work. In the opening pages of his book, he says that the difference between two kinds of dream (the *enhypnion* and the *oneiros*: see Chapter 3) 'is an important distinction which I have already made elsewhere' (1.1.1). What the subjects of his earlier books might have been, we do not know. A tenth-century Byzantine encyclopaedia, the *Suda*, includes a laconic biographical entry for Artemidorus, claiming that he wrote an *Oneirocritica* 'in four books' (a slip for 'five books'?), along with works *On Bird-Augury* and *On Palm-Divination*. But this is very unlikely to be right, since in the *Oneirocritica* Artemidorus firmly denounces palm-diviners as charlatans (2.69.1). It is not impossible that the *Suda* has conflated two different men called Artemidorus (it is a very common name), one of them our dream-interpreter, the other a writer on palmistry. What of his alleged book on bird-augury? The medical writer Galen, in his commentary on the Hippocratic treatise *Regimen in Acute Diseases* (composed at some point between AD 176 and 179) mentions in passing four earlier writers on bird-augury, one of them a certain 'Artemidorus son of Phocas'. This may be Artemidorus the dream-interpreter; it might be our hypothetical

Artemidorus the palmist; it could be someone else altogether. There is certainly no hint in the *Oneirocritica* that our man had any particular interest in bird-divination.

A good deal of ink has been spilled over the date (or rather dates) of composition of the *Oneirocritica*. 'Dates' because, as we will see in a moment, only the first two books were written and published as a pair; the third, fourth, and fifth books were each written separately at later dates, and we have no way of knowing how much time elapsed between the completion of Books 1 and 2 and the completion of Book 5. The early books of the *Oneirocritica* were certainly not composed before around AD 140, since Book 1 includes a reference to the Eusebeian games at Puteoli in Campania, established by Antoninus Pius shortly after the death of Hadrian in AD 138 (1.26.3). However, there is good reason to push the date of these early books down into the later second century AD. Books 1 to 3 are dedicated to a certain Cassius Maximus, a native of Phoenicia (2.70.13) and a man of equestrian rank (4.Pref.1). This man is today widely (and probably correctly) identified with the rhetorician Maximus of Tyre, author of forty-one extant philosophical declamations, and apparently active during the reign of Commodus (AD 180–192).

As for the later books of the *Oneirocritica*, three passages of Book 4 seem pretty clearly to take us down into the early third century AD. Early in Book 4, Artemidorus describes the dream of a certain 'Aristides the lawyer', which foretold his imminent death (4.2.8). This man was clearly known personally to Artemidorus, and he is almost certainly identical to a professional lawyer (*iuridicus*) by the name of Q. Aemilius Aristides, known from inscriptions to have acted as *procurator* at Ephesus between AD 204 and 208/9. Later in Book 4, Artemidorus records dreams of 'Alexander the philosopher' (4.33.3) and 'Paulus the lawyer' (4.80.2); the former is likely to be the Peripatetic philosopher Alexander of Aphrodisias, whose career spans the late second and early third centuries AD, and the latter is probably a jurist who was prominent at the imperial court between AD 205 and 211, and who eventually served as praetorian prefect to Severus Alexander (AD 228–235). A plausible chronology for the *Oneirocritica* would therefore put the early books in the 180s or 190s AD, with the last two books coming in the 210s AD, some time after the (undatable) death of Q. Aemilius Aristides.

The name 'Artemidorus' was extremely common in Roman Asia Minor, and any attempt to identify the author of the *Oneirocritica* with other individuals of that name attested in the late second or early third century AD can only be tentative. But new evidence has recently turned up which may help to place Artemidorus more firmly in the latter part of the reign of Septimius Severus (AD 193–211). At some point during the joint reign of Severus and Caracalla (198–211), a certain 'Artemidorus LAN' is known to have acted as mint-magistrate and 'first archon for the second time' at Daldis. (The significance of the letters LAN is not clear; these may have been the first three letters of his father's name.) This man was responsible for striking three series of local bronze coins, carrying images of Severus, Julia Domna, and the young Caracalla on their obverse ('heads-side': Figs. 2.1–2.3). The Severus type carries on its reverse face an image of the local deity Apollo Mystes playing a lyre, facing the Anatolian goddess Cybele. Given the prominence of Apollo Mystes as Artemidorus' divine patron in the *Oneirocritica* (2.70.13), it is extremely tempting to identify this Severan mint-magistrate with our dream-interpreter. If this identification is correct, Artemidorus would necessarily have been a member of the civic elite at Daldis, of high enough status to have held the chief Daldian civic magistracy (the office

Fig. 2.1. Bronze coin of Daldis with image of Caracalla (AD 198–211). AE 14.62g, 31mm. Gorny & Mosch Giessener Münzhandlung GmbH e-auction 247, 2017, lot 4464 (Photography: Lübke & Wiedemann, Stuttgart).

Photo courtesy of Gorny & Mosch Giessener Münzhandlung GmbH.

Fig. 2.2. Bronze coin of Daldis with image of Septimius Severus (AD 198–211). AE 23.34g, 34mm. CNG E-Auction 363 (11/11/15), Lot 288.

Photo courtesy of Classical Numismatic Group, Inc. (https://cngcoins.com).

Fig. 2.3. Bronze coin of Daldis with image of Julia Domna (AD 198–211). AE 16.37g, 29mm. CNG E-Auction 405 (06/09/17), Lot 313.

Photo courtesy of Classical Numismatic Group, Inc. (https://cngcoins.com).

of 'first archon') twice. It is worth noting that the mint-magistrate Artemidorus did not present himself as a Roman citizen.

A sharper picture of Artemidorus and his interests will gradually emerge over the course of the following chapters: his perspective on his two native cities, Ephesus and Daldis (Chapter 7), his education (Chapter 8), his travels (Chapter 10), and his attitude towards Rome (Chapter 12). But one final point does need the strongest possible emphasis at the outset. Artemidorus was not a professional literary artist. The prefaces and conclusions to each book do show a bit of literary dash—he shoehorns a Homeric tag into his very first sentence, and even risks quoting a bit of Callimachus at the end of Book 4 (4.84.4)—but in general his prose is formulaic and utilitarian, as he himself cheerfully acknowledges (2.Pref.2). His first three books are dedicated to Maximus of Tyre, but this tells us as little about the book's main intended readership as does the dedication of Newton's *Principia* to King James II. The *Oneirocritica* does not seem to be selling itself as a 'do-it-yourself' guide to dream-interpretation, still less a piece of 'popularization' for a non-specialist public; right from the outset, Artemidorus assumes that his readers will be professional dream-interpreters, seeking help in the practical business of interpreting their clients' dreams (1.Pref.2, 1.12.1). Artemidorus is sometimes treated as a representative of the 'Second Sophistic', the great efflorescence of Greek literary and rhetorical culture under the high Roman empire. In fact, Artemidorus has about as much in common with Aelius Aristides or Lucian of Samosata as Delia Smith does with Martin Amis or Ian McEwan.

The Book

As we have already seen, the five books of the *Oneirocritica* were composed in stages. The first two books were originally written as a stand-alone work, dedicated to Cassius Maximus. After a short introductory essay on the nature of dreams and the process of dream-interpretation (1.1–12), the greater part of this original two-book *Oneirocritica* consists of a vast thematic encyclopaedia of all the different elements from which dreams are composed, carefully organized by subject-matter. The two books are almost identical in length (99 and 104 pages of the standard Teubner edition, respectively), and together make up almost two-thirds (63 per cent) of the entire *Oneirocritica*.

Artemidorus was particularly proud of the elaborate and logical structure that he came up with for these first two books (1.10). In the Preface to Book 2, the two features of the *Oneirocritica* that he singles out as most original are 'the logical sequence of the material and the accuracy of my interpretations' (2.Pref.2), and in the Preface to Book 3, he claims that his first two books 'observed an organization and a sequence which have nothing in common with the treatment of the old authorities' (3.Pref.). He claims to have organized his material 'with regard to the natural sequence of things' (1.10.1), an idea which is fleshed out in the Preface to Book 4, where he describes the structure of the original two-book *Oneirocritica* as modelled on the human life-cycle (4.Pref.1):

> I listed all the subjects which can be the content of dreams seen in ordinary experience, observing an order and sequence which followed the human life-cycle from birth to death, and including in each case the analogy which any one thing bears to another and the outcome in which any dream can result.

In fact, the structure of Books 1 and 2 is rather more complex than that. Book 1 is focused on the human body and its characteristic physical activities (exercise, eating and drinking, sex); Artemidorus himself describes the book as concerned with 'all those aspects of human life which are universal and ordinary experience' (2.Pref.1). The book begins, logically enough, with dreams about birth, pregnancy, and raising infants (1.13–16), before proceeding to a systematic account of the different parts of the body from head to toe, with a primary (but far from exclusive) focus on the male body (1.17–50: see Chapter 4). Artemidorus then turns to the various ways in which the body (particularly the youthful or active body) is cultivated and exercised: physical labour, education, agonistic culture, and bathing (1.51–64). Food and nourishment come next (1.65–74), followed by a short miscellaneous section on 'decorative' body-techniques (anointment, dancing, wreath-wearing, 1.75–7). Dreams about sexual intercourse are treated at length (1.78–80: see Chapter 5), followed, naturally enough, by sleep and saying farewell (1.81–2). On the whole, the book makes for an admirably coherent whole, whose structure can be summarized as follows:

1. Preface Dedication to Cassius Maximus
1.1–12 Categories of dreams and methods of dream-interpretation
1.13–16 Birth, pregnancy, babies, and breast-feeding
1.17–50 Parts of the body
> **17–39** The head and its constituent parts, from top to bottom (hair, forehead, ears, etc.)

40-9 The remainder of the body, from top to bottom (shoulders, chest, arms, etc.)

50 Bodily transformations

1.51-64 Cultivation of the body

51-3 The professions (farming, seafaring, cobbling, etc.)

54 Ephebic education

55-63 Agonistic culture: games, music, theatre, and athletics

64 Bathing

1.65-74 Eating and drinking (drinks, vegetables, pulses, etc.)

1.75-7 'Decorative' body-techniques: anointment, dancing, singing, and wearing wreaths

1.78-80 Sex

1.81-2 Sleep and saying farewell

If Book 1 faces 'inwards' towards individual human physicality, Book 2 essentially faces 'outwards', towards the external world of nature, human society, and the gods. Book 2 begins in counterpoint to the end of Book 1, with short chapters on awakening, leaving the house, and greeting people (2.1-2). There then follow a handful of chapters on dress and adornment (2.3-7), whose placement here presumably reflects the fact that one normally dresses early in the morning (contrast 1.75 and 1.77, on 'special-occasion' dress).

The main bulk of Book 2 then follows, with a vast conspectus of the world external to the individual, beginning with weather and the elements (particularly fire and thunderbolts: 2.8-10). The animal kingdom (2.11-22) and the natural world more generally (the sea, farming and plants, rivers and land: 2.23-8) are treated in enormous detail, articulated around the human exploitation of that world (hunting, fishing, farming: see Chapter 6). Human society is represented by law-courts, kingdoms and cities, and warfare and fighting (2.29-32). The gods (including celestial phenomena) occupy nine long and rich chapters (2.33-41: see Chapter 9). At this point, oddly, Artemidorus inserts a handful of miscellaneous 'omissions' (2.42-8), before concluding with a long discussion of dreams about death (2.49-66). The book is rounded off by a further miscellany of unclassifiable topics (2.67-70: flying, trustworthy persons, the human lifespan).

The structure of Book 2 is not as coherent as Book 1, and much of the material in this book (e.g. on celestial phenomena) was intrinsically resistant to being fitted into the 'life-cycle' structure that Artemidorus was aiming at for the *Oneirocritica* as a whole (4.Pref.1). The whole book can be summarized as follows:

2. Preface Dedication to Cassius Maximus
2.1–2 Awakening, going out, and greeting
2.3–7 Dress and personal adornment
2.8–10 'Elemental' phenomena (air, rain, thunderbolts, fire)
2.11–22 Fauna
   11–13 Hunting and terrestrial animals
   14–18 Fishing and maritime/fluvial animals
   19–22 Fowling and creatures of the air
2.23–8 The natural world
   23 Sailing the sea
   24–6 Farming, trees, and manure
   27–8 Rivers and lakes; the land
2.29–32 Human society (law-courts, kingdoms, the city, warfare, and fighting)
2.33–41 The gods
2.42–8 Miscellaneous omissions (ladders, frying-pans, eggs, etc.)
2.49–66 Death
2.67–70 Further miscellaneous topics (teeth, flying, trustworthy people, the human lifespan)

It is unclear how many months or years elapsed before Artemidorus composed Book 3, also dedicated to Cassius Maximus. This book is very much shorter than Books 1 and 2 (32 pages of the Teubner edition, around a third of the length of either of the first two books). It takes the form of a self-consciously unstructured *florilegium* of topics omitted or not treated in sufficient detail in Books 1 and 2 (4.Pref.2). In the Preface, Artemidorus makes only very modest claims for the coherence of his new book (3.Pref.):

> But after writing that treatise I came to think that there were still some gaps in my treatment, but that I should not make any additions to what

I had already written in either of those books. That would be like adding a prosthetic limb to a healthy and handsome body: however handsome the extra limb, it would detract from the original beauty. So I have made this little book for you [Cassius Maximus], as a separate collection of all the omissions on their own, randomly presented and not organized into subject-linked sections.

In fact, the structure of Book 3 is not entirely random; the subject-matter falls into several linked 'clusters', giving the strong impression of a mind moving from topic to topic in a sequence of intuitive leaps. So, for example, after the first chapter on dice (3.1), there follow three chapters on criminal and dishonest behaviour (3.2–4: theft, sacrilege, lying), followed by a series of animals with broadly malign connotations (3.5–8, 3.11–12: quails, ants, lice, worms, bugs; crocodiles, cats, the mongoose), sandwiched around two chapters on other kinds of 'inauspicious' behaviour (3.9–10: fighting, hating, being slain). Similarly, the central part of the book contains an 'intuitive' cluster of chapters on illnesses, disabilities, and injuries (3.39–53: wounds and scars; madness; fear; hernias; disfiguring diseases; etc.). But there is no particular reason to think that any of this was consciously planned out by Artemidorus.

Artemidorus did not originally conceive of this new book as '*Oneirocritica* Book 3'. He saw it as a separate supplementary pamphlet, and hence assigned it its own separate title, or rather pair of titles (3.28.2):

> This third book is not written as a continuation of those previous two, but as a separate entity in itself. For that reason an appropriate title for it will not be 'Book Three', but something distinct—'For the Love of Truth' (*Philalēthes*), or 'Obiter Dicta' (*Enodion*).

Only later, when Artemidorus decided to continue his work with Books 4 and 5, did he reclassify his 'Obiter Dicta' as '*Oneirocritica* Book 3' (4.Pref.3).

These original three books seem to have met with a certain amount of hostile criticism. Artemidorus' essay on the theory of dreams at the start of Book 1 was insufficiently clear; his catalogue of dream-elements was not comprehensive; the original three books did not contain enough general guidance on the interpretation of particular types of dream (compound dreams, recurring dreams, dreams involving myths, etc.). Artemidorus was visibly touchy on the subject (4.Pref.3):

> It turned out that some manifestation of that malign Momus [the personification of 'blame'], kicked out of their company by the gods and demi-gods, was still at work among men, and we must vigorously resist him, recognizing that the greater any achievement is, the more weapons he deploys to counter it. So now too I am aware that some people have criticisms of my books: they allow that what I have written is in no way short of the truth, but complain that not everything has been fully worked out or accounted for, and that some matters of essential relevance to the subject have been omitted.

As a result, some time later—perhaps many years later—Artemidorus was moved to add two further books in response to his critics. (My sense, for what it's worth, is that Book 3 followed Books 1 and 2 relatively quickly—immediate 'addenda and corrigenda', if you like—but that Books 4 and 5 followed only after a much lengthier interval, perhaps a decade or more.) These last two books are entirely different in character from Books 1–3 of the *Oneirocritica*. The first three books had been addressed to Maximus of Tyre, a prominent philosopher not known to have had any particular interest in dream-interpretation; at least in principle, the original *Oneirocritica* was conceived as a book which might fall into the hands of non-specialist readers (however few such readers might have been in practice). By contrast, Books 4 and 5 are addressed to Artemidorus' son, Artemidorus the Younger, himself an aspiring dream-specialist, to help him formulate his own dream-interpretations, and to allow him to respond effectively to critics. In his Preface to Book 4, Artemidorus goes so far as to say that the book is for his son's eyes only (4.Pref.4):

> You must remember that this book is addressed to you, for your own use, and you must not make copies for general distribution. If what I am going to write in this book stays with you alone, it will make you preeminent among all dream-interpreters, or at least second to none: but if it is made public property, it will leave you exposed as having no greater knowledge than anyone else.

This startling injunction has (to my knowledge) no real parallel elsewhere in Graeco-Roman literature. It is of course tempting to see this as simply a rhetorical pose, in order to invest Book 4 with an alluring air of 'secret mysteries revealed'; but Book 4 really does contain a great deal that looks genuinely 'private'. Take this extraordinary chapter, on the use of anagrams as a method of dream-interpretation (4.23):

> On the use of anagrams that outstanding dream-interpreter Aristander and some other old authorities have made complete fools of themselves. In their introductions they explain what is meant by anagrammatic transposition, but at no point give any evidence of making use of it themselves—no transposition of syllables, no subtraction or addition of letters. I mentioned this technique at the beginning of my treatise, and now too I advise you to make use of transposition when you are interpreting someone else's dreams and want to appear smarter than the others. But do not use it under any circumstances when you are interpreting for yourself—it will prove a delusion.

Artemidorus here candidly advises his son to lie to his clients for the sake of his reputation (cf. also 4.20.1, discussed at the start of Chapter 3). Similarly, if less dramatically, Artemidorus often refers allusively to individuals with whom his son is expected to be acquainted: 'our Cratinus' (4.31.1, presumably a friend); 'that young Cypriot dream-interpreter' (4.83.3, perhaps a rival). This really does look like a book intended for his son's eyes only.

Like Book 3, Book 4 is basically a miscellany, around two-thirds of the length of the first two books (65 pages in the Teubner edition). It begins, like Book 1, with a synoptic treatise on dream-interpretation, mirroring and expanding on the essay at the beginning of Book 1 (4.1–4). The rest of the book consists of general guidelines on how to interpret certain broad categories of dreams (things that are braided; dream-prescriptions obtained in incubation-sanctuaries; literary texts in dreams; etc.), and cross-references to the earlier books are very frequent. The book also includes numerous illustrative examples of actual dreams and their outcomes (largely absent from the first three books), some drawn from Artemidorus' own experience, others from earlier dream-books.

Book 5, also addressed to the younger Artemidorus, seems to have been conceived at the same time as Book 4 (4.84.5), but was completed somewhat later; in the Preface to Book 5, Artemidorus apologises for having taken so long to finish it. It is the shortest book of the *Oneirocritica* (24 pages in the Teubner), and consists of a compendium of ninety-five actual dreams and their outcomes that Artemidorus had come across himself in his day-to-day practice. The book is intended as a kind of practical sourcebook of worked-up examples, selected both for their intrinsic interest and their pedagogic qualities (5.Pref.3):

You will find that each dream is given only with a bare statement of the outcome as it actually happened, recorded without scenery or drama. My only intention was to compile from my experience material that you can trust and also find helpful. For that reason I have allowed myself to skip all the possible outcomes for the same dreams which could have resulted from the various fortunes, lifestyles, ages, and circumstances of the dreamers. My first and second, and especially my third book are full of these examples, while my fourth book, addressed to you alone, has refined the subject further, encompassing both technical theory and a hitherto untrodden pathway to interpretation when there is ambiguity. Even so, I think that you still need more experience and practice.

The *Oneirocritica* as we read it today was thus not planned and executed as a single coherent whole, but emerged only gradually and piecemeal as a result of repeated rethinks and additions. Whether Artemidorus systematically revised his earlier books in the light of his later supplements is impossible to say; the only demonstrable example of subsequent revision comes towards the end of Book 2, where he refers the reader forward to a discussion in one of his later books ('We shall consider astrologers who cast horoscopes later': 2.69.1, looking forward to 4.59.2).

More important is the question of how much of the *Oneirocritica* represents Artemidorus' own original research, and how much has been taken over silently from earlier works on dream-interpretation. I see no reason to doubt Artemidorus' explicit claim that he personally collected all the dreams in Book 5 first-hand. But as we shall see, for the earlier books of the *Oneirocritica*, things are not so straightforward.

Artemidorus and his Predecessors

Professional dream-interpreters were a fixture of Greek and Roman society, from the highest to the lowest social levels. In the Homeric poems, the interpretation of dreams is already the preserve of respected specialists. When the Achaean army is ravaged by plague in the opening scene of the *Iliad*, Achilles suggests that they consult 'some prophet or priest, or an interpreter of dreams (*oneiropolos*)' (*Iliad* 1.62–3); Homer later mentions one such *oneiropolos* by name, and he is clearly a man of very high social status (Eurydamas: *Iliad* 5.149–50). Down at the other end of the social spectrum, the Roman satirist Juvenal refers with contempt to female Jewish dream-interpreters in first-century AD Rome who were scarcely distinguishable from beggars (*Satires* 6.546–7). Most ancient dream-interpreters presumably fell somewhere between the two: for a tantalizing glimpse of the ordinary street-level freelance dream-monger, we can admire the rather fine painted shop-sign of an anonymous Cretan dream-interpreter at the Egyptian city of Memphis (Fig. 2.4).

A few of these men and women wrote books about their trade. At the very beginning of his vast work (1.Pref.3–4), Artemidorus reminds us that he stands at the end of a long Graeco-Roman (but overwhelmingly Greek) tradition of books on dream-interpretation.

Most of our recent predecessors, keen on establishing a literary reputation, and thinking that the only way to fame was to leave a treatise on
the interpretation of dreams, have simply copied each other's work—
which is either incompetent rehashing of fine observations made by the
old authorities, or the addition to those concise earlier texts of a whole
bundle of nonsense. They did not write from direct experience, but
simply put down random thoughts on whatever happened to catch
their own individual interest—and this applies equally whether they
had read all of the old books or only some of them (having failed to

Fig. 2.4. Shop-sign of a Cretan dream-interpreter at Memphis, third century BC. *CPI* 1.199. Cairo, Egyptian Museum CG 27567.
Photo courtesy of the P.M. Fraser Archive, Centre for the Study of Ancient Documents, Oxford.

take account of some works which are now hard to find and poorly preserved because of their age). I, on the other hand, have been at great pains to acquire every book there is on dream-interpretation.

We need not lay much weight on the distinction drawn here between the works of the 'old authorities' (finely observed, concise, valuable) and the treatises of Artemidorus' recent predecessors (derivative, poorly organized, ill-informed). This looks very much like the salesmanship of an author trying to stand out in a crowded literary marketplace. But it is noteworthy that, despite his repeated emphasis on direct practical experience (*peira*) as the soundest basis of successful dream-interpretation (see Chapter 3), Artemidorus also insists on the importance of this long Greek literary tradition of dream-wisdom. There is no reason to doubt his claim that he was an eager collector of antiquarian dream-books: he does in fact show knowledge of an impressive range of obscure earlier writers on the subject. The *Oneirocritica* is expressly both a compilation of practical wisdom obtained 'on the job', and a summation of all that is valuable in the existing technical literature.

By my count, Artemidorus refers to some eighteen earlier oneirocritical authors, most of whom are little more than names to us. The earliest in date are probably Antiphon of Athens (2.14.6) and Panyasis of Halicarnassus (1.2.12, 1.64.5, 2.35.1), both of whom seem to date to the late fifth century BC. Whether Antiphon is identical to the well-known Athenian orator and oligarch of the late fifth century is an old and still unresolved problem, which need not trouble us here. Antiphon's book on dream-interpretation was widely read in antiquity: specific bits of dream-symbolism are cited by Cicero, Clement of Alexandria, and others, although none of these can be precisely paralleled elsewhere in the *Oneirocritica*, perhaps suggesting that Artemidorus did not use his work extensively.

A more important point of reference for Artemidorus was the dream-book of Aristander of Telmessus (1.31.1, 4.23, 4.24.3), which demonstrably underlies some important aspects of Artemidorus' theory of dreams (see below). Aristander was the court seer to Alexander the Great and his father Philip II of Macedon; his native city of Telmessus in Lycia was a notorious breeding ground for diviners (Arrian, *Anabasis* 2.3.3), and he also practised other forms of divination, such as bird-augury (*Anabasis* 1.25.6–8). His lost dream-book presumably dates to the late fourth century BC, unless (as some people think) Artemidorus was in fact using a later work, falsely attributed to the famous fourth-century seer. A five-book collection of incubation-dreams (see Chapter 9) attributed to the late fourth-century Peripatetic philosopher Demetrius of Phalerum (2.44.3) may similarly be a later product, spuriously associated with a famous writer of the Classical period; the same is certainly true of the (undatable) dream-books falsely attributed to the mythological Delphic prophetess Phemonoe (2.9.8, 4.2.2) and the legendary Thessalian seer Melampus (3.28.1).

Moving into the Roman imperial period, Artemon of Miletus (1.2.4, 2.44.3) and Alexander of Myndus (1.67.4, 2.9.4, 2.66.1) were both relatively well-known authors of the first century AD. Artemon wrote a work on dreams and incubation-cures in twenty-two books, and Alexander was known for a *Collection of Marvels* and a well-regarded work *On Animals*. Considerably more obscure is Geminus of Tyre (2.44.3), author of a three-book work on incubation-cures, and perhaps a near-contemporary of Artemidorus (if, as seems likely, he is identical to the unnamed 'contemporary' dismissed scornfully at 4.22.3). We are then left with a host of writers of total obscurity: Nicostratus of Ephesus (1.2.12: perhaps early, since he is cited with approval alongside Panyasis), Phoebus of Antioch (1.2.4, 2.9.4, 4.48, 4.66), Apollonius of Attalea (1.32.2, 3.28.1), Apollodorus of Telmessus (1.79.3—another Telmessian), Dionysius of Heliopolis (2.66.1, and probably 4.47.2), Antipater (4.65.2), Menecrates (4.80.1), and an anonymous Cypriot dream-interpreter (4.83.3).

Standing somewhat to one side is the fourth-century philosopher Aristotle, whose extant *On Divination in Sleep* is alluded to in passing by Artemidorus at 1.6. In contrast to the hubbub of lost dream-books listed above, Aristotle's short treatise contains not a word on the practicalities of dream-interpretation or dream-symbolism. Aristotle's purpose is to show that dreams are not sent by the gods (a position with which Artemidorus agrees), but emerge naturally from physiological processes (Artemidorus nowhere expresses a clear opinion on this), and that therefore dreams can predict the future only as a result of chance or guesswork (emphatically not Artemidorus' view). Since Artemidorus was not particularly interested in the origin of dreams, he could leave this entire strand of ancient thought on dreams to one side; it is not even clear whether he knew Aristotle's treatise at first-hand (see further Chapter 8).

We should love to know how Artemidorus' approach to dream-interpretation fitted into the long Greek literary tradition of dream-books, on the levels both of general theory and of specific points of dream-symbolism. Is Artemidorus typical? If idiosyncratic, in what respects? How did the theory and practice of dream-interpretation change between the late fifth century BC (the date of the earliest Greek dream-books) and the early third century AD? And perhaps most importantly of all, how much of the long catalogue of specific items of dream-symbolism in the first two books of the *Oneirocritica* is the result of Artemidorus' own practical experience as a dream-interpreter, and how much has been taken over wholesale from earlier catalogues of this kind?

The short answer is that we have no idea. The works of Artemidorus' predecessors are all but completely lost; in most cases, what we know of these books is confined to what little Artemidorus himself tells us about them. There is no reason to think that any of these books ever enjoyed a wide circulation and readership. Among the tens of thousands of scraps of literary texts that survive on papyrus from Greco-Roman Egypt, only a single tiny fragment of a Greek-language dream-book has come down to us: the sole legible sentence reads 'If (the dreamer) urinates on a statue or a picture, he/she will neglect his/her own affairs' (Fig. 2.5). We have no way of knowing whether this fragment comes from one of Artemidorus' shadowy predecessors, or whether the author is yet another unknown dream-interpreter.

It is worth recalling that in the prefaces to each of Books 1–4, Arte-midorus repeatedly claims that what chiefly distinguishes the first two books of the *Oneirocritica* from earlier works on dream-interpretation is not so much their originality of content, but their rational structure and organization. So in the Preface to Book 3, he says that his first two books 'observed an organization and a sequence which have nothing in com-mon with the treatment of the old authorities, and to the extent of my ability I set out my own views which were sometimes a wholly new approach, sometimes in agreement with others, and sometimes, as appro-priate, in disagreement' (3.Pref.; cf. 1.10.1, 4.Pref.1). It is true that in the Preface to Book 2, he claims that he was 'always careful to avoid simply retracing the steps of the old authorities, except where there was some compelling need, and I omitted no essentially relevant topic, unless those old authorities had already before me treated it with a classic exposition' (2.Pref.1). But in fact, through the whole of Books 1 and 2, he only once simply refers the reader to an earlier work without also summarizing its

Fig. 2.5. Papyrus from Oxyrhynchus with fragment of a Greek dream-book (third century AD). *P.Oxy.* XXXI 2607.

Photo courtesy of The Egypt Exploration Society and the University of Oxford Imaging Papyri Project. © The Egypt Exploration Society; protected by UK copyright law.

content (1.64.5), and his wording in the Prefaces to Books 2 and 3 is quite compatible with the idea that he might from time to time simply be 'retracing the steps of the old authorities'—it all depends on how often he found that his views were 'in agreement with others' (3.Pref.).

That some parts of Books 1 and 2 were silently taken over from earlier dream-books can be shown with reasonable certainty. For example, in Book 1 of the *Oneirocritica*, Artemidorus claims that to dream of plants growing from one's knees is inauspicious, and states a general principle in support of this (1.47.2):

> Anyone dreaming that any sort of plant has grown out of his knees will lose the full use of his knees: and if a sick man has this dream, he will die. This is because plants grow out of the earth, and it is into the earth that the components of our bodies are dissolved.

In Book 3, Artemidorus adds an important qualification to this general principle, which he now attributes to unnamed earlier dream-interpreters (3.46):

> Some people say that if anyone dreams of any sort of plant growing out of his body he will die, because plants grow out of the earth, and it is into earth that the bodies of the dead are dissolved. My own view is that interpretation must be based not solely on the growing of a plant but also on the parts of the body where the plants are seen to grow.

In Book 1, there was no indication that this general interpretation of plant-dreams was not original to Artemidorus. It is only incidentally, in retrospect, that we learn that he has taken it over (with qualifications) from one or more of his predecessors.

There are also a small number of passages in the *Oneirocritica* which read very oddly indeed in the cultural context of the high Roman empire, and seem to fit much more comfortably in the Hellenistic period. In his account of dreams about Greek comedy, Artemidorus distinguishes between Old Comedy and 'the comedy of our own day', the former signifying 'ridicule and quarrels', the latter being characterized by 'good and happy endings' (1.56.5). This passage nicely describes the shift from the riotous obscenity of fifth-century Attic comedy (Aristophanes and others) to the 'New Comedy' of Menander (*c.*344–292 BC), with its domestic themes and happy endings. But Artemidorus elsewhere characterizes Menander as one of the 'old authors' (2.4), which is very hard to square with his reference here to 'the comedy of our own day'. Furthermore, in his account of dreams about a '*basileus*'—a Greek word that can signify both (Hellenistic) king and (Roman) emperor—Artemidorus includes several details that are grossly inappropriate to Roman emperors (e.g. the diadem, sceptre, and purple robe as characteristic 'regal' insignia), but which make perfect sense when applied to Hellenistic monarchs (2.30.1; discussed further in Chapter 12). Rather similar is Artemidorus' analysis of dreams about long hair (1.18), where he says that dreaming of having long hair is auspicious for a *basileus*, since long hair is traditional for such a person. Roman emperors did not usually have long hair, but Hellenistic kings most certainly did: full and shaggy locks were a distinctive element of Hellenistic royal portraiture (in imitation of Alexander the Great's unkempt mop of hair). In all three cases, these 'anachronisms' may well indicate passages of dream-interpretation that have been taken over wholesale from earlier authors with minimal updating.

The manner in which Artemidorus refers to specific earlier dream-books can take us a little further. In very many cases, these earlier authors are referred to only in passing as supporting authorities for particular bits of dream-symbolism. Here, for example, is his sole reference to the dream-book of Antiphon the Athenian (2.14.6):

> Boneless marine animals are only advantageous for criminals, as these creatures too camouflage themselves, blend in to their surroundings, and lurk unseen. For others they signify obstacles and delays because of their adhesive grip, and they predict many slumps in business affairs because they have no bones—and bone is what gives strength to a body. These animals are the octopus, squid, sea anemone, nautilus, musk polypus, purple polypus, and cuttlefish. This last is the only one to benefit those trying to run away, because of the ink which it often employs to make its own escape. Antiphon of Athens also notes this dream.

Is Antiphon the source of this entire section on cephalopods and other boneless sea-creatures? Surely not: he is cited only as authority for the very last item (cuttlefish being auspicious for those trying to run away). We have no good reason to doubt the natural implication of Artemidorus' phrasing, namely that only this final dream-element is drawn from Antiphon—although it is, of course, impossible to tell whether

Artemidorus knew Antiphon's book at first-hand, or only through a reference to it in another dream-interpreter.

In other cases, earlier dream-interpreters are cited for general points of principle, which Artemidorus may or may not opt to follow. This is what he has to say about the swallow (2.66.1–2):

> It is commonly said that the creature signifies untimely deaths, mourning, and great distress, as legend has it that this bird came into being as a result of such tragedies. Both Alexander of Myndus and Dionysius of Heliopolis say that we must go with these legends. Their contention is that, even if a legend is more or less fictitious, our presumption that it is true means that our unconscious mind brings that legend into play whenever it wants to warn us that something analogous to the content of the legend is about to happen. I have found that this rationale fits most legends, but by no means all. And so, on the principle of following in any interpretation not the apparent symbolism of the legends but direct experience of actual outcomes, here too I say that a dream of a swallow is not malign, unless something strange happens to it or it changes to some unnatural colour. Its song is no funeral dirge, but a tune which acts as a prelude and encouragement to the work of the day.

The reference in the first clause is to the bleak myth of the sisters Procne and Philomela. Philomela was raped by her sister's husband Tereus, who cut out her tongue to prevent her reporting the crime; the two sisters took their revenge by killing Itys, the infant son of Tereus and Procne, and fed him to Tereus. Procne and Philomela were subsequently transformed into the swallow and nightingale, whence (according to Artemidorus' predecessors) the inauspicious significance of a swallow seen in a dream ('untimely deaths, mourning, and great distress'). The general principle espoused by Alexander of Myndus and Dionysius of Heliopolis is that if a dream-symbol appears prominently in a well-known myth, its signification is necessarily determined by its place in the myth-narrative. Artemidorus doubts this: he prefers to work inductively from actual observed outcomes of particular dreams, rather than relying on a priori significations of this kind. Another obvious problem with the principle he criticizes here—pointed out by

Artemidorus much later in his work—is that myths come in different variants, which can point in radically different directions. He gives the example of the myth of the phoenix (4.47.2):

> Someone dreamt that he was painting a picture of the bird called the phoenix. The Egyptian said that the man who had the dream fell into such an extreme of poverty that when his father died his complete inability to pay anything meant that he himself bent down to lift his father and carried him out for burial—the phoenix too buries its own father. Now whether the dream did cause that outcome, I do not know, but at any rate that was the Egyptian's story, and on this version of the myth it would have been a logical outcome. But some say that the phoenix does not bury its father, and in fact has no father at all that could be alive, or any other ancestors . . . So if anyone were to tell a man who has had this dream that he will find himself with no parents, on this version of the myth he will not be wrong.

It is, of course, extremely tempting to suppose that the anonymous 'Egyptian' dream-interpreter criticized here is none other than Dionysius of Heliopolis (a native of Egypt); the logic of the dream-interpretation (follow the myth) is precisely the same as we saw in the earlier passage about swallow-dreams.

In only one instance can we be absolutely certain that Artemidorus made extensive use of an earlier dream-book as the basis of his own interpretative principles. This is his symbolic system of spatial polarities for interpreting dreams about the body, expressly attributed in Book 1 to the fourth-century dream-interpreter Aristander of Telmessus. In interpreting teeth-dreams, says Artemidorus, 'the fullest and best set of principles is that proposed by Aristander of Telmessus' (1.31.1). The mouth, or so Aristander claimed, 'must be thought of as a house, and the teeth as the people in the house'. The upper and lower teeth signify superior and inferior members of the household; teeth on the right side are men, while those on the left are women, although teeth on the right can also signify older men or women, and those on the left side younger ones. Incisors signify the young, canines the middle-aged, and molars the old.

As we will see in Chapter 4, Artemidorus employs this symbolic system not only for teeth-dreams, but throughout his long account of dreams about the body (1.17–50). It is highly likely that Aristander too saw his system as applying to all body-dreams, and not just to teeth-dreams. In Book 4 of the *Oneirocritica*, Aristander is cited by name in two successive chapters (4.23, 4.24.3); in the following chapter (4.25), Artemidorus restates the general principle that all 'upper parts' of the body signify superiors and all 'lower parts' denote inferiors. The place-ment of this chapter in a particularly 'Aristander-heavy' part of the *Oneirocritica* surely reflects Artemidorus' dependence on Aristander as the originator of the whole symbolic system. (Artemidorus was clearly not the only dream-interpreter to follow Aristander's system: note 1.48.5, where he refers to the view of 'most dream-interpreters' that feet sym-bolize household slaves.)

It is hard to come to any definitive conclusion about the extent and depth of Artemidorus' dependence on his predecessors. Large parts of Books 1 and 2 could, in principle, have been taken over with minimal alteration from dream-books of the Classical or Hellenistic period (e.g. the relatively 'timeless' sections on animals and the gods in Book 2: 2.11–22, 2.33–41); but plenty of sections in those same books clearly reflect the society and culture of Artemidorus' own day (e.g. chapters on the ephebate, bathing, and gladiators: 1.54, 1.64, 2.32). I see no good reason to doubt that the overwhelming majority of specific dreams reported by Artemidorus (mostly in Books 4 and 5) did indeed derive from his own personal experience, although in a very few cases these may have been well-known 'textbook' dreams taken over from earlier writers (e.g. the dream of the Roman soldier at 4.24.2, discussed in Chapter 12). Artemidorus was, after all, well aware that the meaning of dreams is historically as well as culturally specific: he is notably scorn-ful of dream-interpreters who mechanically follow the old views, with-out paying attention to practical experience and contemporary cultural context (1.64.2).

Conclusion

Self-evidently, Artemidorus the Younger did not follow his father's injunction to keep Books 4 and 5 to himself. But it is very difficult to say whether the *Oneirocritica* ever found a significant readership outside of a narrow circle of professional dream-interpreters, or indeed whether Artemidorus ever intended any part of the *Oneirocritica* (even the notionally 'public' Books 1–3) for wide non-specialist circulation. It is hard to believe that the *Oneirocritica* could have carried much appeal for an elite 'literary' readership: even Maximus of Tyre is unlikely to have relished the prospect of ploughing through hundreds of pages cataloguing thousands of discrete dream-elements, couched in a sober and utilitarian prose-style about as far removed as could be imagined from the elaborate, rhetorical idiom characteristic of 'high' Greek literature of the period.

Aside from anything else, the *Oneirocritica* would simply not have been much use to an elite reader seeking to understand the meaning of his or her dreams. One of the most striking features of the book is the ubiquity of dreamers of modest or very low social status (see Chapter 11). Artemidorus is interested in the meaning of dreams seen by slaves, debtors, craftsmen, actors, and shop-keepers—there are some eighty-nine examples of slave-dreams alone (around half of which are interpreted as foretelling the slave's manumission). He is relatively uninterested in the dreams of the uppermost social classes: although 'the rich' are a fairly common generic category of dreamer, the *Oneirocritica* includes not a single example of a dream seen by an emperor, and only two dreams seen by men of senatorial or equestrian rank (1.73.2, 4.28.2, discussed in Chapter 12 below). The 'demography' of the *Oneirocritica* in fact rather beautifully reflects the ordinary day-to-day clientele of 'the much-maligned diviners of the marketplace' (1.Pref.4), the professional urban dream-interpreters who worked the great cities and festivals of the Greco-Roman East.

Whether or not we think Artemidorus' approach to dream-interpretation is a sound one (Chapter 3) is perhaps not ultimately all that important. The *Oneirocritica* commands our attention because this is one of the very rare surviving texts from Greco-Roman antiquity which is systematically interested—one might say, *professionally* interested—in the hopes, fears, and life-worlds of ordinary members of the sub-elite. How this quirky, credulous, chaotic dream-manual managed to survive into the Middle Ages and beyond is probably not something we will ever know; but we can only be grateful that it did.

3

How to Interpret a Dream

Does Your Dream Need Interpreting?

In Artemidorus' view, not all dreams require interpretation, since not all dreams predict the future. Some dreams are simply the result of an irrational desire, an inordinate fear, or a full or empty stomach (1.1.2, cf. 4.Pref.6):

> For example, it is inevitable that in their dreams a lover will imagine himself with his beloved, that someone frightened will have a vision of what frightens him, then again that a hungry man will dream of eating and a thirsty man of drinking, and for that matter someone who has overstuffed himself will dream of vomiting or choking, because of the blockage caused by indigestion. We can see, then, that these dreams, where the feelings are pre-existent, do not foretell the future but recollect the present.

Dreams of this kind are of no particular interest to the dream-interpreter, since they do not predict anything: they are simply a reflection of the immediate physiological or mental state of the dreamer. Artemidorus calls these uninteresting non-predictive dreams *enhypnia*, and he firmly distinguishes them from *oneiroi*, dreams which predict future events. *Enhypnia* are essentially a sign that there is something wrong with you that you need to get fixed. 'People who lead a moral and principled life', says Artemidorus, 'do not have non-significant *enhypnia*', because their minds 'are not muddied by fears or hopes, and, what is more, they are in control of the pleasures of the body' (4.Pref.7). There is a fairly obvious nod here towards contemporary Stoic ethical thought: the serious person ought to be trying to free himself from precisely the kinds of irrational desires and fears (and stomach-pains) that tend to give rise to non-predictive *enhypnia*.

Artemidorus goes on to divide predictive dreams (*oneiroi*) into two further subcategories: the allegorical, which represent future events in symbolic form, and the directly predictive ('theorematic'), 'where the outcome corresponds literally to the vision' (1.2.1). One might have thought it would be difficult to tell the difference between an allegorical and a theorematic *oneiros*: does a dream of being shipwrecked mean that you will experience a shipwreck (theorematic: 1.2.1) or that you will be released from bondage (allegorical: 2.23.1)? In principle, says Artemidorus, it could mean either, but in practice the question is academic: theorematic dreams tend to be fulfilled instantly, with no time for reflection or consultation (4.1.1). So the dream-interpreter only really needs to concern himself with predictive dreams that take an allegorical or symbolic form, and it is with these kinds of dream alone that the *Oneirocritica* is concerned.

This double classification of dreams (*enhypnia* and *oneiroi*; allegorical and theorematic *oneiroi*) is not found in earlier Greek writings on dreams, and it is possible (though far from certain) that it is original to Artemidorus. As Artemidorus recognizes (4.Pref.6), the words *enhypnion* and *oneiros* are used interchangeably in earlier Greek literature, and he himself does not employ this terminological distinction consistently in the *Oneirocritica*: when his attention slips, he can casually use the term *oneiros* to refer to dreams with no predictive power (1.78.6) and *enhypnion* for predictive dreams (4.33.2). But on the whole this classification of dreams is a perfectly sound and workable one.

It is not always straightforward, says Artemidorus, to tell the difference between an *enhypnion* and an *oneiros*. He gives the example of two men's dreams about oral sex, which he originally interpreted as predictive *oneiroi*, but which then mysteriously resulted in none of the normal outcomes (4.59.1):

Someone dreamt that he was practising cunnilingus on his own wife, and then again someone dreamt that he was being fellated by his wife. Even after a long time none of the outcomes signified by this sort of dream, and which usually result for other people, had happened to them. As there was no obvious reason for this, I was puzzled, and thought it strange that there should have been no outcome for them. But later on I learnt that both men made a habit of these practices and were not keeping their mouths clean. So it was not surprising that nothing happened to them: they were simply seeing in their dreams what regularly gave them arousal.

Artemidorus had naturally assumed that these dreams were allegorical *oneiroi*, since in the normal course of things no one (needless to say) would be gripped by an irrational desire for oral sex with his wife (Chapter 5). But it turned out that both men were in fact the kind of sexual misfits who enjoyed regular oral sex with their wives; their dreams therefore turned out to be ordinary non-predictive *enhypnia*.

A similar 'optical illusion' can arise in the case of dreamers who know something about the principles of dream-interpretation. For such people, perfectly ordinary *enhypnia* can take a superficially symbolic form; their minds 'translate' their desires into the symbols which they know often (in allegorical *oneiroi*) predict the outcome that they desire. A man is in love with a woman; if he knows a bit about dream-interpretation, he may dream about 'a horse, a mirror, a ship, the sea, a female animal, some piece of feminine clothing, or anything else which signifies a woman' (4. Pref.8). But don't be deceived: this is still a non-predictive *enhypnion*, generated purely and solely by the client's existing desire for the woman, which tells you nothing about the future.

It is worth underlining the significance of Artemidorus' casual inclusion of 'desires and fears' among the possible physiological causes of non-predictive (and therefore uninteresting) *enhypnia*. In the modern psychoanalytic tradition, the chief point of dream-analysis is precisely to enable the interpreter to gain psychological insight into the unconscious fears and desires of the dreamer. Artemidorus has absolutely no interest in using dreams to explore his clients' subconscious in this way. If your dream turns out to be simply a reflection of your personal fears or desires (conscious or unconscious), the dream falls outside his purview: he is not your therapist. Nothing could more clearly illustrate the vast intellectual gulf which separates Artemidorus from Freud and his successors.

Experience and Analogy

Once we have established that we are dealing with an *oneiros*, not an *enhypnion*, and we have persuaded ourselves that the dream is allegorical, not directly predictive, we now have to try to work out what exactly the thing is predicting. The clearest statement of Artemidorus' method comes in a passage of remarkable clarity and frankness in Book 4, intended (at least in principle) only for the eyes of his son, the younger Artemidorus (4.20.1):

> You should always try to assign a cause (*aitiologein*) and accompany any interpretation with a stated reason and some credible explanations: otherwise, even if you are quite accurate in your interpretation, giving a bare declaration of the outcome stripped of all its surrounding material will make you seem less professional. But you must not let yourself be misled into thinking that the causes (*aitiologiai*) you assign do actually determine the outcomes. Some people have frequent dreams with the same outcome, and we know that there is some logical pattern to these outcomes from the fact that they always turn out the same, but we cannot find the causes (*aitiai*) why that outcome is as it is. That is why it is our opinion that outcomes are arrived at on the basis of practical experience (*peira*), but explanations of their causes (*aitiologiai*) are simply the best that each of us can come up with from his own resources.

For Artemidorus, the only truly reliable guide to interpreting a dream is practical experience (*peira*) of other dreams of the same kind and their outcomes. As an experienced dream-interpreter, you know from long empirical experience that a dream of an oak tree often in fact signifies an old man, or something else to do with time (2.25.2). Since the outcome is consistent, there must be some logic underlying the relationship between dream-symbol and outcome. You therefore infer a cause (*aitia*): your inference is that oaks signify old age because oak trees are long-lived. This assignment of a cause (*aitiologia*) may be right, or it may be wrong: you do not know. It is simply the best you can come up with from your own resources. Of course, when you are dealing with a client, you should always assign a plausible and rational cause, and not just say 'I have often observed that this turns out to be the case', since you want to look like you know what you are talking about. But the analogic argument that you offer to your client is really nothing more than a plausible guess.

This position is upheld with admirable consistency throughout the *Oneirocritica*. In the Preface to Book 4, summarizing the contents of his first two books, Artemidorus writes as follows (4.Pref.1):

> I listed all the subjects which can be the content of dreams seen in ordinary experience . . . including in each case the analogy (*anaphora*) which any one thing bears to another and the outcome in which any dream can result. In this my reliance was not on bare conjecture from similarities (*eikasia*), but on practical experience (*peira*) and the evidence of actual dream-fulfilments. And where the old authorities had sown the seeds of interpretation without developing them fully in their writings, I developed their preliminary work into a precise and accurate analysis. And I included all matters that now had new outcomes or were themselves new phenomena.

That is to say, Artemidorus determined the most likely outcomes of the countless dream-elements discussed in Books 1 and 2 on the basis of actual observed dream-outcomes, both those observed by Artemidorus himself and those recorded by his predecessors (since *peira* encompasses both one's own experience and that of others). In no case, he claims, did he rely simply on logical conjecture or analogy. He did include in each case an attempt to explain the link between dream-symbol and outcome, and those explanations took the form of analogies: oak-symbol leads to age-related outcome, because oaks are long-lived. But those analogies have no explanatory or predictive force. They are, he claims, simply a retrospective attempt to account for actual observed outcomes, which may or may not be correct.

One's understanding of a specific dream-element is therefore never complete, but is always by definition subject to an ongoing process of refinement through *peira*. Artemidorus warns his son that new observed outcomes may always lead the dream-interpreter to modify his original analogic explanations, however plausible they might have seemed (4.65.2):

> You should certainly trust that dreams which have come true before will have a similar outcome again, but you must also allow the thought that they may now have some new significance. In that way

you will not end up simply resting content with the historic outcomes, but will be trying always to find something new which is consistent with the old. It would be ridiculous to follow the practice of most others, which is to take account only of what has been written or said in the past.

Earlier outcomes are your best guide to predicting the meaning of a dream, but they are not fully reliable. Even if a dream-symbol appears to have been fully and satisfactorily accounted for by your predecessors, it is always possible that experience will throw up new evidence, which may lead you to modify their position. Aside from anything else, since cultural practices change over time, the connotations of particular dream-elements are also subject to change. In the earliest times, public baths did not exist, so early dream-interpreters rightly saw no negative symbolism in bath-dreams (1.64.1). Later on, after public baths had been invented but were not yet in daily use, dream-interpreters rightly saw baths as inauspicious, since people only bathed 'when they had finished a military campaign or ceased from some great labour'. Some modern writers, says Artemidorus, 'follow that old view and interpret on the same criteria, but they are way off track and not following the signs of direct experience [peira]' (1.64.2). By Artemidorus' own day, public bathing had become a standard and pleasurable part of daily life (at least for the better-off), and so bath-dreams now tend to signify wealth, success, and health.

Since experience is cumulative, you should beware of placing too much weight on single examples that do not fit into a wider pattern, which may be 'outliers' generated by something unusual about the status or condition of the individual dreamer (1.45.4):

> If the penis is doubled, that signifies that all the referents will be doubled also, except for the wife or lover: these will be lost, as it is not possible to make use of two penises at the same time. I know of a man, at the time a slave, who dreamt that he had three penises. He was set free, and then had three names instead of the one, taking the extra two names from the man who had freed him. But this was a one-off occurrence: we should not base our interpretations on rare examples, but on those which observe a general pattern.

Artemidorus is particularly uncomfortable with attempts to determine the meaning of a dream-element purely on the basis of analogy or a priori plausibility. Late in Book 2, he criticizes the approach of two earlier dream-interpreters (Alexander of Myndus and Dionysius of Heliopolis), who think that those dream-elements that also appear prominently in Greek myth should always be interpreted in relation to their symbolic significance in the myth (more on this in Chapter 2). Well, says Artemidorus, that may be true sometimes ('I have found that this rationale fits most legends, but by no means all'), but it is most definitely not true a priori. It is, he says, far safer to stick to 'the principle of following in any interpretation not the apparent symbolism of the legends (*to pithanon tōn legomenōn*) but direct experience (*peira*) of actual outcomes' (2.66.2).

On one level, of course, the *Oneirocritica* is nothing but a collection of analogies: dream element x predicts outcome y because x is analogous to y in such-and-such a way. In principle, Artemidorus' intellectual position is that these analogies are nothing more than plausible guesses on the basis of repeated empirical observation: i.e. dream element x has in the past consistently predicted outcome y, and we plausibly infer that the cause of this is that x is analogous to y in such-and-such a way. The logic of Artemidorus' position strictly requires that one should never use a pattern of analogy alone to speculate about what a particular dream-element might be predicting, when practical experience is lacking.

But in practice, as we might expect, Artemidorus often finds himself tempted to drift into analogic reasoning. On several occasions, when he is dealing with an inconveniently voluminous category of dream-symbol (materials, 1.50.6; crafts, 1.52.2; things carried by the dead, 2.57.2), Artemidorus will give a handful of specific examples of observed outcomes, and then casually recommend that we resort to analogy for anything else that appears to fall into the category: 'Dreams about fruits not treated here should be interpreted by applying the principle of analogy on the pattern of the examples given above' (1.73.5). From time to time, Artemidorus seems to suffer a fit of conscience, and worries whether he might be in danger of falling into an 'analogic trap' (for which he seems to have been taken to task by his critics: 4.Pref.5). So just after proposing a suspiciously neat and coherent taxonomy of gladiator-dreams, he hastens to assure us (not, I have to say, very convincingly) that 'this account I give here is not based on plausible conjecture (*pithaneuomenos*) or any argument from probability (*to eikos*), but on my own frequent observations from direct experience (*peira*) of the actual outcomes in each case' (2.32.4).

Only once, I think, does Artemidorus openly bend the knee to Baal. Having described the symbolic significance of various different kinds of trees, he says that 'as for the other trees, one should base one's interpretations on the principles I have already set out, always keeping to an analogy with the outcomes predicted: the interpretation of dreams is really no more than the comparison of similarities (*homoiou parathesis*)' (2.25.5). 'Gotcha', as they say. But let us not be too hard on Artemidorus. Had he rigorously honoured his commitment to empirical reasoning, very many clients would have had to be sent away disappointed ('*peira* provides no information about the tree you dreamed of; I do not know what your dream predicts'). Even the most ethical dream-interpreter has to pay the bills.

Other General Principles: *Stoicheia* and the 'Person'

I suppose we ought to think of Artemidorus' radical empiricism as something of an intellectual pose. In an ideal world, the dream-interpreter would operate in a cold empirical laboratory, rigorously avoiding the use of analogy or inference, working solely from experience (*peira*) of earlier dream-outcomes. In fact, as we have seen, even Artemidorus could not sustain the pose for all that long. In practice, Artemidorus also employs a whole range of 'rationalist' principles in his dream-interpretation—ways, that is, of predicting what a dream-symbol is likely to mean, without having to rely exclusively on practical experience.

The first and most important of these 'rationalist' principles is Artemidorus' theory of the six *stoicheia* or 'elements' (1.3; 4.2.1–10). Dream-content, as we have seen, predicts real future events in the dreamer's life. These future events can be divided into two broad categories: good and bad, profitable and unprofitable, auspicious and malign. Artemidorus thinks we can determine a priori which of those two broad categories of event the dream-content will tend to predict, by looking at whether the dream-content conforms to (or diverges from) real observable phenomena in the waking world. Conformity is good, and divergence is bad.

All dream-content, argues Artemidorus, can be described in terms of whether or not it aligns with one or more of six possible characteristics or 'elements' (Greek *stoicheia*). All phenomena in the waking world exist either by *nature* (Element 1) or through convention (i.e. culture). 'Cultural' phenomena can be further subdivided into those sanctioned by written *law* (Element 2) or purely by *custom* (Element 3), collective or individual. In practice, all cultural phenomena (and some natural ones) take place at a discrete or characteristic *time* (Element 4), and men can perform actions with or without *art* or *skill* (Element 5). Finally, all phenomena have a discrete *name* (Element 6). If a dream's content conforms to these 'elements', it is auspicious; if not, it is not.

This sounds rather abstract, but a few practical examples will illustrate the usefulness and flexibility of the schema. By nature, people only have one nose. If you dream of having two noses, or no nose, the dream is likely to be inauspicious, because the dream-symbol is contrary to nature (Element 1: 1.27, 4.27.3). Similarly, water is cold by nature, so to dream of drinking cold water is always auspicious (Element 1); to dream of drinking hot water is usually malign, unless it is your personal custom to drink hot water, in which case it is auspicious (Element 3: 1.66.1). Figs are auspicious if you dream of them in season, but inauspicious when dreamt of out of season (Element 4: 1.73.3). Since Artemis is the quintessential virgin goddess, a dream of Artemis is malign for a brothel-keeper (art or profession, Element 5: 4.74); but for those who are afraid of something, Artemis is auspicious, because her name resembles the Greek word *artemēs*, 'safe and sound' (Element 6: 2.35.3).

This principle of 'conformity to elements = auspicious' is observed consistently throughout the *Oneirocritica*. Artemidorus is of course well aware that it is not fool-proof. As he specifically highlights in his two essays on the theory of dream-interpretation (at the start of Books 1 and 4), it is very hard to come up with general guidance as to what to do when a dream-symbol conforms to one 'element' but diverges from another. A man dreamt that he beat his mother, and the dream turned out to be auspicious (4.2.7): the dream-symbol was contrary to law (Element 2), but accorded with art (Element 5), since the man was a potter by profession and one's mother is like the earth. But how to know which element 'trumps' the other in any given case? Artemidorus does claim that 'when two sorts of custom are involved, the more widely observed custom prevails over the less' (4.2.8), but it is not hard to find exceptions to this rule-of-thumb scattered throughout the *Oneirocritica*. No doubt Artemidorus had not really thought the problem through.

There is of course a far deeper problem with the theory of the six *stoicheia*, namely that it is precisely the kind of unprovable a priori argument that Artemidorus sees as particularly dangerous for the dream-interpreter, who ought to be relying on empirical observation. If you pressed him to account for the apparent contradiction between these two parts of his dream-theory, I imagine he would reply that conformity to one or more *stoicheia* can only ever indicate in general terms whether the dream will be auspicious or malign; the precise character of the future event can only be determined by *peira* and explained by analogy. This is fair enough; but he certainly ought to have addressed the problem explicitly.

Another general principle in the *Oneirocritica* is the notion that the precise nature of the correspondence between dream-symbol and future event is strongly dependent on the specific person of the dreamer (Chapter 11). A single dream-symbol may predict many different things, depending on the sex, age, social and legal status, financial means, and profession of the dreamer (1.9). Your mental state at the time you were dreaming also matters (1.12.3: were you happy or unhappy at the time?), and it can make a big difference whether you took pleasure in the dream-experience (1.80.3, 4.4.2, 5.87).

Towards the end of Book 4, Artemidorus offers an extended illustration of this personal variable, 'which by itself can serve to give you practice in the concept of analogy (*he tōn homoiōn epinoia*)' (4.67.1). A pregnant woman dreams that she gives birth to a serpent. What does it mean? If the woman is wealthy, her child will become a great orator, because a serpent has a forked tongue, as orators do. If the woman is a slave, her child will become a runaway slave, because a serpent does not move in a straight line. If the woman is the daughter of a prophet, her child too will become a prophet, because serpents are sacred to the divine prophet Apollo. Artemidorus gives no fewer than seven different interpretations of the same dream, varying depending on the dreamer's social and economic status, health, character, and her husband's profession (4.67).

That the meaning of a dream depends on the person of the dreamer may not strike us as terribly surprising. But it is worth emphasizing how radically circumscribed Artemidorus' concept of the person is. He shows very little interest indeed in the specific personal experiences of the dreamer, let alone what we would describe as the dreamer's 'personality'. (In this, once again, he stands in the starkest possible contrast to the psychoanalytic tradition of dream-interpretation, which is interested in little else.) The 'person' is a crucial variable for Artemidorus in determining the meaning of a dream; but 'personhood' for Artemidorus is essentially a matter of your objective position within a web of social relationships, not your individual quirks and quiddities. If you are a slave, the dream predicts one thing; if you are a craftsman, it predicts something else. He is not remotely interested in what kind of relationship you had with your mother.

Why Do Dreams Mean What They Mean?

All of this adds up to a fairly coherent set of practical rules for the dream-interpreter. First make sure you are dealing with an allegorical *oneiros*, not a non-predictive *enhypnion*; then rely (if you can) on *peira* in determining what outcome is predicted by the dream-symbol, using analogy to account for the relationship between symbol and outcome. Conformity to the six *stoicheia* will help determine whether the dream is auspicious or malign; finally, make sure to pay attention to the status and social position of the dreamer.

What is lacking so far is any explanation of why it might be that dreams can in fact (sometimes) foretell future events. Here Artemidorus gives us very little help indeed. Just about all we can say for certain is that he did not believe that dreams come from the gods, but that they are instead the autonomous creation of the dreamer's mind (*psychē*). The clearest statement of this position comes in Book 4 (4.59.3):

> Dreams with something of a literary element to them are never seen by ordinary people (by which I mean the uneducated), but only by the intelligentsia and those who have had some education—and this is the clearest demonstration one could have that dreams are

products (*erga*) of the mind (*psychē*), and do not come from any external source.

Artemidorus' choice of words elsewhere in the *Oneirocritica* is wholly consistent with this. At the beginning of Book 1, he tells us that 'an *oneiros* is a movement (*kinēsis*) or complex moulding (*plasis polyschē-mōn*) within the mind or soul (*psychē*), which indicates what will happen in the future, whether good or bad' (1.2.3). He seems to conceive of the *psyche* as something that possesses its own separate identity and agency: so when the mind 'wants to signify' something to the dreamer, it 'presents' it to the dreamer in symbolic form (3.22.3; 4.27.1). Occasionally this hardens into an explicit soul–body dualism (5.40, cf. 1.80.3, 5.43):

A man dreamt that he was shedding his flesh like a snake sloughing its old skin. He died on the following day. This is the sort of imagining (*phantasia*) produced by the soul (*psychē*) when it is about to leave the body.

When his argument absolutely compels him to take a clear position on whether the gods have a role in the production of predictive dreams, he rather fudges the issue, perhaps in order not to give the impression of overt impiety (1.6):

Dreams which visit people who have no particular worries, and foretell some future event, good or bad, are called 'god-sent' (*theopempta*). I am not now concerned to join Aristotle in the debate whether the cause of dreaming is something outside us, originating from god, or there is some internal causation working on our mind and creating purely natural events in it. Rather, the term 'god-sent' here has the usual application we give it to all things unexpected.

Even in cases when a person has specifically requested a dream from a god, and has 'received' a dream shortly thereafter (Chapter 9), Artemidorus is very careful to leave it open whether the dream does in fact come from the god, or from within the dreamer's mind: 'the god—or whatever else is the cause of dreaming—presents to the dreamer's mind, which is itself pro-phetic by nature, dreams which point to some future outcome' (4.2.12).

All of this leaves us with the strong impression that Artemidorus was simply not interested in engaging with the long-running philosophical debate on whether divination through dreams was possible, and if so, how. As to 'whether' dreams predict the future: well, he knows through experience that they do. When it comes to the 'how', he is pretty sure that dreams are not sent by the gods (though he occasionally hedges his bets), and so logically dreams must be the creation of the dreamer's mind (*psychē*). And that, it seems, is about as far as Artemidorus was prepared to go.

Assessing Artemidorus

The absence of a coherent theory of causality is not a problem specific to the *Oneirocritica*, or even to ancient dream-interpretation more generally. We run up against the same problem in dealing with the entire ancient tradition of divination. One will search in vain for any ancient attempt to account for the precognitive significance of patterns of bird-flight, the form of animal livers, or the outcome of dice-throws, let alone shapes that appear in cheese (2.69.1). Yet augury (bird-divination) and haruspicy (entrail-divination) were employed both by states and individuals throughout antiquity on a scale that is hard to overstate. Millions of Greeks and Romans used divination to help them make decisions about the future, without feeling the need to provide a full naturalistic or theistic explanation for how the process actually worked.

Nonetheless, Artemidorus' refusal to ground his approach to dream-interpretation in an explicit theory of causality is awkward for modern readers, since we do not, on the whole, subscribe to his belief that dreams predict the future. We may therefore be strongly inclined to think—however interesting and important the *Oneirocritica* might be as a source for Roman social history—that Artemidorus himself was a quack preying on the gullible, and his actual dream-interpretations are, more or less by definition, unreasonable and absurd.

There is certainly plenty of material in the *Oneirocritica* that seems to fall squarely into the category of mumbo-jumbo. Artemidorus is distressingly fond of numerology, wordplay and false etymologies. The modern reader may well feel inclined to impatience when informed, in all seriousness, that to dream of having a haircut (*karēnai*) indicates that you will be happy (*charēnai*) (1.22.1), or that a dream of an eagle (*aetos*) signifies the current year (*a*=1, *etos*=year) (2.20.4, 5.57). We find these dream-interpretations ridiculous, because we do not tend to believe that the meaning of a thing is encoded in the sounds of the word that designates it.

But it is worth remembering that, even here, Artemidorus' 'method' stands right in the mainstream of ancient thought (see Chapter 1). The Greeks and Romans were entirely comfortable with the idea that homophones or near-homophones indicate a profound symbolic connection between things or concepts. At Rome, a fig-seller vocally hawking his Caunian figs ('*Cauneas!*') could be taken as a bad omen for a journey (*caue ne eas*, 'beware you don't go'!) (Cicero, *On Divination* 2.84). In Classical Athens, no less a figure than Plato can perfectly seriously explain that bird-divination (*oiōnoïstikē*, from *oiōnos*, 'bird') is concerned with predicting the future, because birds furnish human opinion (*oiēsis*) with sense (*nous*) and empirical knowledge (*historia*) (Plato, *Phaedrus* 244c)—a considerably more fanciful etymology (*oiō-/no-/ïs-tikē*) than anything in the *Oneirocritica*.

We might also recall that Artemidorus' passionate belief in the unconscious significance of puns and wordplay was shared by Freud, who engaged in precisely the same process of linguistic (or rather phonetic) analysis as a means of dream-interpretation—although of course for him it was the dreamer's unconscious, not the future, that was revealed by the relevant word or slip of the tongue. During his siege of Tyre in 332 BC, Alexander the Great is said to have dreamed of a dancing satyr (Greek *satyros*); his dream-interpreter Aristander interpreted this as predicting Alexander's imminent capture of the city (*sa-Tyros*, 'Tyre is yours'). Artemidorus' enthusiasm for this interpretation (4.24.3) is fully matched by Freud's, for whom this was 'the most beautiful example of a dream-interpretation handed down to us from antiquity'. None of this is to defend Artemidorus' use of wordplay as a system of dream-interpretation; it is merely to say that his method does not make him an isolated lunatic.

A more serious criticism of Artemidorus' method—one that has also been levelled against Freudian psychoanalysis—is that his range of associations, symbols, analogies and equivalences is so wide and flexible that almost anything can be bludgeoned into standing for almost anything else.

When he tells us that a certain number of 'days' in a dream can equally well mean 'months' or 'years' (and vice versa), our hackles rise (2.70.9, cf. 5.30); when he assures us that being burned alive can signify recovery from illness, because the verb for being burned alive (*kata-kaiesthai*) is a compound verb, and one is healed by medicinal 'compounds', our patience may well run out altogether (2.52, cf. 4.22.4).

Nonetheless, it is not true that dream-elements can stand for *literally* anything else. Dreams in the *Oneirocritica* only ever predict events that are in some way within the immediate purview of the observer: 'people have not had predictive dreams about matters never in their thoughts' (1.2.11). Artemidorus never offers dream-interpretations in the form 'If you dream of a frog, it will rain tomorrow', or 'If you dream of an elephant falling over, there will be an earthquake in Italy'. In almost every case, the phenomena predicted by dreams are things that you will do or suffer yourself: you will be manumitted, your master will beat you, you will go on a long journey. At most, the dream may have an impact on a close relative or a close friend (e.g. 4.30.4: a woman's dream predicts that her sister will die), but Artemidorus is absolutely clear that such 'other-party' dreams are only possible 'as long as the dreamer knows this person with at least some degree of familiarity' (1.2.5; the same qualification in Aristotle, *On Divination in Sleep*, 464a27).

He does, it is true, accept in principle that there might be such things as 'public' and 'cosmic' dreams, which predict events bearing on an entire civic community or on the natural order as a whole (eclipses and so forth: 1.2.5, 1.2.11–12). But this is hedged round with nervous qualifications. Dreams that have an impact on public affairs will by definition only be seen by kings or senior civic magistrates, since it is necessary that dreams should 'have outcomes for the dreamers themselves' (1.2.11); they will never be seen by ordinary people, unless many thousands of people have the same dream at once (1.2.12). He gives no examples of verifiable 'cosmic' dreams, and does not tell us under what circumstances they might appear. In practice, he records not a single example of a 'public' or 'cosmic' dream in the *Oneirocritica*.

This is, I think, an important absence. It shows that Artemidorus recognized—whether or not he had formulated the principle to himself in such clear terms—that dreams normally offer precognition only of the dreaming subject's own future actions or experiences. (This is essentially

Aristotle's view, for whom dreams can be predictive inasmuch as they give limited foreknowledge of the dreaming subject's own actions: *On Divination in Sleep*, 463a21–31.) And this potentially opens the door to a more sympathetic reading of Artemidorus' belief in the predictive powers of dreams. Peter Struck has recently suggested that we might think of precognition through dreams (and other forms of divination) as an ancient analogue to our own concept of intuition. 'Intuition', Struck suggests, is the culturally specific way in which we tend to categorize that kind of knowledge which we possess about the world that comes not through self-conscious reason, but through some untraceable accumulation of hints and hunches. Dream-divination—at least in principle—might not be all that different; one could think of a 'precognitive' dream as a dream which provides (in symbolic form) a usefully coherent account of things that you may have correctly inferred or intuited in the waking world, without quite being aware that you have done so.

It is easy enough to find examples of 'predictive' dreams in the *Oneirocritica* that can be rationalized in this way as examples of 'intuitive knowledge'. Artemidorus tells us of a young man from Paphos who dreamed that he 'applied make-up to his face as women do, and then took his seat in the theatre; he was caught in adultery and disgraced' (4.41.1). Another man 'dreamt that he had the name of Serapis inscribed on a bronze tag hanging round his neck like an amulet'; he immediately contracted a peritonsillar abscess and 'died of a disease affecting that part of him adjacent to the amulet' (5.26). Both dreams are precognitive, but they do not predict a random bolt from the blue: the first man may have had a sense that his adultery was about to be found out; the second may well have had a suspicious tickle in the throat.

But this line of argument clearly ought not be pushed too far. Plenty of Artemidoran dream-interpretation claims a far more precise knowledge of the future than could conceivably be put down to intuition. In the dream mentioned above, about the man who dreamt of having the name of Serapis inscribed on an amulet hanging round his neck (5.26), Artemidorus tells us that he died on the seventh day because the name Serapis has seven letters in it. There is no way of rationalizing this away as 'intuition' or 'subconscious inference': it is, I fear, pure snake-oil. Some dreams foretell what are in effect bolts from the blue; even if the dream-interpreter did indeed 'predict' the relevant outcome (rather than rationalize it away retrospectively, as we may darkly suspect), this can really be nothing more than an extravagant coincidence (5.66):

> A man dreamt that someone said to him, 'Sacrifice to Asclepius!' On the following day he met with a terrible accident. He was thrown from a vehicle which overturned, and his right hand was crushed. And so this was what the dream was telling him, that he should take precautions and make an apotropaic sacrifice to the god.

Our final assessment of Artemidorus' methods of dream-interpretation will depend on whose standards we choose to apply. By the standards of ancient divinatory practice, Greco-Roman beliefs about the relationship between names and things, and even Freudian theories of the workings of the subconscious, the *Oneirocritica* stands up pretty well: even if many of the specific predictions claimed by Artemidorus do not stand up to scrutiny, he was clearly neither a fool nor a fraud. If we apply more rigorous standards of causal reasoning, or even if we try to rationalize Artemidoran dream-theory as a culturally specific form of intuitive precognition, his approach falls dramatically short.

But perhaps this is not the most helpful way of approaching the *Oneirocritica*. We could quite reasonably decide that we have no particular interest in the question of whether dreaming of fighting a Thracian gladiator actually foretells acquiring a rich but devious wife (2.32.3); we might even decide not to take any great interest in whether Artemidorus had any reasonable justification for thinking that it might do so. We might instead pose the question in the following form: from what ethical point of view, and in what social context, can fighting a Thracian gladiator and marrying a rich but devious woman be seen as 'going together'? This is, in essence, the question to which the following nine chapters will attempt to provide an answer.

4

The Body

As we saw in Chapter 2, the first book of the *Oneirocritica* is essentially concerned with the human body and its cultivation. In his long 'tour' of the human body (1.17–50), Artemidorus offers us an incomparably rich and detailed picture of the symbolic meanings of the different constituent parts of the male and female body, which will be filled out in the later books of the *Oneirocritica* (essentially in Books 3–5: Book 2 is largely concerned with the external world of nature and society). It is, as we have already seen (Chapter 2), very hard to tell how much (if any) of this web of symbols and connotations is distinctive to Artemidorus. Certainly very much of the body-symbolism found in the *Oneirocritica* stands squarely in the intellectual mainstream of Graeco-Roman thought: its closest analogue in extant Greek literature, the *Physiognomy* of Polemo of Laodicea (AD *c*.88–114), offers a rather similar tour of the human body, albeit to a very different intellectual end (judging personality-type by scrutiny of physical body-type). What makes Artemidorus so precious a source for ancient body-symbolism is not so much his originality as his sheer comprehensiveness. Perhaps only here can we fully appreciate the remarkable intellectual coherence with which social values were inscribed on the male and female bodies of antiquity.

Status, Gender, and Age: The Three Dimensions of the Body Proper

The chief way in which the various parts of the human body take on symbolic meaning for Artemidorus is through a set of polarities based on orientation. The key categories are above and below, right and left, and front and back. Each of these three pairs carries a different set of primary associations. The vertical relationship (above and below) symbolizes the social hierarchy: the upper connotes superiority and mastery, the lower subordination. The relationship between right and left is primarily one of gender: the right signifies male, the left female. Right and left can also connote age (right is older, left is younger), and the right is often seen as auspicious, and the left as malign. Finally, the relationship between front and back generally reflects age: the front signifies younger, the back older. But the back also has malign connotations, being associated with death. As a result, when age is being conceived as a positive characteristic in the *Oneirocritica* (wisdom, superiority) it is typically associated with the right-hand side; when it is conceived as a negative characteristic (infirmity, death) it is typically associated with the back.

These three physical dimensions of the body thus reflect three different dimensions of the social order: status, gender, and age. In practice, of course, these three categories overlap: the 'mastery' inherent in being upper is usually associated with the male. But they are not simply reducible to one another: the right-hand side never explicitly symbolizes higher social status or dominance, and upperness never represents 'superior' age.

This set of polarities is certainly not distinctive to Artemidorus, although it is employed in his work more extensively and with greater conceptual precision than in any other extant ancient text. In a rare acknowledgement of his dependence on an earlier classificatory system, he tells us that this entire framework goes back to the great diviner Aristander of Telmessus (fourth century BC: see Chapter 2), who developed it as a system for interpreting dreams about teeth (1.31.1):

The fullest and best set of principles is that proposed by Aristander of Telmessus. They are as follows. The top teeth signify the superior and important members of the dreamer's household, and the bottom teeth the lower orders. The mouth must be thought of as a house, and the teeth as the people in the house. The teeth on the right side of the mouth signify the men, and those on the left side the women, except in some rare cases, for example when a brothel-keeper's household consists entirely of females, or a gentleman farmer's household consists entirely of males. In these cases the teeth on the right side signify the older men or women, and those on the left side the younger. And the teeth called 'incisors' (that is, the front teeth) signify the relatively young; the canine teeth signify the middle-aged; and the molars, which some call the 'grinders', signify the old.

We do not know whether Aristander applied these same relational principles to the entire human body, but Artemidorus certainly does (4.25):

> Generally, you should take the upper parts of the body as relating to the
> better and more respectable class of people, and all the lower parts as
> relating to inferiors and the lower orders. In the head upper and lower
> apply to the eyelids, the teeth, and the lips; in the whole body to what is
> above and below the waist. Within this, all parts on the right side relate
> to males or older people, and on the left to females or younger people
> of either sex.

By far the most important of these three spatial polarities in the *Oneirocritica* is that of right and left. As we have seen, the right is always
associated with the male, and the left with the female; there is also a
secondary association with age, the right signifying older, the left younger.
These associations hold good for every part of the body. Dreaming of
being bald on the right side of the head signifies the death of male
relatives, the left side female relatives (1.21.2). 'The right eye signifies
a son, a brother, and a father, and the left eye a daughter, a sister, and a
mother. And if there are two sons, two daughters, or two brothers, the
right eye signifies the older son or brother and the older daughter, and
the left eye the younger daughter and the younger brother or son'
(1.26.6). 'The right hand signifies a son, a father, a male friend, anyone
whom in common parlance we call "so-and-so's right hand": and the left
hand signifies a wife, a mother, a sister, a daughter, a female slave' (1.42.2,
also 1.2.9). The right breast signifies a son, and the right shoulder signifies
a brother (5.37). These associations also apply to objects outside the
body. So when Artemidorus is talking about the walls of a house, he says
that 'the central wall signifies the master, the wall on the right his
children, and the wall on the left his wife' (2.10.2). Since the Greeks
conceived of east and west as lying on the right and left sides respectively,
the east side of a house signifies death for one's older relatives, the west
side death for the younger ones.

Even when the right and left parts of the body do not expressly signify
gender, there is a clear overlap with typical gender roles. So Artemidorus
tells us that another unnamed expert in dream-interpretation has suggested that 'the right hand signifies earning, and the left hand what has

already been earned, as the right hand is ready to take things, and the left hand is suited to keeping things safe' (1.42.2). I think it is legitimate to take this as a gendered distinction, since it is the husband who earns, and the wife who preserves the household property. As Artemidorus says elsewhere, 'Seeing a key in a dream signifies for anyone intending to marry that his wife will be trustworthy and a good housekeeper' (3.54).

The right is also consistently auspicious in the *Oneirocritica*, while the left is consistently malign. But it is noteworthy that these positive/negative associations of right and left seem to have been particularly associated not with right- and left-hand elements of a single object (e.g. right eye and left eye), but with *movement* towards the right or left. If a god gestures with his right hand to someone who is sick, that signifies recovery; a gesture of the left hand denotes the opposite (5.89, 5.92). A vision of Zeus moving to the east (=right) is auspicious, to the west malign (2.35.1), and a rainbow is auspicious only when it appears to the right (=east) of the sun (2.36.14). In the Greek language, to do something 'to the right' (*epi dexia, dexiōs*) means to do it correctly, and 'to the left' (*ep' aristera*) incorrectly (e.g. Herodotus, *Histories* 2.36.4), and so the reversal of these normal directions of action is consistently inauspicious. Greeks normally wore their cloak 'to the right', throwing one end of the fabric over the left shoulder, and pulling the other end round the back and over the right hip, leaving the right arm free. Wearing your cloak 'to the left' (*ep' aristera*), says Artemidorus, 'is malign for all, and signifies that in addition to unemployment the dreamer will have to endure ridicule and mockery' (3.24). The same principle applies to writing (3.25):

> Writing from right to left signifies that the dreamer will do something criminal, or use deceit and trickery to make an insidious attack on someone else and do him wrong: and it often signifies turning to adultery and secretly fathering bastard children.

By comparison with the rich symbolism of right and left, the spatial relationship of upper and lower is relatively straightforward, simply signifying social status (see Chapter 11). For slaves, a dream of decapitation signifies freedom, for 'the head is master of the body, and the removal of the head signifies that the household slave will be separated from his master and set free' (1.35.5); likewise, for a member of a ship's crew, decapitation signifies death for his immediate superior in rank (1.35.7). Feet, at the lowest point of the body, signify slaves (1.48.1–2), and also children, 'because children assist their parents in the same way that their servants do, and look after their needs like household slaves' (1.48.5). Knees therefore represent freedmen, because 'they do the same service as the feet, except that as they are higher than the feet it makes sense that they represent freedmen rather than slaves' (1.47.3). For 'upper' body-parts to drop to a lower level signifies a drop in social status: 'I know of someone who dreamt that his eyes dropped out and fell to his feet. He did not go blind, but he married his daughters to his household servants, thus bringing about that conjunction of higher and lower' (1.26.9).

This same symbolism of upper and lower is also mobilized by Artemidorus in his long analysis of dreams about flying. Flying above the earth in an upright position—a crucial qualification, as preserving the body's normal orientation of higher and lower—is generally auspicious, because it represents status-elevation (magistracies for the rich, transfer to a more important household for a slave, and so forth: 2.68.1–3). Likewise, 'it is auspicious for a slave to dream of flying inside his master's house: he will then have a position above many in the household' (2.68.5). But all this only applies if the body is in its normal position: most malign and ill-omened of all is 'flying with head pointing down to the earth and feet up to the sky: this foretells substantial misfortune for the dreamer' (2.68.6).

Finally, the polarity of front and back, although not extensively used by Artemidorus in the *Oneirocritica*, is perhaps the most interesting and problematic of all. As we have seen, for Artemidorus (following Aristander) the front teeth signify younger people, and the back teeth older people (1.31.1). He explains the rationale behind this in his discussion of baldness (1.21.2):

If someone dreams that the back of his head is bald, he will experience poverty and serious destitution in his old age. Everything at the back is significant of future time, and baldness equates to destitution.

The back therefore connotes what is older because it is symbolic of future time, a notion that also appears (without the reference to old age) in Artemidorus' account of dreams about having your head on backwards (1.36):

> To dream that your head is turned round, so that you are looking at things behind you, prevents any intended emigration from your native land, because it foretells a change of mind about leaving your country, and it also prevents any other form of intended action: it is telling you not to look at immediate satisfaction, but at what will satisfy you in the future.

The back side of the body is therefore inauspicious, as having an association with death (1.49):

> We consider the back and all that is to the rear of the body to be significant of old age—hence some people rightly call these parts 'Pluto's province'. So whatever condition these parts have in someone's dream will also be the condition of his old age.

This association of future time with things that are 'behind' the observer may strike us as counter-intuitive, since we generally assume that the future is in front of us, and it is the past that lies behind. In fact, the Greeks and Romans also generally placed the future 'in front of' the observer, much as we do. As Maurizio Bettini once brilliantly observed, it seems to be *only* in the sphere of Graeco-Roman dream-interpretation that the future is conceived as lying at one's back: likewise, the emperor Domitian once dreamed that a golden hump grew on his back, which signified the *future* prosperity of the Roman empire, after his own death (Suetonius, *Domitian* 23). As Bettini argued, this reversal of the usual Graeco-Roman spatialization of time probably reflects the importance (in dream-interpretation) of the idea of *knowledge* of an otherwise obscure future:

> If the future is seen as something that must be known [i.e. in a predictive dream], then its position has to be turned around at once; it can only be at the back. The future is the unseeable, the unknowable par excellence. And that which cannot be seen has an excellent chance of standing behind the one who is looking for it... Formally, we could

say that knowledge stands in a hierarchy above the spatial location of future and past and that, whenever it enters into play, the usual localization gets inverted at once.

The Gendered Body

Late in Book 4, Artemidorus is discussing dreams of being transformed from a woman to a man and from a man to a woman (4.83.2):

> It makes no difference for a woman whether she dreams of having a beard, a man's genitals, a man's dress or hairstyle, or anything else specifically male: the outcome will be the same. It is similar for men. It makes no difference whether a man dreams of complete bodily trans-formation into a woman, or only of having female genitals, female dress or footwear, or hair braided like a woman's: the outcome will be the same.

Transformation-dreams are a good way into thinking about which parts of the body (and which physical properties of the body) might have been particularly evocative of masculinity and femininity to Artemidorus and his clientele. Perhaps counter-intuitively, the genitalia seem not to be particularly strong gender-markers in this context; Artemidorus records not a single case of a woman dreaming of having male genitals or vice versa. (The genitalia are also absent from Polemo's discussion of mascu-linity and femininity in his *Physiognomy*.) The closest thing to a genital-switching dream comes in Book 4, and in fact only describes the malign consequences for the male genitals of dreaming of a (theatrical) gender-switch (4.37):

> Someone dreamt that he was playing the role of a man pretending to be a woman in a comedy: he contracted a disease of the genitals. Someone else dreamt of seeing eunuchs: he too suffered a disease of the genitals. The first was because of the androgynous name of the role, the second because of what had been done to the people he saw.

Far more important are dreams about growing a beard (for a woman) and being pregnant or breast-feeding (for a man). In each case, the gender-switching dream is auspicious for an unmarried person, since it signifies sympathy with his or her future spouse (1.14.1, 1.16.2, 1.30.2; cf. 2.3.5, on men wearing women's clothes). However, there is a striking asymmetry between women's beard-dreams and men's pregnancy/breast-feeding dreams. Gender-switching dreams are, in general, auspicious for women, since gaining a masculine body-part signifies an increase in strength and confidence. If the beard-growing woman is involved in a law-suit, 'she will refuse to be belittled, and will stand up to it like a woman with virile attributes' (1.30.2). Similarly, for a female prostitute, changing into a man is auspicious, since she will have the strength to endure more sex than previously (1.50.4: see Chapter 11). For analogous reasons, gender-switching dreams are generally inauspicious for men. For a man in physical training, changing into a woman signifies illness, 'as women are more delicate than men' (1.50.3). For most men, dreaming of being pregnant indicates sickness (1.14.1). Breast-feeding is even worse, particularly for men in hyper-masculine occupations like athletes and gladiators: 'for an athlete, a gladiator, and anyone in physical training it foretells sickness, as it is the bodies of the weaker sex that have milk' (1.16.2). Artemidorus gives the example of a man who specialized in the most brutally violent and 'manly' of all sports, the *pancratium* (no-holds-barred bare-fist fighting), for whom, consequently, the feminization of his body was particularly disastrous (5.45):

A pancratiast dreamt that just before the games he had given birth and was breast-feeding his own baby. He lost his bout and thereafter gave up the sport: his dream had shown him undertaking a woman's role rather than a man's.

Hair in general is one of the more strongly gendered elements of the body. Female and male hairstyles (short or long, unbraided or braided) are particularly obvious symbols of gender (1.18, 2.6, 4.83.2). Hair on the chest is strongly indicative of masculinity, and so lots of chest hair is good for a man, but bad for a woman: 'A shaggy chest that is thick with hair is auspicious and profitable for men, but for women it prophesies widowhood. When the man for whose sake they take care of their bodies is gone, women are more neglectful of themselves and become hairy' (1.41.1). A beard is a wholly positive thing for a man, signifying masculinity and success: a man who dreamt he had a burning beard ended up having a famous and illustrious son, 'because a son is the pride of his father just as a beard is the pride of a face' (5.47). A beard is good for a creditor, since it gives him a formidable appearance (1.30.1), and losing one's beard signifies damage and disgrace (1.30.4).

As will already be clear from the gender-switching dreams discussed above, the constituent parts of the body are very often gendered and assigned positive or negative value in terms of their physical properties ('hardness' etc). Just as with the spatial polarities discussed in the first part of this chapter (upper and lower, right and left, front and back), Artemidorus here seems to operate with another three basic pairs of polar opposites: firm or soft, dry or moist, vigorous or limp (all of which are also key characteristics of 'masculine' and 'feminine' bodies in Polemo's *Physiognomy*). These properties are not explicitly theorized by Artemidorus, although he does include a brief (and not very illuminating) chapter on the significance of things that are hard, things that are soft and vigorous, and things that are soft and limp (4.12).

In his systematic analysis of the body in Book 1, Artemidorus always treats natural firmness as something auspicious. Success is associated with shoulders that are 'full' and 'fleshy' (1.40: *pachys, eusarkos*), and with arms and hands that are 'well-toned' (1.42.1: *eutonos*); 'full' cheeks are auspicious (1.28: *pachys*), as is a 'fleshy' forehead (1.23: *eusarkos*). Hardness on the palm of the hands is also good, as signifying regular employment (1.42.6)—a nice example of the generally favourable picture of labour in the *Oneirocritica* (a deeply idiosyncratic position in Graeco-Roman literature: see Chapter 11). By contrast, he says, 'dreams of thighs grown fat (*pialeos*) have been seen to have unpleasant consequences for the rich, signifying for the most part heavy expenditure on sex, or it could be not so much expenditure as actual harm' (1.46). 'Fleshiness' implies firmness, and is therefore good, but 'fatness' implies softness, which is bad. It is no surprise that manliness (*euandria*) is symbolized by 'firm' parts of the body, the forehead (1.23), the shoulders (1.40) and the knees (1.47.1), as well as—predictably—the penis (1.45.1).

The association of dryness with the male and moistness with the female was entirely standard in ancient thought (e.g. Aristotle, *Generation of*

Animals 766b33), and Artemidorus clearly agreed. It is striking that men seem never to dream simply of having breasts; such dreams always involve breast-feeding, that is to say, being 'moist' in a characteristically female way (1.16.2, 5.45). We are told that walking on the sea is auspicious for anyone intending to marry, since the sea is 'like a wife because it is moist' (3.16.1). However, dreams of having sex with the moon-goddess Selene are inauspicious because of her excessively 'moist' character, signifying a fatal bout of dropsy (1.80.3). Similarly, mud or clay symbolizes a catamite (*kinaidos*)—a man who enjoys being anally penetrated, i.e. a man who willingly plays a feminine role—'because it is moist and loose' (3.29).

Artemidorus consistently assumes that it is good for the body and its parts to be active and vigorous. Unnatural growth of hair on any part of the body is always inauspicious, because hair signifies that the relevant body-part is being unnaturally underused. Although some earlier dream-interpreters believed that a hairy tongue was auspicious for some dreamers (e.g. orators), Artemidorus firmly denies this: 'nothing grows hair unless it is idle and unused, and the tongue should not be idle' (1.32.2). Similarly, to have hair growing on the wrists or palms is bad, because it signifies inactivity and unemployment (1.42.6). Perhaps most striking of all, hair on the penis is profoundly malign, since it indicates that the penis (which ought to be active and vigorous) is not being put to appropriate use (5.65):

> A man dreamt that a thick mat of hair had suddenly grown on his penis and covered it with hair all the way to its very tip. He became an overt catamite (*kinaidos*), ready to indulge in any gross form of sexual gratification, but just not putting his penis to the normal male use. And so that part of him was left so idle that it actually grew hair for lack of friction with another body.

The body of the *kinaidos* is thus a particularly interesting limiting case for Artemidorus' theory of the body's physical properties. If the ideal (male) body is firm, dry, and vigorous, the body of the *kinaidos* is loose, moist, and idle. The point is not, I think, that the *kinaidos*' body is inappropriately feminine (though note 2.12.14, where he is grouped with hermaphrodites); firmness and vigour are just as important for the healthy female body as for the male body. It is rather that the body of the *kinaidos* serves as a kind of polar opposite to the ideal body of either gender, embodying every undesirable physical characteristic to the fullest possible extent.

The Absent Vagina

These last reflections lead us naturally on to the physical centre of Artemidorus' reflections on the human body and its meanings: the penis. We might begin with the puzzling fact that Artemidorus' systematic tour of the human body in Book 1 makes no space for the female genitalia. Why not? It is true that Artemidorus is generally more interested in the male body than the female body in Book 1, but he does carefully discuss the pregnant body (1.14), lactation (1.16), the differences between male hair and female head-hair (1.18), and women's breasts (1.41). If particular physical characteristics are common to both men and women, he often distinguishes their significance for male and female dreamers (1.18, 1.26.8, 1.28, 1.30.2, 1.41, 1.44.3). But when we arrive at the genitals, suddenly only the penis is in question (1.45). Artemidorus tells us at some length what it means for a man to dream of having breasts, breast-feeding, being pregnant, having a woman's hair or wearing women's make-up; yet he mysteriously fails to tell us what it means if a man (or woman) dreams of having a vagina.

This reflects a near-total silence about the female genitals in the *Oneirocritica*. They appear in passing in a list of female characteristics that a man might dream of adopting (4.83.2: having female genitals, female dress or footwear, or hair braided like a woman's), and, rather colourlessly, as the location of phallic penetration in an incest-dream (5.63). We also hear of a man who dreamt that his wife pulled up her clothes and showed him her genitals as a sign of contempt (4.44); even here, I think it is rather the aggressive gesture of genital display (conventional in Greek society, rather like 'giving someone the finger'), instead of the female genitalia themselves, that is really in question. Menstruation is never mentioned at all.

This absence cannot be coincidental. The extraordinary *under-signification* of female genitalia in Artemidoran dream-symbolism is best explained in relation to the equally extraordinary *over-signification* of the penis. Artemidorus' long chapter on the penis (1.45) is, one might have thought, completely useless for the working dream-interpreter, because the penis symbolizes more or less everything. It can connote every possible relationship within a household: it corresponds to parents (male and female), 'since it embodies the generative principle'; children (male and female), 'because of itself it starts the creation of children' (also 5.15, 5.86); a wife or lover, 'because it is made for sex'; and siblings or any other blood relative, 'since the whole principle of a family depends on the penis'. It represents strength and manliness, 'because it is itself the cause of these attributes'. Moving out from the household into wider society, the penis represents personal identity in the form of one's given name (1.45.4, 5.91); it connotes respect for one's status, because its name (*aidoion*) is cognate with the word for respect (*aidōs*); it symbolizes both profit and loss, because it both grows and shrinks; and it evokes rational speech (*logos*) and education (*paideia*), because, 'like reason itself, there is nothing more creative than the penis'. It reflects both mastery and being mastered by another, since the penis is one's 'taskmaster'.

The penis, then, stands symbolically at the absolute centre of human society, signifying 'the whole field of kinship and social activity' (Foucault). It is the lynchpin of the household and the family; it symbolizes wealth, status, reputation, mastery, and even rationality and human speech itself. As we shall see in the next chapter, Artemidorus' conception of human sexuality will be entirely structured around phallic penetration: the only part of a sexual act invested with symbolic meaning is the insertion of a penis into a bodily orifice. Alone among body-parts, the penis has an existence and agency independent of the rest of the body in the *Oneirocritica* (Fig. 4.1). We are told of a man who dreamed of 'feeding bread and cheese to his penis as if it had a life of its own' (5.62); we also hear of a woman who dreamt that her husband's penis had been separated from the rest of his body, 'and that she was holding it in her hands, looking after it, and taking every care to preserve it' (5.86). Its significance even 'colonizes' the entire central part of the human body: both the groin and the thighs simply signify the same thing as the penis by dint of proximity, above and below (1.46). The absence of the female genitalia from the *Oneirocritica* is—or so I would suppose—the consequence of this symbolic hypertrophy.

Fig. 4.1. Epitaph of Philogeiton (Roman imperial period, unknown provenance). *Supplementum Epigraphicum Graecum* 53, 2107; Pierre Bergé & Associés, *Archéologie Fayez Barakat*, 14/12/2009, lot 93.
Photo © Pierre Bergé & Associés.

The Disabled Body

Artemidorus concludes his account of the body in Book 1 with a broad generalization about what kinds of bodies should be seen as auspicious or malign (1.50.8):

> In my observations physical beauty, a handsome figure, and bodily strength are auspicious for all alike, as long as these attributes do not exceed human norms, since to dream that one is preternaturally beautiful, handsomely built, or strong has the same outcome as

dreaming that one is ugly, crippled, or enfeebled, all of which signify death for the sick, and for those in good health unemployment and chronic illness.

As this passage implies, bodily dysfunction, whether physical or mental, is an abhorrent and inauspicious thing in the *Oneirocritica*. There is hardly so much as a hint of sympathy for the disabled, who can expect to be stared at and mocked in public. Seeing a disabled person in a dream may simply signify death: a man dreamt that his daughter was a hunchback, and consequently his sister died (4.29). The repugnance provoked by physical disability is particularly clear in Artemidorus' exposition of the seven different possible outcomes of a dream of giving birth to a snake (4.67: see Chapter 3). The first three outcomes are positive (the dreamer's child becomes an orator, a sacred official, a prophet), the next three negative (the child becomes a sexual predator, a robber, a runaway slave), and last (and presumably worst) of all comes the disabled child (4.67.7):

Another woman had the same dream, and the son born to her became a paralytic. Snakes need to use their entire body to effect movement, and the same is true of humans who are palsied. The woman was sick when she had the dream, so it makes sense that the child conceived and carried when its mother was sick did not maintain its nervous system in a healthy state.

Snakes are slithery and devious, like the sexual predator; they move in unpredictable zig-zags, like the runaway slave; and their whole body twists and turns as they move, like the boy with cerebral palsy.

Worse still, disability and disease are casually and persistently ethicized in the *Oneirocritica*. In one particularly clear section, physical incapacity and illness are explicitly treated as symbolically evocative of moral failings (3.51):

To imagine that one has the same physical symptoms as any of one's acquaintances—for example a problem with the same foot or the same hand or any other part of the body, or generally the same disease or the same pain—signifies that one will also share the moral faults of the other. Diseases of the body and the crippling of any of its parts symbolize mental lack of control and irrational desires, so it stands to reason that anyone sharing the physical symptoms will also share the moral faults. I know of someone who was lame in his right leg, and dreamt that his household slave was lame in the same leg and limped as he did. What happened was that he caught the slave on top of the mistress with whom he himself was smitten: and so this is what the dream was telling him, that the slave would share his own failing.

Artemidorus does not feel the need to provide a rationale for this link between disease and physical disability on the one hand, and moral faults ('mental lack of control and irrational desires') on the other; he simply assumes that the connection is obvious.

Moreover, in Artemidoran dream-symbolism, any form of physical disability or blemish is interchangeable for any other. A long and complex dream in Book 5 of the *Oneirocritica* draws the connection between different kinds of physical deformity, and moral fault, in a particularly telling manner (5.67):

A man dreamt that he was holding on to a barber's mirror which was standing in the street near the marketplace, and was urgent to see his reflection in it. He was not given permission, but even so he looked in the mirror there and then and saw his image completely covered in spots. He had fallen in love with a prostitute, and with nobody's permission had abducted her and kept her with him. They had a child who was blighted not only by his parentage but also because he was cross-eyed. The barber's mirror signified that the woman was a common prostitute available to anyone, and she was in an uneasy relationship with her abductor because there were people trying to stop him taking the woman off to live with him. After seeing his reflection, the man had a child born to him who was otherwise his own image, but spoiled, because of the spots which he had in the dream.

A mirror normally symbolizes a spouse (2.7.1), so a barber's mirror (a 'public' mirror) naturally connotes a prostitute. Barbers' mirrors were usually fixed to the wall (Plutarch, *On Listening to Lectures* 8 [42b]; Lucian, *The Ignorant Book-Collector* 29), and so the removal of the mirror to the marketplace and the man's insistence on seeing his reflection even without permission symbolizes his violent abduction of the prostitute. To see someone else's face in a mirror, or a distorted or blemished version of one's own face, is inauspicious for one's children, who will either be bastards, sired by other men, or diseased (2.7.2). Hence because the man saw his face covered in spots, his son was born cross-eyed, a disability which was seen in the ancient world as both risible and slavish (Petronius, *Satyricon* 39, 68). The interest here derives from the twofold connection between moral defect (abduction of a common prostitute) and physical defect (spots/strabismus), and between physical blemish (the father's spots) and innate disability (the son's crossed eyes).

The quintessential space of the disabled in the *Oneirocritica* is the public street and the marketplace. Disability and disfiguring diseases are expected to attract people's attention, and more in disgust than sympathy (3.47):

Scabies, leprosy, and elephantiasis make poor men more notable, more regarded, and conspicuous for the increase in their substance: that is because these diseases attract attention to those who suffer from them. And they bring secrets to light for the same reason. For the rich and powerful a dream of having these conditions brings them public offices. It is always more auspicious for someone to dream that he himself has the scabies, leprosy, or elephantiasis, or any similar condition such as white leprosy or mentagra. To see someone else suffering from them signifies distress and anxiety, because the sight of anything repulsive or disfiguring afflicts the minds of those who see it and depresses them.

Likewise, when mental illness is evoked in the *Oneirocritica*, it is always associated with public visibility and mockery. 'Giving renditions of songs in the marketplace or the streets signifies disgrace and ridicule for a rich man, and for a poor man insanity' (1.76.6). It is true that, for Artemidorus, dreams of madness are auspicious for all categories of dreamers; but the rationale underlying these positive outcomes leaves a remarkably bleak impression of the lives of the mentally disabled in the Greek city. To dream of being mad is good for an aspiring politician, since he will have a large public audience; it is good for teachers, since children follow after madmen in the streets; it is good for the poor, because everyone gives alms to a madman; and it is good for the sick, because madmen are always out moving about in public (3.42.1; for madness and excessive movement, cf. 1.76.2). We are evidently in the same unforgiving world as that of the madman Carabas of Alexandria, vividly evoked by the Jewish philosopher and historian Philo (*Against Flaccus* 36–8):

> There was a certain madman named Carabas, whose madness was not wild and bestial—the kind that is dangerous both to the sufferer and those who approach him—but gentler and milder. He spent his days and nights naked in the streets, in both hot and cold weather, as the plaything of idle children and youths. They drove this wretched man to the gymnasium, and set him up in a high place where everyone could see him. They stretched out a papyrus-stalk and put it on his head like a diadem, dressed his body with a door-mat in place of a cloak, and one of them found a little stick of the local papyrus-reed lying in the street, and gave it to him in place of a sceptre. When he had received all the insignia of royalty and was dressed up like a king like some pantomime-artist in the theatre, the young men hoisted staffs on their shoulders and stood on either side of him like spear-bearers. Others then approached as if to pay homage, plead a case before him, or consult him on public affairs.

Very many different kinds of disability and physical blemish are evoked by Artemidorus: being deaf and mute (1.76.3), lameness (3.51, 5.3), hernias (3.45), scars (3.40), skin diseases (3.47), cerebral palsy (4.67.7), being hunchbacked (4.29), paralysis (5.51), and others. But incomparably the most prominent kind of disability in the *Oneirocritica* is blindness. The greater part of the very long chapter on eyes in Book 1 is dedicated to dreaming of going blind (1.26.1–6), and most of the rest of the chapter is concerned with dreams that signify you will go blind (having many eyes, having someone else's eyes, having eyes on the wrong part of your body). Elsewhere, a startling number of different things connote future blindness for the dreamer: the sun disappearing (2.36.4), flying (2.68.7), moles (3.64—the animal, not the skin-condition), lighting a lamp from the moon (5.11), giving birth to two baby girls (5.44), carrying gold (5.90). Numerous other kinds of eye-conditions appear in the *Oneirocritica*,

Fig. 4.2. Confession-stele from Silandus in Lydia (AD 236). *Supplementum Epigraphicum Graecum* 38, 1237. Manisa Museum, Turkey.

Photo: P. Thonemann.

either as underlying conditions or as dream-outcomes: short-sightedness (1.26.1), ophthalmia (2.36.2, 5.9), unspecified eye disease (2.36.3), cataracts (3.39), sore eyes (4.24.4), and crossed eyes (5.67). Almost 10 per cent of the 'historical' dreams in Book 5 have blindness or another eye disease as their outcome (nine out of ninety-five).

The prevalence of blindness in Artemidoran dream-interpretation presumably reflects the realities of life in Roman Asia Minor (Fig. 4.2). Total or partial loss of vision—whether caused by infection, cataracts, or glaucoma—must have been, if not quite as ubiquitous as toothache, a perfectly ordinary part of the experience of ageing in the Roman world. Unlike other disabilities, blindness in Artemidorus has no negative moral connotations, and is not interchangeable with other disabilities or ill-nesses: it is simply a likely outcome of all sorts of dream-events. This appears to reflect a genuine difference in the way that the blind were treated (or are described as being treated) in the real world compared to other disabled persons. In the *Oneirocritica*, the blind are not abandoned to the mercy of the street and the marketplace: they tend to have someone else to help them walk (1.26.10), usually their children (1.26.1) or their slaves (5.20). A dream of blindness can even be said to be auspicious for the destitute, since 'a good number of people come forward to help a blind man, which gives him relief from his troubles' (1.26.2).

Conclusion

In introducing his chapters on the parts of the human body, Artemidorus asked for 'a little indulgence from those who are irritated by the fine distinctions I make' (1.16.3). There was no need to do so. His tour of the human body and its associated symbolic meanings is one of the richest and most compelling parts of the *Oneirocritica*, and this chapter has barely scratched the surface of what an imaginative cultural historian could make of it. A particularly prominent theme of this chapter has been the ways in which gender roles are inscribed, often in slightly unexpected ways, on the human body; this will also be a central motif—albeit from a slightly different perspective—in Chapter 5.

5

Sexuality and Gender

The Truth about Sex

The three long chapters on sex-dreams towards the end of Book 1 of the *Oneirocritica* (1.78–80) have long been recognized as one of the most intellectually coherent and historically important parts of Artemidorus' work. In the opening pages of *The History of Sexuality 3: The Care of the Self*, Michel Foucault correctly identified the *Oneirocritica* as the only extant text from the ancient world 'that presents anything like a systematic exposition of the different forms of sexual acts'. Artemidorus, in Foucault's view, saw the sexual act 'first and foremost as a game of superiority and inferiority', defined by the single act of phallic penetration. The crucial question for Artemidorus was, Who penetrates whom? The key to the symbolic 'meaning' of a sexual act in the *Oneirocritica*, Foucault argued, is not the biological sex of the participants, but their relative social status. Sex is 'good' if the relationship penetrator/penetrated corresponds to a relationship of domination/submission outside the bedroom; if not, it is not.

This brilliant insight has rightly become a central plank of modern understandings of ancient sexuality. In the 1980s and 1990s, it played a major role in the demotion of 'homosexuality' and 'heterosexuality' as categories for understanding sexual preferences and behaviour in the ancient world. By taking sex out of the realm of personal preferences, and tying it so intimately to broader social hierarchies, Foucault succeeded in bringing sexual behaviour right into the mainstream of ancient social history.

Artemidorus' account of sex-dreams is, as we shall see, something of a structuralist tour de force. These three chapters have so often been treated as a uniquely privileged source for Greco-Roman assumptions about sexuality that it is worth wondering how closely they really reflect the 'standard ancient view' (if there was such a thing). John Winkler, for example, believed that we can use the *Oneirocritica* 'to reveal the basic principles of meaning employed by Greek-speaking men around the Mediterranean basin in ancient times to interpret sexual acts', and very firmly nailed the historical value of the text to this assumption of 'typicality':

> The value of his text for us depends on our confident realization that it represents not just one man's opinion about the sexual protocols of ancient societies but an invaluable collection of evidence—a kind of ancient Kinsey report—based on interviews with thousands of clients.

This is, I think, a difficult position to defend, for two reasons. First, the assumption that Artemidorus' chapters on sex-dreams are in fact the result of rigorously inductive reasoning—based *solely* on 'interviews with thousands of clients'—is a very fragile one. That is not to say that these chapters are an entirely a priori construction. My working assumption (here and elsewhere) is that Artemidorus started from what he thought were a few really telling real-life examples, some drawn from his own experience, others from earlier dream-interpreters; from these, he then engaged in some heroic generalization and systematization. As every-where in Books 1–3 of the *Oneirocritica*, it is difficult to tell what is based on data, and where Artemidorus is quietly filling in the blanks.

Second, and more importantly, Artemidorus was not compiling a database of sexual behaviour; he was compiling a database of *dreams* about sexual behaviour and their purported outcomes. This matters, because the sexual protocols of dreams may, *but need not*, directly reflect the sexual protocols of real life. Sex with one's mother is very prominent in the Artemidoran sexual schema: it carries a phenomenally rich and complex set of symbolic meanings, some good, some bad. In real life, sex with one's mother was taboo, full stop. It is *possible* that in real life the biological sex of the participants in a sexual act was always less important than the relative social status of penetrator and penetrated: but this cannot simply be assumed from Artemidorus' choice to prioritize this aspect of sexual relations.

Unnatural Urges

Artemidorus begins by noting—as he occasionally does elsewhere (1.31.1, on teeth; 1.42.2, on hands)—that sex-dreams pose particular problems of subdivision (*diairesis*) (1.78.1). He divides sex-acts in dreams into three basic categories: (1) sex-acts that 'accord with nature (*physis*), law (*nomos*), and custom (*ethos*)'; (2) sex-acts that are 'contrary to law (*nomos*)'; and (3) sex-acts that are 'contrary to nature (*physis*)'. These categories need a bit of unpacking.

(1) Sex-acts that accord with 'nature, law, and custom' consist of the following: (a) penetrating one's wife or mistress (1.78.2); (b) penetrating a prostitute (1.78.3); (c) penetrating a woman one does not know (1.78.4); (d) penetrating a female slave, and penetrating or being penetrated by a male slave (1.78.5); (e) penetrating a female acquaintance (1.78.6); (f) being penetrated by a male acquaintance (1.78.6); (g) masturbating oneself, or (if one is a slave) masturbating one's master (1.78.7). In almost every instance, the dreamer is assumed to be male; the only exception is 1.f, where the dreamer can be male or female.

(2) Sex-acts that are 'contrary to law' fall into two basic subcategories: (a) incest, and (b) giving or receiving oral sex. 'Contrary to law' certainly does not mean 'illegal': oral sex was not illegal. 'Contrary to law' instead signifies something like 'contrary to universally accepted custom', or 'socially unacceptable'. Incest-dreams are further subdivided into (a.i) penetrating or being penetrated by one's son (1.78.8); (a.ii) penetrating one's daughter, with brief analogic comments on penetrating a sister, brother, or friend (1.78.9); and (a.iii) penetrating one's mother (1.79.1–6— an enormously detailed discussion, taking up more than a third of the entire account of sex-dreams). Throughout, the dreamer is assumed to be male: Artemidorus does not tell us what an incest-dream signifies for a female dreamer. Under the heading of dreams about oral sex, Artemidorus discusses (b.i) being fellated by one's mother, by one's wife or mistress, by a friend, relative or child, or by someone one does not know, and (b.ii) performing fellatio or cunnilingus on someone else, male or female, known or unknown (1.79.7); it is unclear whether the dreamer in this last case is conceived only as male. The classification of all

categories of oral sex as 'contrary to law' is one of the more surprising features of Artemidorus' taxonomy; Artemidorus later admits to having been flummoxed by the dreams of two men who—from his perspective—had very bizarre sexual tastes indeed (4.59.1):

> Someone dreamt that he was practising cunnilingus on his own wife: and then again someone dreamt that he was being fellated by his wife. Even after a long time none of the outcomes signified by this sort of dream, and which usually result for other people, had happened to them. As there was no obvious reason for this, I was puzzled, and thought it strange that there should have been no outcome for them. But later on I learnt that both men made a habit of these practices and were not keeping their mouths clean. So it was not surprising that nothing happened to them: they were simply seeing in their dreams what regularly gave them arousal.

(3) Under sex-acts that are 'contrary to nature', Artemidorus recognizes five categories of dreams: (a) having sex with oneself, either auto-penetration or auto-fellatio (1.80.1; cf. 5.31); (b) a woman penetrating another woman (1.80.2); (c) penetrating a goddess, and penetrating or being penetrated by a male god (1.80.3; cf. 5.87); (d) penetrating or being penetrated by a corpse (1.80.4); (e) penetrating or being penetrated by a wild beast (1.80.5). In every case except 3.b and 3.d (where it makes no difference if the dreamer is male or female), the hypothetical dreamer seems to be male. But what exactly does Artemidorus mean by 'contrary to nature'? Elsewhere in the *Oneirocritica*, phenomena described as 'unnatural' (*para physin*) tend to be physical impossibilities, like having two noses (1.27), becoming pregnant as a result of fellatio (1.79.7), or a sparrow changing colour (2.66.2). Some of the sex-acts listed here seem fairly clearly to fall into that category: auto-penetration is the most obvious case, and perhaps also inter-female penetration (since penetration is assumed to be impossible without a penis). But other instances are more problematic. There is nothing physically impossible about penetrating a corpse: the Greek tyrant Periander is said by Herodotus to have had sex with his dead wife Melissa (*Histories* 5.92). Artemidorus seems here to be blurring together sex-acts that are actually *impossible* (auto-penetration, female penetration) and sex-acts that are *outside*

normal human experience, whether because of their extreme moral deviance (necrophilia, bestiality) or their purely mythological character (having sex with a god).

Overall, then, Artemidorus' tripartite categorization of sex-acts is a rough-and-ready combination of the normative and the pragmatic: (1) sex-acts that fall within the realm of ordinary human experience, and are ethically acceptable; (2) sex-acts that fall within the realm of ordinary human experience, but are ethically unacceptable (incest, oral sex); and (3) sex-acts that are outside the realm of ordinary human experience (physically impossible, only attested in myth, or deviant in the extreme), which may or may not be ethically acceptable.

All of this is of course a structuralist's dream: one could make a lovely Venn diagram out of it. But before we turn to the actual meaning of specific sexual acts, we should emphasize two further general (and closely interconnected) points. First, as we have seen, the dreamer of a sex-dream is almost always assumed to be male (only three exceptions, 1.f, 3.b and 3.d). It is true that male dreamers, both as a hypothetical category and as 'real-life' dreamers, enormously outnumber female dreamers throughout the *Oneirocritica* (see below, this chapter). But the under-representation of female dreamers in these chapters is particularly dramatic, especially given the prominence of women in the *content* of sex-dreams. A dream of being fellated by one's mother is very bad indeed for a male dreamer, signifying 'the death of the dreamer's children, the complete loss of his property, and serious illness' (1.79.7): but what does it mean if a mother dreams of fellating her son? Artemidorus does not tell us.

Second, 'sex' for Artemidorus is reducible to a single action: phallic penetration of a bodily orifice. Although in these chapters Artemidorus alternates between a non-specific verb for 'sexual intercourse' (*migēnai*) and a specific verb for 'penetration' (*perainein*), in practice it is penetration (vaginal, anal, and oral) that he has in mind throughout. As Foucault puts it,

> No caresses, no complicated combinations, no phantasmagoria: just a few simple variations around one basic form—penetration. It is the latter that seems to constitute the very essence of sexual practice, the only form, in any case, that deserves attention and yields meaning in the analysis of dreams.

The only exceptions to this 'phallocentric' (or rather 'penetration-centric') approach to sex are Artemidorus' brief comments on masturbation (1.78.7) and his passing recognition that oral sex can be performed on either a man or a woman (1.79.7). As a consequence, the only kind of sex between women that Artemidorus recognizes as a meaningful dream-element is a woman performing phallic penetration on another woman, classified as 'contrary to nature' presumably because it is a physical impossibility (1.80.2: unless Artemidorus has dildos in mind). Other varieties of lesbian sex—just like foreplay of all kinds—are simply passed over in silence, either as symbolically uninteresting or as implicitly 'unclassifiable' within Artemidorus' interpretative schema. (This last point is worth emphasizing, since it is sometimes incorrectly assumed that Artemidorus regarded all sexual acts between females as 'unnatural': this is, I think, a serious misreading of what he actually says.)

Power, Pleasure, Positions

When we turn to the symbolic significance of sex-dreams, the first thing that will strike a modern reader is that the gender of the two parties involved in a sex-act is not *in itself* a significant determinant of the dream's meaning. (Vaginal and anal penetration are nowhere explicitly distinguished, and seem, from Artemidorus' perspective, to be interchangeable.) Instead, whether a sex-dream is auspicious or malign depends, above all, on the relative social statuses of the penetrator and the penetrated. If the penetrator is socially superior, the dream is auspicious, because sexual dominance and social dominance 'conform'; if the penetrator is a social inferior, the dream is malign, since the sexual relationship is 'in conflict with' the social relationship. So when interpreting sex-dreams involving slaves, the gender of the slave is not a salient variable (1.78.5):

> To have sex with one's own slave, female or male, is auspicious, because his slaves are the possessions of the dreamer: so they signify that the dreamer will take natural pleasure in his possessions as they increase in number and value. But to be penetrated by a household servant is not auspicious: it signifies that one will be held in contempt and harmed by that servant.

Likewise, to dream of being penetrated by another man may be good or bad, depending on his age and wealth relative to the dreamer (1.78.6):

> For a man it is auspicious to be penetrated by someone richer and older, as it is usual to receive benefits from such people: but penetration by someone younger and indigent is malign, as it is usual to confer benefits on such people.

In practice, of course, gender and social status normally coincide, since women are assumed to be socially inferior to men. A man normally 'rules' over his wife, as the penetrator *ex hypothesi* 'rules' over the penetrated; it is therefore good for a man to dream of penetrating his wife, so long as she is appropriately willing and submissive (1.78.2):

> To dream of having sex with one's wife, if she is willing, submissive, and not resistant to intercourse, is auspicious for all alike. A wife represents the dreamer's craft or business, from which he derives his pleasure, or else whatever he manages and controls, as he does his wife. The dream signifies profits from these sources—sex gives pleasure, and so does profit. But if his wife resists or will not make herself available, the opposite is signified.

This principle of *mutual willingness* is a significant one in Artemidorus' interpretation of sex-dreams. Non-consensual sex is malign for both the penetrator and the penetrated: 'to be forcibly penetrated by one's son signifies that the dreamer will have harm done to him by his son, harm which will also cause pain to the son' (1.78.8). Conversely, taking pleasure in a sexual encounter is always auspicious for both parties, as Artemidorus explains early in Book 4, where he advises paying close attention to 'the emotional response of the dreamer in the actual dream' (4.4.2):

> A man whose son was sick dreamt that he penetrated his son and took pleasure in it: the boy lived, because when we speak of 'possessing' someone that can refer both to sexual intercourse and to continued ownership, and this outcome was understood as the result of the father's pleasure. Someone else with a sick son dreamt that he penetrated his son, and was distressed that he did so: this boy died, because

we use the term 'corruption' equally of both sexual violation and death, and this outcome was understood as the result of the father's distress.

Similarly, if you enjoy being penetrated by a god, the dream signifies benefits from your superiors; if not, it signifies things which will alarm and upset you (1.80.3). The principle is nicely illustrated in a 'real-life' dream recorded in Book 5 (5.87):

A man dreamt that he was sexually penetrated by Ares. He developed a condition in his anus and rectal passage which could not be cured by any other means, and he submitted to surgery to effect the cure. Ares signified the surgical knife, as we often refer metaphorically to a knife as an 'Ares', and the pleasure the man took in the intercourse indicated that the surgery would not be fatal.

Along with mutual willingness goes the idea of a 'natural' position for sex, which has a strong influence on whether the dream is auspicious or malign. Most of Artemidorus' thinking on the symbolic significance of different sexual positions is clustered in his long account of dreams about sex with one's mother, the outcomes of which 'vary with the various modes of contact and bodily positions adopted' (1.79.1–6). Most favourable is the 'face-to-face' position, which, he says, 'some call the position according with nature (*kata physin*)' (1.79.2). Since this position is 'natural', its connotations are broadly positive: 'the dream has a sick man back on his feet and signifies that he will regain the state which nature intended, as nature is the universal mother of all things, and "as nature intended" is what we say of healthy people, not the sick' (1.79.3).

This 'natural' sexual position is explicitly treated by Artemidorus as analogous to mutual consent and pleasure, since both signify the easy and unquestioned exercise of natural authority (1.79.3):

Just as anyone having sex in accordance with the law of Aphrodite, with a compliant and willing partner, is given authority over every part of her body, so a politician or statesman having this dream ('face-to-face' sex with one's mother) will preside over all the affairs of his city.

Virtually every other sexual position discussed by Artemidorus is profoundly inauspicious. If the mother presents her backside, the dreamer 'will have backs turned on him'; if both parties are standing up, the dreamer will be impoverished (he will lack even a bed); if the mother is kneeling or lying on her front, that signifies destitution, because of her motionlessness. Although Artemidorus thought that dreaming of being 'ridden' by your mother (face-to-face, with the mother on top) had its auspicious aspects (see Chapter 11), he was clearly in a minority: most interpreters took this dream as presaging death (1.79.5).

The categorical malignity of all sexual positions other than 'face-to-face' has the interesting consequence that, according to Artemidorus' own symbolic logic, male-on-male penetration will 'usually' tend to be inauspicious, since, as he blandly says, 'intercourse between men usually involves one party turning his back on the other' (1.78.8). So although penetrating your mother can signify all sorts of good things (depending on the position adopted), penetrating your father is always and uncon-ditionally bad, because he will (usually? necessarily?) present you with his back (1.78.8):

> If anyone dreams of penetrating his own father, he will be exiled from his own homeland or estranged from his father: either the father himself, or the people of his country (the equivalent of a father), will turn their back on him.

I suspect this is why, when Artemidorus analyses dreams about being penetrated by a man unrelated to the dreamer (1.78.6, quoted above), he chooses only to discuss being penetrated, not doing the penetrating. A dream of being penetrated by a man can be unconditionally good (if the penetrator is of higher status than you); but a dream of penetrating another man is always at best ambivalent, because of the negative connotations of the back turned towards you.

Artemidorus goes on to provide a 'naturalistic' explanation for the uniquely favourable connotations of face-to-face sex. To have sex with one's mother in any other position is to commit *hybris* ('violence, degradation'), because each living creature has one and only one 'natural' position for sexual intercourse (1.79.6):

> That men's invention of all these other modes of sexual congress is down to abuse (*hybris*), unbridled lust (*akolasia*), and drunkenness

(*paroinia*), when nature (*physis*) has taught them only the face-to-face position, can be seen from the behaviour of the other animals. All species have their one habitual method of copulation, and they do not deviate from it, because they are following the dictates of nature. So for example some mount from behind, like the horse, donkey, goat, bull, stag, and the other four-footed animals; some first join their mouths, like snakes, doves, and weasels; some do it gradually, like the ostrich; some, like all birds, get on top of the females and use their weight to force them down to the mating position; and some, like fish, have no contact at all, but the females gather up the sperm which the males have extruded. So it is reasonable to suppose that men also have a specific position, which is face-to-face, and that they have invented the others when giving rein to abuse and lust.

This is strong language, and, I think, constitutes a strong argument in favour of the basically heteronormative character of Artemidorus' sexual ethics. Although male–male sexual relations are common enough in the dream-symbolism of the *Oneirocritica*, sex between men is effectively absent from the waking world of dream-outcomes: we find only a man penetrating a male slave (1.78.7), a fleeting mention of boy-prostitutes (4.66), and three contemptuous mentions of men who enjoy being anally penetrated (the catamite or *kinaidos*: 2.12.14, 3.29, 5.65). It is worth noting the symbolic connection that Artemidorus draws between male–male anal penetration and physical injury (*blabē*): 'anyone dreaming of penetrating a friend will turn him into an enemy, for injuring him without previous cause' (1.78.9). Roman Asia Minor in the second century AD was no prelapsarian paradise of sexual liberation.

Women's Dreams

As we have seen, although women are ubiquitous as the *object* of sex-dreams in the *Oneirocritica*, they are only twice envisaged as the possible *subject* of a sex-dream (1.78.6, 1.80.2; also 1.80.4, where the dreamer can be male or female). This is no momentary blind spot. Women are a distinctly marginal class of dreamer throughout the *Oneirocritica*: they appear as 'real-life' dreamers only some twenty-five times in total (and often, as at 4.67, in ways that provoke some scepticism about their existence). When one reflects that Artemidorus includes fifteen real-life dreams seen by athletes or their fathers (a vastly smaller demographic than women), this is not an impressive haul. Even as a hypothetical category of dreamer, women are very far from prominent: only some forty-three dream-elements in the whole *Oneirocritica* (around 2 per cent of the total) carry a meaning specific to female dreamers, to which we might add a further fourteen dream-elements which are said to mean the same thing for both men and women. The marginalization of women as dreaming subjects even extends to the manner in which Artemidorus introduces his 'real-life' female dreamers. Male dreamers are often identified by their real names and professions; but when it comes to female dreamers, Artemidorus follows the old Greek social convention of not identifying women by their given name, but only in relation to their husband or father ('the fuller's wife', 4.33.4; 'the wife of Diognetus', 4.83.1).

Women are certainly not the only social group to be sidelined in this way. Children, despite their large presence as the objects of parents' hopes and fears, are an even more striking absence among the dreamers of the *Oneirocritica* (only 1.16.2, 1.30.3, and—less specifically—1.50.2). Perhaps Artemidorus did not see children as capable of having predictive dreams at all. But given Artemidorus' willingness to give extensive airtime to the dreams of non-elite social groups (artisans, the poor, and slaves: Chapter 11), the under-representation of women among the dreamers of the *Oneirocritica* is especially eye-catching.

'A person's dreams', says Artemidorus, 'will not present him with a vision of things he has never thought about: even at the personal level people have not had predictive dreams about matters never in their thoughts' (1.2.11). To judge from the women's dreams in the *Oneirocritica*, women's thoughts ran on some very predictable tracks indeed. With monotonous regularity, women's dreams rotate around the themes of childbirth, children, and their relationship with their husband or lover. Among the 'real-life' dream-outcomes in Book 5 (nine of which pertain to female dreamers), we find a woman giving birth to triplets (5.12: all three died), a woman whose son dies (5.37), a woman whose husband leaves her (5.53), a woman unintentionally committing incest with her son (5.63), a woman falling out with her lover (5.80), a woman giving birth to a son, divorcing her husband, and raising her son alone (5.86). Elsewhere, Artemidorus reports women's dreams foretelling that their children will be lost (4.33.4) or become sick (4.24.4), or even that the woman will kill her own child (4.39). Repetitive though these dreams are, some of them have a terrible poignancy (5.73):

> A woman who longed for children dreamt that she saw seven birthing stools floating in the sea. The outcome was that she did have pregnancies, but could not fulfil the role of a mother: the seven children to whom she gave birth all died prematurely when still in their swaddling clothes.

The 'archetypal' woman's dream in the *Oneirocritica* is the dream of giving birth to an animal. Dreams of this kind are very common elsewhere in Greek and Roman literature: one thinks of Clytemnestra's dream of giving birth to a snake (Aeschylus, *Libation-Bearers* 527–35), or of Pericles' mother's dream of giving birth to a lion (Herodotus, *Histories* 6.131). It is clear from Artemidorus' four examples of animal-birth dreams (fish, eagle, snake, goose) that these dreams were a favoured playground for dream-interpreters to show off their ingenuity. Artemidorus lists three possible outcomes of giving birth to an eagle, depending on the social status of the mother (2.20.3: all positive); he gives seven possible outcomes of giving birth to a snake, explicitly in order to give the younger Artemidorus 'practice in the concept of analogy' (4.67: some good, some bad); the 'old authorities' are said to have discussed the significance of a dream of giving birth to a fish (2.18.2). Towards the end of Book 4, Artemidorus paraphrases at some length the ideas of a 'young Cypriot dream-interpreter', who analysed a dream of giving birth to a goose 'into a number of rival outcomes' (4.83.3), no doubt as a theoretical exercise like Artemidorus' account of snake-birth dreams.

In the intervals between child-bearing, child-rearing, and servicing their husbands, the women of the *Oneirocritica* are presumed to engage in productive household labour. (For Artemidorus' views on work more generally, see Chapter 11.) The standard variety of women's work is textile-weaving (4.40):

Here is a dream you can store away to demonstrate that work has the same meaning as life. A woman dreamt that she had finished the web on her loom. She died on the following day. She had no more work to do, which meant no more life to live.

Artemidorus describes the different types of loom in surprising detail, suggesting that the technology was entirely familiar both to him and his readers (3.36). He assumes that women's household work is undertaken for the benefit of their male relatives (2.24.2):

A pickaxe (*axinē*) and a hoe (*amē*) signify women and women's work—women's work because their function is to bring things in for the benefit of the man who has them in his hands, and women because of the gender of the words for them.

The point here is presumably that a man wields a pickaxe or hoe in a 'pulling' or 'gathering' motion, just as he uses his wife (whom he has 'in his hands') to accumulate household goods.

It is worth reflecting on Artemidorus' claim that the words for these two tools (*axinē* and *amē*) in themselves indicate their symbolically 'feminine' character. (On gender-signifiers in the *Oneirocritica*, see also Chapter 4.) In Greek, as in Latin and German, all nouns have one of three grammatical genders: masculine, feminine, or neuter. In Artemidorus' system of equivalences between dream-objects and real-life outcomes, when a dream-object signifies a person, the grammatical gender of the dream-object very often determines the biological sex of the person that it signifies in real life (e.g. 1.74.2, 1.77.5, 2.12.12, 2.31.1, 3.12, 3.33—but examples are legion). Only three times does Artemidorus bother to make this rationale explicit (2.24.2, 3.35, 4.83.3); usually he leaves it implicit, presumably as being too obvious to be worth mentioning. His habitual silence on the subject is revealing, and suggests that he and his readers were used to seeing grammatical gender as implying a slight 'sexing' of the objects concerned.

One of the most impressive parts of Artemidorus' account of sex-dreams—intellectually impressive, not morally impressive—involves a virtuosic symbolic connection between grammatical gender and what he regards as 'normal' relations between the sexes. He is talking about dreams of face-to-face sex with one's mother (1.79.3):

> This dream is auspicious for every artisan and labourer. A man's trade is commonly called his 'mother', so coupling with this 'mother' can only mean keeping busy and earning a living from one's trade (*technē*). It is auspicious too for every politician and statesman, because a mother symbolizes one's homeland (*patris*). So just as anyone having sex in accordance with the law of Aphrodite, with a compliant and willing partner, is given authority over every part of her body, so a politician or statesman having this dream will preside over all the affairs of his city (*polis*).

A mother signifies one's trade (*technē*), homeland (*patris*), and city (*polis*), three nouns of feminine gender. Face-to-face sex with a willing partner ('in accordance with the law of Aphrodite') is seen as involving dominance of the female (the penetrated) by the male (the penetrator). Hence dreams of this kind are wholly auspicious, since the 'normal' power relationship between the sexes (men have authority over women) corresponds both to a power relationship in a sex-act (consensual face-to-face penetration) and to a power relationship in the public sphere (rule over a *polis*). This casual assumption that men naturally 'rule' over women is pervasive in the *Oneirocritica*: for a man to dream of consensual sex with his wife is auspicious, because she represents 'whatever he manages and controls, as he does his wife' (1.78.2). One of the least attractive parts of the *Oneirocritica* is a chapter on delivering and receiving beatings, where the exercise of physical violence is a symbolic reflection of dominance and authority in social relationships (2.48):

> Beating people is only auspicious if the beating is done to those over whom one has authority. The exception is one's wife: if she is beaten, that means that she is an adulteress. All others receiving a beating do so to the benefit of the man dealing the blows. But it is not auspicious to beat those over whom one does not have authority: this foretells some punishment under the law. To be beaten oneself is not auspicious if this beating is done by the gods, by the dead, or by those under one's authority... I myself have observed such an outcome in my own

experience. I dreamt once that I was being physically abused by my wife. On that day an offensive man came up to me. I was annoyed and put in a foul mood, and it was only to be expected that someone abused by an inferior who owed him respect should be displeased or aggrieved by the incident.

This is one of only three dreams in the *Oneirocritica* dreamed by Artemidorus himself (1.19, 2.59.2). And aside from the fact that she bore him a son (the younger Artemidorus), this is, I think, the one and only thing that we know about Mrs Artemidorus—that she was, in her husband's considered view, 'an inferior who owed him respect'. One wonders what she would have made of her husband's cheerful claim that a horse resembles a wife 'in that it prides itself on its beauty and supports a mount' (1.56.7, cf. 4.Pref.8).

6

The Natural World

Nature and Culture

Towards the end of Book 2 of the *Oneirocritica*, Artemidorus gives a long account of dreams about flying. Naturally enough, dreams of flight usually signify travel abroad. If you dream of flying neither too low nor too high, but at a height from which you can see the features of the land below, the character of the landscape reflects the kinds of experience you will have on your travels (2.68.4):

> So, for example, plains, ploughland, towns, villages, fields, all forms of human activity, lovely rivers, lakes, a calm sea, harbours, ships running before a fair wind—all these sights prophesy an auspicious time abroad. But glens, ravines, wooded valleys, rocks, wild animals, river torrents, mountains, cliffs—these foretell nothing but a malign experience of travel abroad.

Imaginary 'bird's-eye views' of the world have a long history in Greco-Roman thought, from the Shield of Achilles in Homer's *Iliad* (18.468–617) to the Dream of Scipio in the sixth book of Cicero's *De re publica*. But panoramic visions of the earth from above seem to have had a particular vogue in the Antonine and Severan periods (mid-second to early third centuries AD). Bird's-eye perspectives become increasingly common in Severan art, the most famous example being the *Forma Urbis Romae*, a vast marble map of the city of Rome fixed to an interior wall of the Vespasianic Temple of Peace in Rome. The Greek satirist Lucian of Samosata, writing under the Antonine emperors, was especially fond of bird's-eye views of the inhabited world, which play a prominent role in his *Icaromenippus* (especially chapter 12) and Charon (especially chapters 6 and 15). In his Meditations, the emperor Marcus Aurelius reflects that 'when your talk is about mankind, view earthly things as if looking down on them from some high point above—flocks, armies, farms, weddings, divorces, births, deaths, the hubbub of the law-courts, desert places, various foreign nations, festivals, funerals, markets; all the medley of the world and the ordered conjunction of opposites' (7.48, expanding on Plato, *Sophist* 216c).

Artemidorus' own aerial vision of the world sets up a sharp division between auspicious and malign landscapes. Positive connotations attach to landscapes that are *flat* (plains, fields, rivers and lakes, a calm sea) while *rugged* terrain of all kinds (ravines, mountains, cliffs) is seen as inauspicious. Similarly, it is *cultivated* nature, transformed and tamed by human activity, that foretells success (ploughland, towns and villages, a sea that carries ships), while *uncultivated* nature (wooded valleys, rocks, wild animals) connotes only danger.

Artemidorus was no Romantic; he saw no grandeur or sublimity in wild landscapes. When he has cause to speak about dreams of uncultivated landscapes, exactly the same picture emerges: mountains and forests are bad, marshlands are only good for those who make their livelihood there, and you are best advised to get back into flat and unwooded terrain as fast as possible (2.28.1):

> Marshland is only beneficial for shepherds: for others it is indicative of unemployment, and for travellers it puts obstacles in their path, because there are no roads through it. Mountains, valleys, glens, ravines, and forests signify for everyone discouragements, fears, upsets, and periods without work; for slaves and criminals, tortures and beatings; and for rich men loss of property, because there is felling in those places and always something being lost. It is always more auspicious to dream of traversing these places, finding the paths in them, and getting down from them to the plains—and to wake up when one is no longer in that terrain.

The crossing of mountain-ranges—'traversing these places, finding the paths in them, and getting down from them to the plains'—was a necessary evil for Artemidorus and the inhabitants of western Asia Minor. The single most heavily used Roman road in the province of Asia was probably the great west–east highway running inland from Ephesus along the Maeander valley; within half an hour of leaving

Ephesus, anyone travelling along this road necessarily had to cross over the thickly wooded hills of Mt Thorax. The only constructive human activity that Artemidorus recognizes as characteristic of mountainous zones is the felling of trees. The geographer Strabo (writing around the turn of the era) describes the great mountain ranges of western Asia Minor as 'good for game and timber' (14.1.12, 33), and this reflects the normal Greco-Roman view of mountains and woodland as simply a resource to be exploited. Mountain-dwelling hunters and wood-cutters must have been a common sight at Artemidorus' native Daldis: an inscription of the second century BC records the existence of two so-called 'hunters' settlements' (*katoikiai kynēgōn*) in the wooded hills to the north of Daldis (*SEG* 57, 1150).

This unsentimental view of the natural world runs through the entire *Oneirocritica*. The positive values that Artemidorus ascribes to landscape, flora, and fauna are almost entirely instrumental. If an animal, plant, or natural feature is useful to humans, its symbolic significance is positive; if not, it is not. One of the more startling features of his lengthy analysis of animal-dreams in Book 2 is that each of its three major subsections—on land animals, fish, and birds—is prefaced by a short account of dreams about suitable hunting equipment: staked nets, traps, and snares (2.11.2); fishing-nets, lines, and hooks (2.14.1); birdlime and cloud-nets (2.19). Artemidorus does not feel the need to justify this: he simply assumes that one's main reason for being interested in animals is in order to catch and eat them.

Animals

Artemidorus' taxonomy of the animal kingdom (2.11–22) is unmistakeably that of a layman, not a scientist. His discussion is divided into three broad sections, on terrestrial animals (2.11–13), fish (2.14–18), and birds (2.19–22). The first section, he tells us, will be subdivided into those animals with two feet, no feet, and four feet (2.11.3); in fact, only the latter two groups are treated in detail.

Quadrupeds fall into two categories: the tame and domestic animals (2.11.3–12.5—dogs, sheep, goats, horses, etc.) and wild animals (2.12.6–17—lions, bears, elephants, etc.). In virtually all cases, domesticated animals are auspicious, and wild animals are malign. Although there are a handful of exceptions (e.g. goats are bad, 2.12.2), Artemidorus is prepared to elevate this to the status of a general principle: 'as a common rule, you should take all tame and domesticated animals as referring to one's family and friends, and all wild animals as referring to one's enemies, or a disease, an unpleasant time, or a business failure' (4.56.6); 'there is an analogy between all wild animals and one's enemies' (2.12.10).

After a brief account of footless land-animals (2.13: snakes), Artemidorus turns to sea-creatures (2.14–18), encompassing a few other characteristically 'watery' animals (frogs and sea-birds, 2.15 and 2.17). Although the total number of sea-creatures listed here is truly spectacular (some sixty distinct species in 2.14 alone, no doubt reflecting the rich sea-fishing industry at Ephesus: see Chapter 7 below), the symbolism of fish is strikingly underdeveloped by contrast with either land-animals or birds. Artemidorus' procedure here is to group sea-creatures into certain broad categories—small fish, colourful fish, fish without scales—and then offer a single symbolic meaning for the entire category (fish without scales 'signify the dreamer's hopes slipping away from him', 2.14.8). Artemidorus' instrumental view of animals is especially clear in this section: the meaning of fish is determined by how easy it is to catch them (2.14.2, 2.14.7–8), or whether they upset your stomach (2.14.5), and fresh fish are always better than dead fish, 'either catching them alive oneself, buying them from others, or eating them served at one's table' (2.18.1).

Finally, Artemidorus turns to birds (2.20–1) and other flying creatures (2.22), beginning with raptors (2.20.2–6), then a miscellany of other birds (2.20.6–2.21). Artemidoran bird-symbolism is more complex than for any other category of living thing, reflecting the rich Graeco-Roman tradition of bird-observation and bird-lore. Both Artemidorus and his readers were clearly intimately familiar with the peculiar habits of dozens of different bird-species: as Jeremy Mynott puts it in his wonderful *Birds in the Ancient World*, 'how many people now would know from personal experience about the migratory habits of cranes and quails (2.20.8, 3.5), the different predatory strategies of hawks and kites (2.20.6), or the vocal range of ravens (2.20.6, 4.32, 4.56.4)?' To take only a single example, here is Artemidorus on the symbolism of cranes and storks (2.20.8):

Fig. 6.1. A white stork at Ephesus.
Photo courtesy of Kemal Buluş.

Cranes and storks seen congregating in flocks signify attacks by brig-
ands or enemies. If they appear in a dream in winter, they bring on a
storm, and if in summer, a drought. Seen in isolation and singly, cranes
and storks are auspicious for travel abroad and return from travel,
since these birds set off on their own travels and migrate at the turn of
the seasons. And they are auspicious also for marriage and the procreation of children, because they produce their young from a monogam-
ous union: storks are particularly apposite for the procreation of
children because of the care that the offspring take of their parents.

The storks still visit Ephesus every year between March and September
(Fig. 6.1)—their huge nests are strung along the tops of the ruined
Roman aqueduct at nearby Selçuk—but it is hard for us today to imagine
quite how dramatic an event their great annual migrations between the
Danube and East Africa must have been for the ancient inhabitants of
the Aegean basin. When Homer wishes to evoke the densely packed
ranks of Achaean spearmen pouring forth onto the plain of Scamander,
it is the endless migrant flocks of cranes and storks that spring to his
mind (*Iliad* 2.459–65):

Like the great flocks of flying birds—geese, or cranes, or long-necked swans—in an Asian water-meadow, by the streams of Kaÿstrios, which wheel this way and that in their wings' glory, and the meadow echoes to their cries as they settle in tumult: so the many companies of men poured out from their ships and their huts onto the plain of Skamandros.

We have Patrick Leigh Fermor to thank for an incomparable description of the 'straggling interminable armadas' of storks heading south across the Balkans in their September migration; the cranes, so he was told, were an even more eerie sight as they crossed high over the Cretan mountains, 'that endless caravan lasting for hours stretching beak to tail from one edge of the sky to the other so high above Mt Ida as to be almost out of sight, but accompanied by a strange unearthly sound like a far-away conversation'.

On the whole, Artemidorus' account of animal-dreams in Book 2 is not a very satisfactory one. The subject is just too complex and capacious to fit neatly into his tripartite schema (tame and wild terrestrial, marine, avian). Some categories of animal (notably sea-fish) end up being treated at a length completely incommensurate with their symbolic interest, while other animals slip between the cracks of his schema and have to be slotted in awkwardly later on. Mice and weasels, for example, turn up only as an afterthought in Book 3 (3.28.1). Their omission from the main section on animal-dreams in Book 2 presumably reflects the fact that mice are 'domestic' (house-dwellers) but not domesticated, and hence are neither 'tame' nor 'wild': Artemidorus neatly interprets them as signifying household slaves, who are neither family and friends ('tame'), nor enemies ('wild'). Insects and arachnids fail altogether to fit into Artemidorus' taxonomy: venomous spiders, scorpions, and centipedes are squeezed in briefly after venomous snakes (2.13.6); bees, wasps, locusts, and flying beetles appear at the end of the discussion of birds (2.22); various other bugs are bundled together pell-mell early in Book 3 (3.6–8: ants, lice, worms, bedbugs, mosquitoes); and cicadas end up getting a chapter of their own (3.49), largely based on the rich mythology of the cicada (Plato, *Phaedrus* 258e–259d).

How should animal-dreams be interpreted? In Book 4 of the *Oneirocritica*, where Artemidorus tries to formulate systematic guidelines for interpreting broad categories of dreams, he gives the following general rule (4.56.1):

> You must also set the characteristics of animals alongside their human counterparts, and look in every case at the correspondence of mentality and habit. So, for example, those animals which are proud, bold-spirited, enterprising, and formidable—such as the lion, tiger, leopard, elephant, eagle, harrier—foretell men of the same type.

The basic principle is straightforwardly anthropomorphic: each animal corresponds to a particular kind of person, based on a resemblance of habits, appearance, or both. So small venomous creatures (widow spiders, water-snakes, lizards) signify 'small men who are easy to ignore, but still have the capacity to do people harm' (4.56.2). Nocturnal creatures are inauspicious, not because the night-time is bad in itself, but because people who are active at night tend to be adulterers or thieves (4.56.4, 3.65). Where habits and appearance point in two different directions, the animal can signify two different kinds of person (4.56.5): a leopard is noble in its habits, but patterned in appearance, so can signify either a powerful nobleman or a duplicitous person (2.12.7; 4.56.1–2). Likewise, a partridge is beautiful in appearance, and so can signify an aesthete or a beautiful woman (4.56.2); but it can also signify 'godless, impious women who never show any loyalty to the men who support them, since partridges are hard to tame, speckled, and the only birds with no respect for the gods' (2.46).

The classification of animals in terms of human characteristics was a standard feature of Greek thought in Artemidorus' day: in his *Physiognomy*, Polemo of Laodicea (AD *c*.88–144) included a long list of correspondences between animal species and human personality-types ('the partridge is evil, strong, deceitful, and disputatious'). In practice, this simple approach ('interpret animals as if they are people') is applied only sporadically in Artemidorus' extended survey of the animal kingdom at 2.11–22. Some categories of animal do indeed usually stand directly for kinds of person—so most birds correspond to a particular personality-type or profession (swans are musicians, pelicans are coarse foolish men, pigeons are whores: 2.20.7–9), as do many of the land-animals, both domestic and wild (lions signify one's superiors, bears signify women, monkeys signify rogues and cheats: 2.12.6–2.13). But other categories of animal tend not to be anthropomorphized in this way. Fish are the most striking example: in the whole of the long chapter on fish-dreams (2.14, also 2.16, 2.18), not one type of fish stands in directly for a kind of person. Multicoloured fish signify not deceitful people (as leopards do), but 'deceptions and intrigues' in the abstract (2.14.3); morays, eels, and congers signify not slippery people, but 'wasted labour and hopes unfulfilled' (2.14.7). Even the amiable dolphin, sacred to Apollo, lover of music, signifies only 'that a wind will blow from the direction of the dolphin's appearance' (2.16, similarly Pliny, *Natural History* 18.361).

It is hard to say why Artemidorus was so unwilling to see dream-fish as 'symbolic people'. This category-distinction is not unique to Artemidorus: in Greco-Roman metamorphosis-myths, humans are very often transformed into birds, rather less often into quadrupeds, insects, or other land-animals, and (dolphins aside) almost never into fish. No doubt the muteness of fish (emphasized at 2.14.2) was one significant factor: in his *Physiognomy*, Polemo characterizes fish as 'ignorant, timid, without evil, and silent'. Unlike quadrupeds and (particularly) birds, whose songs and grunts were conceived by ancient thinkers as closely analogous to human speech, fish are stubbornly uncommunicative, and are thus situated at a further remove from human society (Aristotle, *History of Animals* 4.9). Dream-animals speak to the dreamer fairly often in the *Oneirocritica* (2.12.18, 2.13.1, 2.20.2, 2.69.2, 4.32), but fish never do. Symptomatically, the closest Artemidorus comes to a direct analogy between a fish and a person is when he tells us that 'if a pregnant woman imagines giving birth to a fish, according to the old authorities the child she produces will be dumb' (2.18.2).

The habits and appearance of particular species are the most normal determinants of animal symbolism, but they are not the only operative features. Here, for example, is Artemidorus on dreams about bears (2.12.8):

> A bear signifies a woman, because the mythographers who have written about metamorphoses say that Callisto the Arcadian was transformed into this animal. It also signifies disease because of its savage nature, and movement and travel abroad, because it shares its name (*arktos*)

with the constellation which is in constant movement. And then again it can foretell circulation confined to the same locality, because this constellation is always revolving in the same place and never sets.

The meaning of a dream-bear may be determined in the normal 'habit-based' manner: bears are savage, so the outcome for the dreamer will be unpleasant. But Artemidorus is also happy with the idea that its meaning may derive from Greek myths about bears (an unusually feeble connection: because a woman was once transformed into a bear, a bear can symbolize a woman), or even by the behaviour of the constellation *Ursa Major* (the Great Bear; cf. 2.11.4, dogs and the 'dog star'). (Artemidorus later expresses some qualms about myth-based readings of animal-dreams: see 2.66 on the swallow, discussed in Chapter 2.) Likewise, as so often in the *Oneirocritica*, etymology and wordplay can always trump any other principle of interpretation: a weasel signifies a law-suit, because the letters of the Greek words for weasel (*galē*) and lawsuit (*dikē*), when considered as numerals (*alpha* = 1, etc.), both add up to 42 (3.28.3). A similarly arbitrary procedure determines the meaning of dreams about wolves (2.12.11):

A wolf signifies a year, because of its name (*lykos*). A poetical word for 'years' is *lykabantes*, derived from a particular aspect of the animals' behaviour: when crossing a river they always follow one another in an orderly line, just as the sequence of the seasons brings about the completion of a year's cycle. A wolf also signifies an enemy who is violent, predatory, malicious, and openly aggressive to the dreamer.

The term *lykabas* does indeed turn up in Homer's *Odyssey* (14.161, 19.306), meaning either 'year' or 'month' (the context does not make it clear). The true etymology of the term is in fact uncertain, though I think we can be fairly confident that Artemidorus' suggestion ('wolf-crossing', from *lykos*, 'wolf', and *bainein*, 'to go') is way off the mark. Although this procedure is certainly not restricted to animal-dreams in the *Oneirocritica*, we can only be struck by Artemidorus' willingness to let this obscure etymology determine the primary meaning of the dream-element.

Plants

For all of its problems, Artemidorus' account of animal-dreams is a masterpiece of organization and intellectual coherence by comparison with his treatment of plants. Artemidorus evidently struggled to decide where to fit plants into his 'life-cycle' approach to dream-symbolism in his original two-book *Oneirocritica* (see further Chapter 2), and his treatment of plants ends up split across four discrete sections of Books 1 and 2. His first discussion of plant-dreams comes in his account of 'trade-dreams' at 1.51–2, which begins, naturally enough, with farming, the chief occupation of most people in the ancient world (1.51.2):

> To cultivate, sow, plant, or plough the land is auspicious for those intending to marry and for those without children. A field for plough-ing can only mean a wife, and seeds and plants the children—wheat for boys, barley for girls, pulses for miscarriages. For everyone else a farming dream signifies hard labour and misery. And if anyone in the dreamer's house is sick, that person will die: seeds and plants have earth heaped over them, and so do the dead. Dreams of reaping, fruit-picking, or pruning, if seen when those activities are out of season, mean the postponement of all business and initiatives until that proper time and season has come.

This symbolic interpretation of wheat, barley, and pulses (boys, girls, miscarriages) reflects both the grammatical gender of the relevant Greek words ('wheat' is masculine, 'barley' feminine, and 'pulse' neuter—a common principle of dream-interpretation in the *Oneirocritica*: see Chapter 5) and a standard Greek culinary hierarchy (wheat for the rich, barley for the masses, beans for the poor: cf. 1.69).

Artemidorus' second discussion of plants comes in his section on food and drink, where he treats in sequence vegetables (1.67), legumes and cereals (1.68–69), meat (1.70–71), cakes (1.72), and fruit (1.73). The third section comes a few chapters later, where he tackles a slightly different selection of plants in his account of dreams about wreath-wearing (1.77: mostly flowers and herbs, but also dates, olives, oak, and others). That Artemidorus should dedicate a lengthy chapter to wreath-dreams is

unexpected and very interesting; that such a large proportion of Artemidoran plant-symbolism should end up being concentrated in this
chapter is truly startling (more on this shortly).

His fourth and final stab at the topic comes mid-way through Book 2,
where he returns a second time to agriculture-dreams (2.24.1), awkwardly acknowledging the overlap with his earlier account in Book 1
('I have already spoken of the significance of sowing, planting, and
ploughing in the section on trades; I shall now deal with other things
which relate to agriculture'). After a short discussion of tools associated
with arable agriculture (2.24: plough, yoke, sickle, etc.), he turns to trees
and shrubs (2.25, also 4.57), focusing on non-fruiting trees (cypress,
pine, box, etc.) to avoid overlap with his earlier discussion of fruit.
Artemidorus rounds off this second discussion of agriculture with a
section on manure (2.26), before moving on to other matters.

Inevitably, this scattered account leads to a fair amount of repetition
and inconsistency. The olive turns up three times, each time with a
slightly different set of connotations (1.72.2, 1.77.5, 2.25.1); in Book 4,
when Artemidorus briefly returns to the symbolism of trees and shrubs,
the olive means something else again (4.57.1: death for the sick), and
when an olive tree appears in a dream in Book 5, it has yet another new
connotation (5.18: philosophy).

In Book 4, Artemidorus offers a few general principles for the interpretation of tree- and plant-dreams. Some of these principles are very
simple and literalistic: slow-growing trees (oak, olive, cypress) bring
things to pass slowly (4.11.1); tall plants (cypress, pine, vine-prop) tell
the dreamer to take a long view (4.11.3); long-lived trees signify tardiness
(4.57.2). Practical usefulness is the main thing that determines whether a
given plant is auspicious or malign: 'in general all cultivated fruiting trees
are more auspicious than the wild varieties, and the evergreen fruiting
trees more auspicious than the deciduous ... trees which do not fruit are
less auspicious, except for those whose work is directly or indirectly
dependent on them' (4.57.1). Artemidorus conceives of plants in entirely
instrumental terms, as material for food (1.67–73), wreaths (1.77), or (in
the case of trees) ship-building and other construction-work (2.25.2–3).
Wild and uncultivated plants are therefore completely absent from the
Oneirocritica: even thorns and brambles are only considered in their
function as hedges for closing off a property (4.57.3, cf. 3.33). His

treatment of non-fruiting deciduous trees in Book 2 illustrates the principle nicely (2.25.3):

> Planes, black poplars, elms, beeches, ash-trees, and all similar trees are advantageous only for people setting out to war, and for carpenters— for the former because weapons are made from their wood, and for the latter because carpenters' work depends on them. For others they are indicative of poverty and deprivation, because these trees bear no fruit.

Aside from practical usefulness, the other main determinant of the meaning of a plant-dream is mythology—only occasionally brought into play for animals, but very common in the interpretation of plant-dreams. As Artemidorus puts it, 'trees have the same meaning as their fruits and as the god to whom any given tree is sacred' (4.57.1). Associations with particular gods, myths or festivals determine the significance of barley-bread (1.69: gift of gods), apples (1.73.1: Aphrodite and Eris), pomegranates (1.73.4: Persephone), narcissus-flowers (1.77.2: Narcissus), celery (1.77.4, 5.7: Nemean games), myrtle (1.77.5: Demeter and Aphrodite), vine and ivy (1.77.8: Dionysus), laurel (2.25.2: Apollo and Daphne), fir (2.25.2: Boreas and Pitys), white poplar (2.25.3, 5.74: Heracles), asphodels (3.50: Hades), and olives (5.18: Athena). When no relevant divine association comes to mind, Artemidorus turns to wordplay as a last resort: the pea (*pisos*) signifies persuasion (*peithō*) (1.68), and 'melons (*pepones*) are auspicious for friendships and reconciliations, because in the poets *pepon* is used as a term of endearment: but for business deals they mean failure, because anything which flops is called a melon' (1.67.3).

As we saw earlier on, Artemidorus normally sees animals through the eye of the hunter, fisherman, and fowler; similarly, his view of plants is in almost all respects a 'farmer's-eye view'. Farmers are a very common category of dreamer in the *Oneirocritica* (twenty-two times in Books 1 and 2 alone); they are usually conceived as primarily arable farmers, though more specialized cultivators are occasionally specified (1.67.3, 'vine-growers'; 2.37.7, 'farmers who cultivate fruit-trees'). The outcome of malign dreams, as one would expect, is usually crop-failure (five times in Books 1 and 2), reflecting the prime anxiety of the working farmer. Artemidorus casually assumes that his readers will be familiar with the rhythms of agricultural life: early in Book 4, when he is casting around for an example of dream-elements specific to particular times of year, it is the scythe and hoe that come to mind (4.2.6).

A fairly common dream-pattern in the *Oneirocritica* is the image of a cultivated plant (usually wheat) growing from a part of the dreamer's body (1.24.2, 3.46, 5.18, 5.39, 5.63, 5.84). That this was in reality a fairly common dream-type in antiquity is suggested both by its frequency in the *Oneirocritica* (particularly among the 'real-life' dreams of Book 5), and by Artemidorus' uncharacteristic hesitancy about what the dream signifies (3.46): the observed outcomes of this dream seem not to have fitted into a satisfyingly neat pattern. One of these plant-growing dreams gives a vivid picture of the dangers of life in the remote Anatolian countryside (5.84):

> A man dreamt that stalks of wheat had grown out of his chest, and then someone came along and pulled them out as if they had no business to be there. The man had two sons, and they met with a cruel fate: they were living out on the farm, and a band of robbers attacked and killed them. The stalks of wheat signified his sons, and their removal signified the taking of his sons' lives.

The typical farmer of the *Oneirocritica* seems to be an independent small-holder, sometimes with his own dependent work-force (1.31.1: a farmer with an all-male household), although the fears of eviction that plague some farmers may indicate lease-holding (2.9.6, 2.53.2). Shepherds are very seldom mentioned as a class of dreamer, and never in a way that suggests they were among Artemidorus' regular clientele (2.28.1, 3.34.2, 3.50.1). Gardens, curiously enough, have strongly negative connotations, apparently because they were seen as profligate or frivolous enterprises (the only plants specifically associated with gardeners are mallow and oleander: 1.77.4): a garden-dream, says Artemidorus, 'is particularly advantageous for brothel-keepers, because of the quantity of seed which is deposited there and the occasional nature of the work: but it exposes all women to the charge of indecency and lasciviousness' (4.11.2).

A Farmer's Dream

Although farmers often appear as a hypothetical class of dreamer in the *Oneirocritica*, only two 'real-life' dreams recorded by Artemidorus are explicitly attributed to farmers. One is the dream just discussed, of the man whose sons were killed by bandits while living on an outlying farm; the other is an unusually rich and beautiful dream, which draws together many of the themes of this chapter (5.74):

A man dreamt that he had been transformed into a huge forked tree, one part white poplar and the other part pine, and then all sorts of birds settled on the poplar, and gulls, cormorants, and all other types of seabird on the pine. The man had fathered two sons, one of whom became a professional athlete because of the white poplar, and travelled the world coming into contact with all sorts of men and different races, and the other, although the son of a farmer, became a shipowner of some note in the seafaring world. The dreamer himself lived out a prosperous life to a great old age.

Metamorphosis into a tree is not in fact treated elsewhere by Artemidorus. But the vast size of the tree is clearly a good sign: it signifies that the dreamer will flourish, and live to an advanced age (cf. 4.11). The two forks of the tree refer to the dreamer's two sons, whose future careers are symbolized by the two species of tree. The white poplar—one of the largest trees to grow in the Aegean—was sacred to Heracles (Pausanias, *Description of Greece* 5.14.2; Vergil, *Aeneid* 8.276–7), and its boughs were used for victory-wreaths at athletic contests, notably the Tlapolemeia on Rhodes (2.25.3). The pine-tree is said elsewhere by Artemidorus to refer to a ship, 'because of the wood used in ship-building and the pitch and resin which come from these trees' (2.25.2). As we have seen, birds in Artemidorus almost always symbolize persons, and so the birds that settle on the two branches of the tree represent the sorts of people who the farmer's two sons will come across in their professional lives: men of all races for the athlete, and other professional seamen for the ship-owner (gulls and cormorants: 2.17).

We have no way of knowing whether this is a real dream, or whether it has been invented (or at least tidied up) by Artemidorus to illustrate his methodology. I am not sure that it matters very much. What matters for us are the symbolic connections which Artemidorus regards as natural or plausible to draw between particular plants and animals and particular outcomes in the human world. These connections are determined by a set of implicit rules, some (not all) of which are highly specific to the Greco-Roman symbolic imagination. Here is a selection of those rules, in no particular order:

1. Plants, animals, and landscapes can all be divided into two broad categories: 'tame/domestic/cultivated' and 'wild/uncultivated'. Things falling into the former category are auspicious, the rest malign.
2. Animals resemble people, and their habits and appearance indicate what kinds of people they resemble. But some animals resemble people more closely than others: birds are particularly close to humans, and fish are furthest away.
3. The positive value of a plant or animal lies in its instrumental usefulness, whether as food, building material, or something else. Useless plants are not interesting.
4. The symbolic character of a plant is very often based on an association with a particular deity or myth; such associations are considerably rarer, and more problematic, for animals (2.66).
5. One of the key determinants of the symbolic character of a plant is the particular social context in which that plant is worn as a wreath (1.77, and often elsewhere). This one is really surprising. Of course, everyone knows that the Greeks and Romans went in for vegetal wreaths: just summon up a visual image of a Greek athlete or a Roman emperor. Civic honours, athletic or military victory, religious office, and a whole range of social statuses could all be expressed through the conferral or wearing of wreaths (see further Chapter 10, on athletic wreaths). But it is still startling to find Artemidorus assigning wreath-symbolism such a central role in determining the significance of particular plant-species. To judge from the *Oneirocritica*, white poplar trees—and roses, celery, dates, myrtle, and many others—only 'mean' anything at all by dint of their use in wreaths.

For us, the chief value of Artemidorus' treatment of plants and animals lies in its status as a uniquely extensive 'lay' account of the natural world. His interpretation of dream-symbols from the natural world is not remotely scientific; rather, it reflects what he expects his contemporaries to associate with particular animals and plants, and so gives us a wonderfully clear picture of the ordinary day-to-day animal- and plant-lore of his day (vines do not flourish near cabbages, 1.67.3; white poplar has something to do with Heracles, 2.25.3). Bird-symbolism in the *Oneirocritica* may strike us as particularly rich, varied, and well-informed—but that is no less than we ought to expect; the casual knowledge that ordinary Greeks and Romans had about birds and their habits is a perpetual surprise and rebuke to the modern reader (the spectacular ornithological carnival of Aristophanes' *Birds* is the best-known example). Unsentimental, radically utilitarian, mildly epicure: Artemidorus brings us as close as we are ever likely to get to the mainstream of ancient Greco-Roman attitudes towards the natural world.

7

Cities of Dreams

Cities without History

For all Artemidorus' interest in the natural world—wild and cultivated plants, domestic and undomesticated animals, the physical landscape—the characteristic human habitat of the *Oneirocritica* is unambiguously an urban one. Farmers and land-owners are a reasonably common category of dreamer in the *Oneirocritica*, but it cannot be said that the lives and lifestyles of the rural population are depicted with any great vividness. In the compendium of ninety-five 'real' dreams in Book 5 of the *Oneirocritica*, only one explicitly has the countryside as the setting for either the dream-vision or the outcome—and it is a rather inauspicious example (two sons, temporarily resident on a remote outlying farm, killed by bandits: 5.84). Artemidorus assumes throughout that the normal sphere of human affairs is the Greek city.

The picture of cities and civic life that Artemidorus provides is very clearly a direct reflection of the realities of the Greek *polis* of his own day. This may seem like a banal point; but in the context of wider Greek literary and intellectual traditions of the Antonine and Severan periods, it is a startling idiosyncrasy. In no other Greek author of the Roman imperial period is the Greek past—above all the Greek *polis* of the Classical period—so totally absent. Artemidorus has no interest in Classical Athens or Sparta: Athens is mentioned once in passing (1.8.2), Sparta never. He never invokes the Persian or Peloponnesian Wars, or the victories of Philip II or Alexander III of Macedon; Marathon and Plataea do not stir his soul; there is no sign he cares much about panhellenism, Classical Greek democracy, or even collective Greek identity. The glorious Classical past of 'true and pure Greece' does not weigh heavily on the Greek *polis* of the *Oneirocritica*.

As we will see in Chapter 12, Rome and the Roman state were not a major focus of loyalty for the people of the *Oneirocritica*; the Roman provinces are, I think, never mentioned at all. Nor does Artemidorus show any interest in the old regional 'ethnic' groups of Asia Minor (Ionians, Lydians, Carians, etc). For Artemidorus, collective identity and a sense of belonging derive purely and solely from one's membership of a living, vibrant *polis*-community, whose ancient history is of no particular interest or importance. Patriotism—love for your home city—is taken as a given, but not because that city is ancient or famous, but because human flourishing depends on living in a city that is populous, well-governed, and wealthy (4.60):

> When dreaming of cities, it is more auspicious to see those which are more familiar, such as home-cities or those in which a successful time has been spent, rather than others. It is less auspicious to see foreign or unfamiliar cities. Likewise, it is auspicious to see any city which is populous, well-governed, and full of the luxuries and all other indicators of a great or prosperous city. But it is not auspicious to see any city, either one's own or other people's, which has been deserted or ruined.

The *Polis* and its Spaces

When Artemidorus thinks of the *polis* as a physical entity, his mind is attracted not so much to types of building (in which he shows very little interest) as to kinds of civic spaces. It is true that early in Book 1 he defines public dreams (*dēmosioi oneiroi*) as those which are concerned with 'harbours, walls, marketplaces (*agorai*), gymnasia, and civic monuments (*koina anathēmata*)' (1.2.5), but in practice it is public spaces, not civic structures, that carry symbolic significance for him. City-walls, for example, appear nowhere else in the *Oneirocritica*.

For Artemidorus, the quintessential arena of *polis*-life, which also carries the most wide-ranging symbolic connotations, is the *agora*, the open public space that served as the city's marketplace, meeting-place, and political centre (3.62):

> A marketplace (*agora*) signifies disturbance and commotion because of the crowd that gathers there. For those who make their living in the

marketplace a dream of a marketplace seething with people and full of noise is auspicious: but an empty and silent marketplace foretells unemployment for them, and for everyone else lasting security. A marketplace which has been sown with a crop is obviously out of bounds to all, whatever the crop sown. Some people say that such a prodigy signifies famine for a city which enjoys prosperity and prosperity for a city experiencing famine. Theatres, streets (*plateiai*), suburbs (*proasteia*), temple precincts, promenades (*peripatoi*), and all public spaces have the same meaning as a marketplace.

As the final sentence indicates, the various public spaces of the Greek *polis* are symbolically interchangeable with one another: what matters is that they are open, accessible, and filled with crowds and noise. The visibility of human action in the *agora* and other public spaces means that these spaces signify public disgrace or public acclaim, depending on what one dreams of doing in them. It is inauspicious to dream of defecating 'in a god's temple, in the marketplace (*agora*), in the street (*plateia*), or in the bath-house' (2.26.4), since this foretells public disgrace; similarly, for a rich man to dream of singing in the *agora* or in the streets (*plateiai*) predicts disgrace and ridicule (1.76.6). By contrast, to dream of being sacrificed 'at the altar of a god, or in public view in the assembly (*ekklēsia*) or the marketplace (*agora*), is auspicious for all, and especially for slaves: they will gain their freedom to public acclaim and recognition' (2.51). For Artemidorus and his clientele, *polis*-life was life lived in the open air, under the judgemental or approving eyes of one's fellow-citizens—a conception which, as we shall see shortly, is also central to Artemidorus' picture of civic offices in the Greek city.

Civic festivals, processions, and theatrical performances were occasions of particularly intense symbolic interest to Artemidorus' clients, since it was here that presenting *la bella figura* to one's fellow citizens was most socially important. Predictably enough, anxiety-dreams in the *Oneirocritica* often take these great public events as their setting: one of Artemidorus' clients dreamt of urinating in full view of his fellow-citizens as they took their seats at the theatre (4.44.2), and another man translated his anxiety about being caught in adultery into a dream about attending the theatre in full make-up (4.41.1). (The world of the theatre is discussed further in Chapter 10.) Mass civic festivals saw the entire body of citizen men and women on full public display, fretting about their appearance and reputation, as in this remarkable dream focused around a religious or civic procession of some kind (5.53):

> A woman dreamt that the slave-girl (*therapaina*) who did her hair borrowed from her the portrait of herself which she owned, painted on a panel, and also her clothes in order to take part in a procession. The immediate result was that by her sly insinuations the slave-girl caused the woman's husband to leave her, and brought financial loss and abuse on the woman herself.

The logic of the dream is obvious enough. For a respectable citizen woman, a great civic procession of this kind is one of the proudest moments of the year, when she gets to show herself off at her finest. What could be more humiliating than for her slave-girl to attend the procession in her place, wearing her clothes, and carrying a painting of her mistress to underline exactly whose slave she is? It is no surprise to find that the dream predicts public disgrace for the woman concerned.

One of the most evocative pictures of civic life in the *Oneirocritica* comes in Artemidorus' analysis of dreams about night-time festivals (3.61):

> All-night carnivals, festivals held at night, and celebrations into the small hours are auspicious for marriages and partnerships, and signify prosperity and acquisition of property for the poor. And likewise it has been observed that they remove their fears and troubles from those who are troubled or afraid of something: there is no way that one will party all night if one is not in full celebratory mood. These festivities do show up adulterers and the women with whom they commit adultery, but no punishment will follow, because what goes on at these all-night carnivals, however uninhibited, is common knowledge among all participants and in a way licensed behaviour. For prosperous people of some distinction in life such a dream brings them embarrassment and scandal which will ultimately cause them no grief.

Nocturnal festivals were a time when the rigid social hierarchy and sexual morality of the Greek *polis* was temporarily lifted. The poor forget their poverty, the anxious forget their troubles, and sexual promiscuity and uninhibited behaviour carry no disgrace—nights when, as the Hellenistic poet Callimachus puts it, a man can kiss 'whichever girl or boy he wants to' (F227 Pfeiffer). Night-time carnivals, tellingly, are one of only a very few dream-elements in the *Oneirocritica* which carry no inauspicious connotations for any category of dreamer, rich or poor.

Masters of the City

At the top of the social hierarchy of the Greek *polis* stand the city's magistrates, priests, and high civic officials. In Book 2, Artemidorus gives a short list of characteristic civic offices that one might dream of holding (2.30.2–6). First comes the office of 'general' (*stratēgos*), here referring not to a military command, but to the chief civic magistracy. Here, as so often, Artemidorus reflects the local realities of the Roman province of Asia in the second century AD. In the cities of western Asia Minor (but not in other parts of the Greek world), the chief executive officials were typically a board of *stratēgoi*, who proposed motions to the assembly, managed public finances, and administered local justice. Throughout the *Oneirocritica*, when Artemidorus is referring to a high civic magistrate, he usually calls him a *stratēgos* (1.2.12; 2.30.2; 4.49; 4.84.1; 5.36).

Next comes the civic secretary (*grammateus*), also a high official in many cities of Asia, Ephesus included (*Acts of the Apostles* 19:35). Artemidorus regards this office as a tiresome one: to dream of being a *grammateus* 'signifies having to concern oneself with other people's affairs which have no personal relevance, and result only in wearisome work for the dreamer with no benefit whatsoever. For someone who is sick this civic office foretells his death, because it is the secretaries who do the carrying out' (2.30.2). This last analogy probably refers to the role of the secretary in introducing motions to the civic assembly (*I.Ephesos* 21, 24B).

Artemidorus then gives a list of four more junior administrative offices (2.30.3): the *astynomos* (superintendent of public works), *paidonomos* (supervisor of boys), *gynaikonomos* (supervisor of women), and *agoranomos* (market-supervisor). The first of these administered municipal works such as roads and fountains, while the second and third (often associated with one another: Aristotle, *Politics* 1300a4) oversaw the conduct of male and female children and adult women. In Asia Minor, the *gynaikonomos* is more widely attested in the Hellenistic period than under the Roman empire, but the office certainly survived down to Artemidorus' day in some cities (such as Miletus: *I.Didyma* 84). The *agoranomos* was the overseer of the civic marketplace, with particular responsibility for managing the food supply and setting the price of staple foodstuffs. Like the office of civic secretary, this was not a desirable function: for most people, to dream of becoming *agoranomos* 'signifies troubles and scandals: even if the *agoranomos* gets things done and spends money without making any personal profit, he will inevitably be criticized, as it is impossible to do the job without incurring criticism' (2.30.3).

This list of magistrates is fairly representative of what would have found in any large or middling city of Asia Minor in the second of third century AD. Perhaps the most surprising omission, both here and elsewhere in the *Oneirocritica*, is the city council (*boulē*) and its members (*bouleutai*), who are almost entirely absent: *bouleutai* never appear as a distinct class of dreamers, and the *boulē* only appears once, as one of the things potentially symbolized by the hearth-goddess Hestia (2.37.16):

> Hestia, both the goddess herself and statues of her, signifies for politicians their city council (*boulē*) and treasury, for private citizens life itself, and for a magistrate (*archōn*) or king (*basileus*) the power of their office.

Throughout the *Oneirocritica*, civic magistrates (*archontes*) are, as here, repeatedly classed alongside kings or emperors (*basileis*—the term can denote both a king and the Roman emperor). As an emperor is to a soldier, and a master is to his slave, so the civic magistrate is to the private citizen (2.12.6). A large snake signifies a king, the master of a house, or a magistrate 'because of its power' (2.13.1). A ram connotes 'the master of a house, a magistrate, or a king', because (or so Artemidorus wrongly believes) the Greek word for 'ram' (*krios*) is cognate with an old Greek word for 'lord' (*kreiōn*) (2.12.1). Kings and magistrates, like the gods, should always be trusted if they speak to you in a dream, because 'to rule is to have the power of a god' (2.69.1).

The authority of the civic magistrate means that civic office can also be treated as analogous to other positions of absolute dominance: the power of gods over men, or the power of a father over his household. It is, we are told, auspicious for a rich man or a grandee to dream of becoming a god: 'the dream foretells the highest public office available to a man of his status, since just like the gods, magistrates too have the power to do people good or harm' (3.13). A dream recorded in Book 5 depends on the analogy between a civic magistrate and the head of a household (5.36):

A man dreamt that he was debarred from the gymnasium by the chief magistrate (*stratēgos*) of his city. His father threw him out of the house. A father has the same significance in a house as the chief magistrate has in a city.

In one remarkable dream recorded by Artemidorus, the twofold comparison between high civic office, the power of the gods, and the person of the Roman emperor is rendered absolutely explicit (4.49):

Any dream of a change for the better is auspicious for the rich, even if someone dreams of changing into a god—but there must be no deficiency in the transformation. For example, someone dreamt that he had become Helios, the Sun-god, and was walking through the marketplace (*agora*) wearing a crown with eleven rays. He was appointed chief magistrate (*stratēgos*) of his city, but died after eleven months in office because his crown did not have the full number of rays.

The man dreamed of walking through the city's *agora* wearing a radiate crown, a diadem or head-band with projecting rays. The radiate crown was a typical attribute of the sun-god Helios in Greco-Roman iconography, and normally had twelve rays, symbolizing the twelve months of the solar year (hence the malign significance of wearing a crown with only eleven rays). But by the late second and early third centuries AD, when Artemidorus was writing, the radiate crown had also become a standard divine attribute of reigning emperors (it is very common in imperial coin-portraits: Fig. 7.1). Since the only human entitled to be depicted wearing a radiate crown was the emperor, it is hard not to see the dream as representing the symbolic elevation of the

Fig. 7.1. Silver *antoninianus* of Caracalla (AD 213–217), RIC IV Caracalla 312C. AR 4.85g, 22.5mm. ANS 1944.100.51525.
Photo courtesy of the American Numismatic Society.

dreamer to 'imperial' status; no doubt the dreamer saw the radiate crown as a generic symbol of power and prominence, translated to the dreamer's own civic context.

For this particular dreamer, high office in his native city was symbolically represented by dramatic public visibility—walking through the *agora* wearing a brilliant imperial crown. Civic magistrates lived their lives on full public display: to dream of being transformed into a woman is inauspicious for a man who is active in politics (*politeuomenos*), not because women are ineligible for office, but 'because for the most part women keep themselves at home, and so this dream will strip the dreamer of all public office' (1.50.3). In the first book of the *Oneirocritica*, Artemidorus records a revealing dream of his own, concerned with a fellow-member of the civic elite of western Asia Minor, presumably at Daldis or Ephesus (1.19):

> I myself once dreamt of an acquaintance of mine, who had been appointed to public office and was blessed with every other good fortune: in my dream I saw him being escorted in the city by the squad (*taxis*) assigned to his support, but the hair on his head was dry and in need of a cut. I deduced that the dream was indicative of grief coming his way, and a few days later he was deposed from his office, which cost him a lot of money and a lot of grief.

As the dream implies, when Artemidorus visualized the success and social esteem of his acquaintance, he pictured him not actually engaged in the exercise of his office (whatever it was), but being escorted in formal procession (*propempomenos*) through the streets of his native city with an entourage of attendants. Greek magistrates did not have the same formal retinue of heralds, lictors, and scribes (collectively known as *apparitores*) enjoyed by civic magistrates in the Roman West, but at least some Greek civic officials had a regular support-staff of public slaves (*dēmosioi*), and that is probably what is referred to here. (The man may perhaps have been an *eirenarchēs*, 'officer of the peace', who would have had a formal staff of 'pursuers', Greek *diōgmitai*, under his command.)

During their tenure of office, senior priests and civic magistrates in Greek cities were visually distinguished from ordinary citizens, both by their accompanying entourage and also by special clothing (often luxurious purple-dyed robes) and headgear (often a golden or gilded wreath). Dreaming of having a big head is auspicious for a rich man who has not yet held office, since 'it foretells some public office, when he will need to wear a wreath, a headband, or a diadem' (1.17). Similarly, for the rich, a dream of being struck by a thunderbolt 'is not harmful to those who will wear a gold wreath because of their tenure of a magistracy or priesthood, but in fact foretells that their conduct in office as magistrate or priest will be all the more distinguished' (2.9.5). To dream of wearing a golden or gilded wreath is, says Artemidorus, 'auspicious for the rich, for politicians, and for candidates for public office', but is malign for a slave, unless the dream also features the ordinary 'accompaniments of a gold wreath, by which I mean purple-bordered clothing and an attendant entourage'—that is to say, the other visual trappings of a high civic magistrate (1.77.7, cf. 2.30.6). Similarly, purple clothing is auspicious for the rich, and 'foretells honours and recognition, because wearing purple is a privilege appropriate to their status'; but for the poor, it foretells imprisonment, because 'anyone wearing purple absolutely requires a diadem or wreath and a full entourage of attendants and guards' (2.3.4).

The prominence associated with public office leads to some odd correspondences in the *Oneirocritica*. To dream of suffering from a disfiguring disease such as scabies, leprosy, or elephantiasis foretells a civic magistracy for a rich or powerful man, since these diseases 'attract attention to those who suffer from them' (3.47.1: see further Chapter 4). No less striking is Artemidorus' claim that dreams of crucifixion (elevation to a high place) can predict appointment to high office: 'to dream of being crucified in a city signifies some public office corresponding to the place where the cross has been erected' (2.53.2). He gives a specific example from his own native Daldis (4.49):

> Location often plays its own part in the outcomes. An example is the case of the man who dreamt that he was crucified (a dream of cruci-fixion signifies fame and wealth—fame because someone crucified is lifted very high, and wealth because of the food he provides for large numbers of birds): in Daldis Menander dreamt that he was crucified in front of the temple of Zeus Polieus ['of the City'], and he was appointed the priest of that same god, to his greater distinction and wealth.

As is abundantly clear from the dreams discussed above, civic magis-tracies were desirable not so much for the actual power that they brought, but rather for the honour and prestige that they brought to the individual. A man was expected to seek public office not in order to fulfil a political programme, but in order to boost his public recognition and status. The most prestigious symbolic honours conferred on civic magistrates at the termination of their term of office were painted portraits (often painted on a gilded shield) and bronze or marble statues, and it is no surprise that both forms of honorific monument are invoked in the *Oneirocritica*. Artemidorus tells us that 'a portrait signifies the dreamer's children, his principles in life, and his character—his children because of their resemblance, and his character and principles because all men take pride in their portraits' (3.31). Such painted portraits were often set up in the city gymnasium, as a public space protected from the elements; in Book 5 of the *Oneirocritica*, Artemidorus informs us of a man who 'dreamt that he went into the gymnasium in his native city and saw there his own portrait, which had actually in real life been set up there in his honour' (5.3). The man dreamt that the frame of the portrait fell apart, and as a result he went lame in both legs. As for statues, Artemidorus simply says that they 'represent the leading men in a city: so whatever statues do or have done to them in a dream predicts that the same will be done by or happen to these civic authorities' (3.63). Dream-ing of being made of bronze is auspicious for athletes and slaves (1.50.5):

> The athlete will be victorious and have a statue made of him, and the slave will be freed, as it is only free men who have bronze statues

erected to them. There is the same significance if someone sees in his dream a bronze image or statue of himself set up in the marketplace (*agora*).

Needless to say, the *agora* was an especially favoured location for honorific portrait statues (whether of victorious athletes or civic magistrates), as being the spot of maximum public visibility in the Greek city.

Elites and Masses

Artemidorus uses a rather varied terminology to refer to politically active members of the Greek civic elite: the 'first men' (*prōteuontes*, 3.63), 'political men' (*politeuomenoi*, 1.50.3; *politeutai*, 1.79.3, 3.16.2), and above all 'leaders of the people' (*dēmagōgoi*, 1.17, 1.77.7, 1.79.3, 3.16.2, 3.42.1). This last term carries none of the negative connotations of the modern 'demagogue': it simply refers to someone who is prominent in civic politics. But this choice of words does reflect a wider assumption in the *Oneirocritica*, namely that the chief distinguishing feature of the politician's activity is his relationship to the people (*dēmos*).

It is true that the citizen assemblies of the Greek city in the Roman imperial period no longer wielded the kind of political authority that they possessed in the democratic cities of the Classical and Hellenistic periods. But voting assemblies of the entire citizen body continued to meet regularly at least down to the later third century AD, and although they could no longer initiate legislation, they could and did make life extremely uncomfortable for civic elites who failed to keep their cities supplied with cheap grain, or who were perceived as profiteering in some way. Dio of Prusa, a leading member of the civic elite at Prusa in Bithynia under Trajan (AD 98–117), gives a vivid picture of the difficulty of keeping a volatile assembly-meeting under control (*Or.* 7.25–6):

The crowd kept up a constant shouting, sometimes cheerful and encouraging, if they wished to praise a speaker, but sometimes incandescent with rage. Their anger was awful to behold, and when they chose to shout against someone, they were so terrifying that some speakers ran around pleading for mercy, while others tore their cloaks in terror. I myself was once almost flung off my feet by their shouting, as if by a sudden tidal wave or thunderbolt falling on me. Then other speakers would come forward, or stand up in the midst of the crowd, and try to deliver either a few words or a long speech to the masses. Some of them they listened to for quite a long time, but others enraged them the moment they started to speak, and they refused to let them get out a word.

The ordinary Greek words for the 'masses' in the Greek city are *plēthos* and *dēmos*, but the term that Artemidorus normally uses is *ochlos*—a term with strong pejorative associations, like the English 'rabble'. What the civic magistrate seeks above all is a warm reception from the *ochlos*. Since people stare at mad people, to dream of being mad is auspicious 'for those who want to be political leaders (*dēmagōgein*) and to rule a crowd (*ochlos*) and for those who present themselves before a crowd: they will be thought that much more deserving of a popular reception' (3.42.1).

The *ochlos* in the *Oneirocritica* is always represented as disorderly and hard to govern. To dream of wearing white clothes usually signifies disorder of some kind, 'because those who face crowds at public meetings are dressed in white' (2.3.2). Similarly, for all those who make their living from the crowd (*ochlos*), and in particular for statesmen (*politeutai*) and politicians (*dēmagōgoi*), a dream of walking on the sea 'foretells both considerable renown and more than usual profit: the sea is like a crowd also because it observes no sort of discipline' (3.16.2, cf. 2.38.1). The successful magistrate is therefore someone who is able to exercise control and mastery over the masses: to dream of moulding people into exist-ence, as from clay, foretells high office for a rich and powerful man (3.17), since he will similarly be able to 'mould' the crowd, and it is auspicious for those who wish to 'lead the crowd' to dream of having many sheep (2.12.1).

A fairly common category of dreamer in the *Oneirocritica* is 'those who make their living (*porizomenoi*) from a crowd (*ochlos*)' (1.64.4, 1.68, 2.15, 3.6, 3.16.2, 3.47.2, 3.48, 3.52). This category encompasses professional musicians (1.64.4) and probably other craftsmen and tradesmen, but sometimes explicitly includes politicians (3.16.2, 3.52).

Civic magistracies in the Roman imperial period did not normally bring a salary, so Artemidorus is presumably speaking loosely of people whose career depends on the approval or disfavour of the general public. Only once, in Book 3, does Artemidorus give a specific example of how the politician can be seen as 'making a living' from the crowd. To dream of sleeping on a dunghill is, he says, auspicious for a rich man (3.52):

> The dream will procure him a magistracy or some other civic honour, because all members of the public (*dēmotai*) make a contribution to the dunghill and add to it, just as some of the tax they pay is handed to the magistrates.

The reference here is to the role played by civic magistrates in the collection of local tolls and market dues, a role which no doubt brought ample opportunities for individual profit.

Civic elites were expected to provide for their native cities with regular large-scale benefactions. Candidates for civic office often promised to pay for specific building works or to provide money donations to the citizen body, and from the early second century AD onwards, these promises could be legally enforced. The 'social contract' of the Greek *polis* in the Roman imperial period laid strong ethical requirements on rich men to engage in regular euergetic giving of this kind. As Artemidorus emphasizes, relative social status in the Greek city is determined by whether one is a habitual giver or a habitual recipient (4.2.12):

> For anyone worried about promotion in his career it is better to be generous and make a gift rather than to receive a gift, unless that gift is conferred by his superiors—it is the wealthy man who can afford to share his wealth, and the poor man who receives the handouts.

Similarly, it is good for a rich man to dream of a river flowing out of his house, since it indicates that he will be a 'successful giver' (2.27.3):

> He will have authority in his city, priding himself on spending much money in the public interest, and many people will flock to his house to present their needs and make their petitions—everyone needs a river.

The giving and receiving of donatives occupies a remarkably prominent place in Artemidorus' analysis of dreams about civic magistracies (2.30.4–6). To dream of making public distributions (*epidoseis dēmosiai*) from one's own resources, whether of cash or foodstuffs, is auspicious for a poor man, 'as it is not possible to make large donations if you have little to give'; it is also auspicious for theatrical performers, since 'those who make civic donations win applause' (2.30.4). To dream of receiving a donative is also auspicious, but not to receive your share is malign: 'this is a direct prediction of death, as donations are no longer made to the dead' (2.30.5). The giving of donatives—either in the form of cash-gifts or banquets—is also something expected of the leading members of private 'colleges' such as trade-guilds or cultic associations (2.30.6):

> To dream of being president or bursar (*epitropos*) of any association or collegiate body brings everyone vexations and unpleasantness in their life, and often financial loss too, especially for those who imagine themselves taking competitive pride in personal expenditure on dinner-parties or donations.

Perhaps the most striking image of all for the relationship between the politically active man and his city comes in Artemidorus' account of sex-dreams in Book 1 (see Chapter 5). Artemidorus is discussing the meanings of dreams about having sex with one's mother in a position 'according with nature', i.e. face to face (1.79.3):

> It is auspicious too for every politician (*dēmagōgos*) and statesman (*politeutēs*), because a mother symbolizes one's homeland. So just as anyone having sex in accordance with the law of Aphrodite, with a compliant and willing partner, is given authority over every part of her body, so a politician or statesman having this dream will preside over all the affairs of his city.

It is noteworthy that this particular dream-interpretation—sex with one's mother foretelling dominance over one's city—is a rare instance where we can say for certain that Artemidorus is reflecting widespread ancient views: the former tyrant Hippias of Athens interpreted a dream of sex with his mother as a prediction that he would reconquer his native city (Herodotus, *Histories* 6.107), and Caesar is said to have had the same dream the night before he crossed the Rubicon (Plutarch, *Caesar* 32.9).

Ephesus and Daldis

The picture of the Greek *polis* and civic life offered in the *Oneirocritica* was clearly based above all on Artemidorus' two native cities, the great metropolis of Ephesus and the sleepy Lydian hill-town of Daldis (Chapter 2). In a handful of cases, we can be sure that Artemidorus is recording dreams of members of the local elite at one or the other city: in Book 4, he describes the auspicious outcome of an unpromising dream of Menander of Daldis (4.49: appointed as priest of Zeus Polieus at Daldis), and the malign outcome of a dream of the lawyer Q. Aemilius Aristides, *procurator* at Ephesus between AD 204 and 208/9 (4.2.8). It was presumably at Ephesus that Artemidorus made the acquaintance of other members of the civic elite of western Asia Minor, such as L. Astranius Ruso of Laodicea on the Lycus (4.1.3) and the philosopher Alexander of Aphrodisias (4.33.3). The obscure dream-interpreters Nicostratus of Ephesus (1.2.12) and Apollonius of Attalea (1.32.2, 3.28.1) may well have been local contemporaries of Artemidorus, assuming that Attalea is the small Lydian city north of Daldis, rather than the homonymous city on the southern coast of Asia Minor.

Twice in the *Oneirocritica*, Artemidorus reminds his reader that the dream-interpreter needs to inform himself of idiosyncratic local customs, since otherwise he might be misled by apparently freakish dream-elements. On both occasions, it is local Ephesian practices that spring to mind: the custom of bull-fighting among the young at Ephesus (1.8.2), and the rigorous entrance-rules at the temple of Artemis at Ephesus (4.4.1):

> A married woman dreamt that she entered the temple and house of Ephesian Artemis and dined there, and not long afterwards she died: death is the penalty for any married woman entering that temple. A prostitute dreamt that she had entered the temple-precinct of Artemis: she was set free and abandoned her prostitution, because she could not have entered the precinct if she had not abandoned her life as a prostitute.

It was a peculiarity of the Ephesian cult of Artemis that married women were permitted to enter the temple-precinct (unlike prostitutes, who were completely excluded), but were barred from the temple itself on pain of death. This local Ephesian custom is also referred to in a Greek novel of the second century AD, Achilles Tatius' *Leucippe and Clitophon*: 'Since deepest antiquity, this temple [of Ephesian Artemis] has been forbidden to married women, and open only to men and virgins; if a married woman enters it, the punishment is death' (7.13.2–3). The famous cult-statue of Artemis at Ephesus is evoked by Artemidorus as one of the possible images of Artemis that might appear in a dream (2.35.3, grouped with the similar cult statues of Artemis Pergaea at Perge and Artemis Eleuthera in Lycia: see Chapter 9), and Artemidorus refers in passing to an extraordinary local ritual performed in the mountains just south of Ephesus, the *dendrophoria* or 'tree-carrying' undertaken by devotees of Dionysus at Magnesia on the Maeander (2.37.8).

Ephesus was one of the great sea-ports of Asia Minor, and played a central role in long-distance maritime trade between Asia Minor and the western Mediterranean. It also had a thriving local sea-fishing industry; a long inscription from Ephesus, dating to the late 50s AD, records the construction of a fish-market and customs-house for collection of the fishery-tax by an association of Ephesian fishermen and fishmongers (*I.Ephesos* 20). There are several echoes of the maritime world of Ephesus in the *Oneirocritica*, perhaps the most vivid of which is the fantastically detailed chapter dedicated to dreams about sea-fish and shellfish in Book 2 (2.14), which distinguishes the symbolic meanings of no fewer than sixty different species, along with seven types of fishing-net and fishing-line. Not only are ship-owners and sea-traders a remarkably well-represented category of dreamer in the *Oneirocritica* (1.14.2, 1.48.2, 1.35.3, 1.80.3, 2.25.2, 2.37.12), but Artemidorus records five specific dreams of ship-owners (*nauklēroi*)— a ship-owner called Diogenes whose bow-officer died (4.24.4); a ship-owner planning on making a journey to Rome (4.22.7); a man whose ship's bilge collapsed (4.30.1); a man whose ship was requisitioned by Roman state officials for compulsory public service (5.16); and a ship-owner whose dream foretold a spectacularly profitable trading mission (2.23.5):

I know of a ship-owner who dreamt that the figures of the gods installed in his ship had disappeared. He was full of fear and thought that the dream must signify death and destruction, but in fact the outcome was the complete opposite and wholly to his benefit: he made a great deal of profit and was able to pay off his debts to the lenders who held his ship as security for the loan, and the result was that he no longer had anyone else with a claim on his ship.

It is hard not to see all this as reflecting the typical clientele of a dream-interpreter based at Ephesus: anxious fishermen and long-distance merchant shippers must no doubt have been among Artemidorus' most regular clients.

Daldis is a considerably more shadowy place in the *Oneirocritica*. I have no doubt that many of the individual dreamers mentioned by Artemidorus were inhabitants of Daldis, although the only man who can be placed there with confidence is the priest Menander (4.49); it is likely enough that other acquaintances of Artemidorus and his son—such as the man referred to in passing as 'our Cratinus' (4.31.1)—were also natives of Daldis.

Nonetheless, there are a few occasions where Artemidorus casually refers to social institutions which we know to have been highly characteristic of Daldis and other small towns of north-east Lydia in the Roman imperial period. One of the most distinctive features of the funerary epigraphy of north-east Lydia is the large number of tombstones erected by private religious or trade-associations (*symbiōseis*) and other non-civic societies or 'brotherhoods' (*phratriai*) for their members. Private associations of this kind appear three times in the *Oneirocritica*, each time in contexts that suggest that the collective identity and solidarity of these groups were particularly significant for their members. In Book 2, deer are said to represent people 'who have lost all self-respect and become faint-hearted cowards', in particular 'deserters, people pursued in the courts, or people resigning from their associations (*symbiōseis*)' (2.12.16). In Book 4, we find what seems to be a classic anxiety-dream about appropriate behaviour at association-meetings (4.44.2):

A man dreamt that at a meeting of an association (*symbiōsis*) or society (*phratria*) of which he was a member he exposed himself to his fellow-members (*symbiōtai*) and urinated on each of them. He was expelled from the society (*phratria*) as having disqualified himself: people indulging in such drunken behaviour naturally meet with hostility and rejection.

These private associations also served as burial-clubs, enabling poorer members to receive the honour of a formal burial and a tombstone. In *Oneirocritica* Book 5, Artemidorus describes a dream in which a man's *symbiōtai* and *phratores* suddenly appeared before him and said 'invite us round to your house and give us a dinner'. The man replied 'I don't have the money or the means to entertain you', and sent them away; on the following day, he was shipwrecked, and barely escaped with his life. Artemidorus explains that 'it is the custom for fellows (*symbiōtai*) of those who have died to visit their homes and dine there, with the reception said to be hosted by the dead man, as a mark of the honour (*timē*) shown by his fellows to the deceased' (5.82). It is striking that Artemidorus feels the need to explain this custom, indicating that it would not have been familiar to most of his readers. Presumably the members of north-east Lydian *symbiōseis* and *phratriai* would normally gather to feast in the home of their deceased member after his death. Even Artemidorus' use of the word 'honour' (*timē*) may reflect a distinctively local Lydian practice. On tombstones from north-east Lydia, both associations and private individuals are, very unusually, described not as 'burying' or 'commemorating' the dead, but as 'honouring' them (the Greek verb is *timān*). The funerary banquet 'hosted' by the dead man may well have been seen as symbolic reciprocation for the 'honour' conferred by the association in erecting his tombstone.

A quite different aspect of social structure at Roman Daldis and other small towns of rural Lydia is vividly reflected in a further dream from Book 5 of the *Oneirocritica* (5.85):

A slave dreamt that he was given a boiled egg by his mistress, and that he threw away the shell and consumed the egg. His mistress happened to be pregnant at the time, and later gave birth to a little boy. She died in childbirth, and on the instruction of his mistress' husband the slave who saw this dream took over the baby and brought him up (*anethrepsato*). This, then, was the sense in which the outer casing was dispensable as being of no value, and the inner content provided the dreamer with the means of sustenance.

The rearing of children by 'nurturers' (*threpsantes*) or foster-parents was unusually widespread in Roman north-east Lydia, and not only for children whose parents died before they reached adulthood. Almost a third of all tombstones from the region include a foster-relative (foster-child, foster-sibling, or foster-parent) among those commemorating the deceased, and fosterage was clearly an absolutely standard part of normal family structures in the region. The dream recorded here shows a male slave being charged with rearing a male child after the mother's death; the final words seem to indicate that the rearing of the young boy was this slave's chief duty within his master's household. Similar situations are widely attested in the funerary epigraphy of Daldis and neighbouring towns. So at Saittai, to the north-east of Daldis, we find a member of the local civic elite (a certain Ti. Claudius Lonchas) erecting a tombstone for a man he describes as 'his father's freedman and his own rearer (*threpsas*)' (SEG 31, 1018), and at the village of Nisyra, south-east of Daldis, a wealthy young man called Lucius was commemorated by (among others) his living mother and father, and a male and female slave, Polycarpus and Epiktesis, who were responsible for 'rearing' the young Lucius (*TAM* V 1, 432).

Finally, one of the most distinctive and idiosyncratic genres of private monument erected by the inhabitants of rural Lydia in the Roman imperial period is that of the so-called 'confession-inscriptions'. These are small stone stelae that record the punishments (often illnesses) imposed on individuals by the gods in response to various sins (false oaths, thefts, infractions of religious norms)—an example is illustrated in Chapter 4 above (Fig. 4.2). The worshipper publicly acknowledges his or her guilt by erecting an inscribed stele in the sanctuary of the god, detailing the sin, the punishment, and the propitiatory actions that he or she has performed. In such texts, we are often told that the god has appeared to the sinner in a dream to demand propitiation. Here is a characteristic example:

Meidon son of Menander held a drinking party in the sanctuary of Zeus Trosou, and his attendants ate meat which had not been offered in sacrifice. The god struck him dumb for three months, and appeared to him in a dream, (demanding) that he erect a stele and write on it what he had suffered; he then recovered the use of his voice.

Although Artemidorus does not explicitly deal with dream-visions of this kind (gods stipulating propitiatory rituals), he does record a 'real-life' dream which fits beautifully into this schema of sin, punishment, and ritual propitiation (2.33.2):

> To polish, oil, or clean statues of the gods, or sweep the area in front of them and wash the temple surrounds, signifies that the dreamer has committed some offence against those particular gods. I know of someone who after this dream forswore himself by the god whose statue he had dreamt of cleaning: this was what the dream was telling him, that he must supplicate the god for forgiveness.

Divine punishments incurred by swearing falsely are extremely common in the Lydian confession-inscriptions, and Artemidorus is here clearly reflecting the distinctive religious mentality and propitiatory practices of Daldis and other highland towns and villages of Roman Lydia.

Conclusion

This chapter could easily have been extended to almost the entire length of the *Oneirocritica* itself. The whole messy, noisy, smelly texture of everyday life in a Greek urban community is there: the barbers' shops and market butchers (5.67, 3.56), the potteries and tanneries just outside the city-limits (2.20.5), children throwing knucklebones and old men playing backgammon (3.1), stinking dunghills (3.52), persistent beggars (3.53), having one's pocket picked in a workshop (2.59.2), the rich ephebes (citizen youths in their late teens) with their right hands tucked neatly inside their cloaks (1.54).

The Greek *polis* of Artemidorus is a community in which the civic elite, necessarily and rightly, play a prominent and visible role. In this sense, there is nothing in the *Oneirocritica* to surprise the reader of contemporary Greek literary texts and public epigraphy or the archaeologist of the Greek city in the Roman period. If there is a distinctive flavour to Artemidorus' picture of Greek civic life—and I think there is—it comes above all in his consistent attention to the spaces and contexts when elite and masses mingled: processions, public meetings, festivals, and the world of the agora. The *Oneirocritica* is certainly not a worm's-eye view of the Greek *polis* of the Severan age; but nor is it the Greek *polis* as seen from the *bouleuterion* or the sophist's study. And that is quite enough to make it a source of rare value for the student of Greek civic life under the Roman empire.

8
Books and Literary Culture

'Give me a place to stand', said Archimedes, 'and I shall move the earth.' 'To be ignorant of what happened before you were born', as Cicero remarked, 'is to remain always a child.' In Socrates' words, 'the unexamined life is not worth living'.

When a writer quotes another writer, it can indicate that he or she has read that other writer's work, but it need not do so. Every culture has its own distinctive stock of maxims, proverbs, and inspirational quotes, some of which come with names attached. (Not always the right name: as Voltaire never wrote, 'I disapprove of what you say, but I will defend to the death your right to say it.') I have lost count of the number of times the uplifting Cicero quote in the previous paragraph has turned up in the personal statements submitted by applicants for Classics degrees at my university. But how many of those eager prospective Classicists have ever opened Cicero's *Orator*, or have any idea of the quote's original context?

Artemidorus, like most Greek prose authors of the Roman imperial period, was fond of quoting Greek poetry. The very first sentence of his work features a quotation from Homer's *Iliad*:

> I have often felt the urge to start on this current project, but what held me back was not any 'concession to fear or weakness of mind', as the poet says [*Iliad* 10.122], but rather, and most particularly, the overwhelming prospect of the scale and complexity of the conceptual problems involved.

These snippets of verse are often integrated into his exposition of particular bits of dream-symbolism. It is, he tells us, auspicious for a rich man to dream of being struck by a thunderbolt, since it signifies that he will hold office as a magistrate or a priest, and will be crowned with an honorific gold wreath for his service (2.9.5):

> For gold resembles fire in its colour, and we read in Pindar that 'gold is like a blazing fire' [*Olympian* 1.1–2].

Now, it is of course quite possible that at the end of a hard day's dream-interpretation, Artemidorus liked to curl up with a much-thumbed papyrus roll of Pindar's victory odes. But I wonder. The words 'gold is like a blazing fire' come from the very first line of Pindar's most famous poem, the victory ode that we now know as *Olympian* 1, commemorating the victory of Hieron of Syracuse in the single horse race at the Olympic games of 476 BC. This poem stood first in the standard 'collected edition' of Pindar's victory odes produced by the Hellenistic scholar Aristophanes of Byzantium around 200 BC, and its opening lines were very close to being proverbial. Here, for example, is the Greek satirist Lucian, in his dialogue *The Cock* (mid-second century AD), in which the poor cobbler Micyllus recounts his dream of becoming rich to his interlocutor Pythagoras, who has been reincarnated as a cock (*The Cock*, 7):

> Micyllus: I saw a vast, vast quantity of gold, Pythagoras; you can't imagine how lovely it was, and how brightly it shone. What is it that Pindar says in praise of it—could you remind me, if you know it—where he says that water is best, then quite rightly reveres gold, right at the start of that finest of all his poems?
>
> Cock: I suppose it's this that you're after—'Water is best, and gold like a blazing fire shining out at night, supreme of all lordly wealth'?

Even Micyllus, a greedy, poorly educated cobbler, can just about dredge up the start of *Olympian* 1. Artemidorus' choice to quote these words tells us as little (or perhaps as much) about his knowledge of Pindar's poetry as would a journalist's choice to start a piece on Austen or Dickens with 'It is a truth universally acknowledged' or 'It was the best of times, it was the worst of times'.

In the *Oneirocritica*, Artemidorus refers to well over thirty Greek prose and verse authors by name. Many of these are earlier writers on dream-interpretation, at least some of whose works he clearly knew at first-hand (see Chapter 2). We may also leave to one side a couple of passing references to the dreams of named individuals who also happened to be authors—the dreams of 'Fronto' (4.22.5: probably the orator M. Cornelius Fronto, AD *c.*95–166) and of 'Plutarch' (4.72.2: perhaps, but not certainly, the philosopher and biographer Plutarch of Chaeronea, AD *c.*46–120).

This leaves us with seventeen 'literary' authors—that is, authors who are not cited as authorities on dream-interpretation—whom Artemidorus gives the impression of having read. The range of genres and periods is startlingly broad: early Greek hexameter poetry (Homer and Hesiod), lyric and elegiac verse of the archaic and classical periods (Theognis, Pindar, Evenus), tragedy and comedy (Euripides and Menander), classical Greek prose (Xenophon), highbrow Hellenistic and post-Hellenistic poetry (Callimachus, Lycophron, Nicander, Parthenius, Heraclides the Younger), and scientific works of zoology and medicine (Aristotle, Archelaus, Aristophanes of Byzantium, Xenocrates of Aphrodisias). How much of this impressive range of literature did Artemidorus know at first-hand?

'The Poet'

By far the most prominent literary author in the *Oneirocritica* is Homer. Artemidorus, like very many of his contemporaries, usually refers to him simply as 'the poet'.

It is hard to overstate the centrality of the two Homeric epics to literary education and culture in the Greek-speaking provinces of the Roman empire. Around a thousand papyrus fragments of the *Iliad* and *Odyssey* survive, roughly ten times as many as those of the next most favoured author (Euripides). Funerary epigrams from Roman Asia Minor, even those from remote rural districts, invariably try (not always successfully) to imitate the diction and vocabulary of the Homeric epics. The Homeristai ('Homer-players'), actors who performed scenes from Homer in full costume with appropriate props, were enormously popular in the Greek East, and Artemidorus clearly assumes they will be familiar to his readers, as in his account of the dream of Apollonides the surgeon (4.2.9):

After imagining himself in a dream as a player in a Homeric re-enactment and wounding many, he then had many patients to treat. The point is that actors in Homeric scenes inflict wounds and shed blood, but without any intention to kill: and the same is true of a surgeon.

Artemidorus quotes directly from the Homeric epics at twelve points in the *Oneirocritica*; he sometimes cites more than one passage at a time, giving us a total of sixteen verbatim quotations from either the *Iliad* or the *Odyssey*. There are also a dozen or so occasions where he discusses particular rare words or myths in a manner that indicates he probably has Homer in mind. No other author comes close to this density of reference in the *Oneirocritica*, and there can be no doubt that Artemidorus knew the Homeric epics at first-hand. But there are some curious features to his use of the Homeric poems that may suggest that his knowledge of Homer was partial at best.

Of the sixteen quotations from Homer in the *Oneirocritica*, one (2.5.1) is a simple reference to the standard Homeric epithet for 'iron', *polykmētos* ('laboriously worked'), which turns up several times in both the *Iliad* and *Odyssey*. Of the remaining fifteen quotations, ten come from the *Iliad*, four from the *Odyssey*, and one appears in both poems. This echoes a general preference for the *Iliad* over the *Odyssey* in Graeco-Roman antiquity: papyrus copies of the *Iliad* outnumber those of the *Odyssey* by around three to one. Of Artemidorus' four quotations from the *Odyssey*, one comes from *Odyssey* Book 4 (1.56.7), and one from *Odyssey* Book 11 (1.1.4). Books 4 and 11 were by far the two most widely read books of the *Odyssey* in antiquity, probably because they featured 'guest appearances' of popular figures from the *Iliad* (Menelaus and Helen, Achilles and Agamemnon).

Similarly, of the eleven quotes from the *Iliad* in the *Oneirocritica*, no fewer than six derive from *Iliad* Book 2. Papyrus fragments of the first two books of the *Iliad* outnumber other books of the poem by a large margin, and Book 2 seems to have been particularly favoured as a school-text in the Roman imperial period: of 57 extant *Iliad* papyri of the Roman imperial period written in 'school-hands', no fewer than 21 (37 per cent) are fragments of Book 2. The massive over-representation of *Iliad* Book 2 in the *Oneirocritica* no doubt reflects Artemidorus' own educational background: this was probably the one book of Homer he had read (and perhaps memorized) during his teenage studies under a *gramma-ticus* at Daldis or Ephesus.

Artemidorus' particular fondness for *Iliad* Book 2 is confirmed by the character of his quotations from this book, as compared to his quotes from other parts of the *Iliad* and *Odyssey*. Early in Book 1 of the *Oneirocritica*, in the course of a discussion of ethnically specific customs, Artemidorus mentions the rarity of bull-fighting in the Greek world (1.8.2):

> Contests with bulls are willingly undertaken in Ionia by the young of Ephesus, in Attica at the Eleusis pageants by 'the young men of Athens in each year's cycle' [*Iliad* 2.551], and in Larissa, a city in Thessaly, by the best of the gentry resident there: but in the rest of the world bull-fighting is an ordeal imposed on men who have been condemned to death.

This line is not quoted by any other ancient author. It is not especially memorable or 'quotable'; it has no particular ethical content, and cannot have been a proverb (as the first lines of Pindar's *Olympian* 1 evidently were). But it does have a peculiar fitness to the context here. In the quoted passage from the *Iliad*, Homer is describing annual bull-sacrifice by the Athenians, not at Eleusis, but at the sanctuary of Athena on the Athenian Acropolis. Artemidorus is talking about bulls; he has cause to mention the Athenians; this line from *Iliad* Book 2 jumps unbidden into his mind, and he drops it in casually, without even troubling to remind us that it comes from Homer. Nothing could more clearly illustrate his deep familiarity with this part of the *Iliad*.

The other quotations from *Iliad* Book 2 tend to support this impression. In his long discussion of animal-symbolism in the second book of the *Oneirocritica*, Artemidorus explains why goats are inauspicious (2.12.2):

> They are especially malign for those sailing the sea: we commonly speak of great waves as 'goats' (*aiges*); the poet has the 'boisterous butting' (*epaigizon*) of a violent wind [*Iliad* 2.148]; and the most fearsome sea is called the 'Aegean' (*Aigaion*). Dreams of goats do not create bonds of marriage, friendship, or partnership, and do not preserve existing bonds,

because goats are not gregarious—they go their separate ways to feed by themselves in precipitous and rocky places, getting themselves into difficulty and causing difficulty for the goatherd. Hence the epithet 'wide-ranging' used by the poet when he speaks of troops to be mar-shalled being 'like wide-ranging flocks of goats' [*Iliad* 2.474].

Once again, there is nothing remotely proverbial about these two brief Homeric quotations. To all appearances, the idea of a 'goat' has triggered Artemidorus' recollection of a rare Homeric word (*epaigizein*) and a pertinent Homeric epithet for goat-flocks, both from *Iliad* Book 2, and he drops them in, as it were, in passing.

But things are different for other parts of the two Homeric poems. Take, for example, Artemidorus' account of dreams of age-transformations— what it means if an old man dreams of turning into a child, or a youth dreams of turning into an adult, and so forth (1.50.2). The general principle here is that transformation into a 'neighbouring' age-class (child to youth, youth to adult, and vice versa) is auspicious, but trans-formation *across* an age-class (infant to adult, youth to old man) is perilous. Artemidorus concludes his account as follows:

> And if a grown man transforms into a child, he will make a silly mess of his business and suffer loss. That line of poetry got it right—'Younger men's minds are always in a flutter' [*Iliad* 3.108].

This quotation is not very apposite to the context. In this passage of *Iliad* Book 3, Homer is not talking about the foolishness of children, but the superior wisdom of the elderly Priam to his younger (but adult) sons; the quotation thus completely fails to illuminate the specific dream-interpretations that Artemidorus has just expounded. It is, though, significant that this particular line of Homer was very widely known and quoted in antiquity. The historian Polybius quoted it as a witticism, presumably addressed by an elder man to a younger man (Fragment 208), and Lucian cites it in his *Heracles*, as the first of a sequence of proverb-like quotations and examples to illustrate the superior wisdom and eloquence of old age (*Heracles*, 4). It turns up in a vast fifth-century AD compilation of 'handy quotes for every occasion' (Stobaeus' *Anthology*, of which more shortly), in a section of literary maxims 'On Youth'. This particular quote seems to have been a standard popular aphorism, like 'youth is wasted on the young', which tells us nothing about Artemidorus' knowledge of Homer.

Another way of approaching Artemidorus' knowledge of Homer would be to ask how well he actually understands Homer's Greek—a poetic language as distant from the Greek of Artemidorus' own day as, say, Chaucer's English is from ours. He believes (2.12.1) that the Homeric noun *kreiōn* ('lord') derives from a non-existent verb *kreiein* ('to lord over'); he thinks that the obscure Homeric word *lukabas* (probably 'year' or 'month') derives from 'wolf-crossing' (*lykos*, 'wolf', and -*bas* from *bainein*, 'to go'), because 'when crossing a river they always follow one another in an orderly line, just as the sequence of the seasons brings about the completion of a year's cycle' (2.12.11: see also Chapter 6). In the Preface to Book 4 (4.Pref.6), he claims that Homer uses the words *enhypnion* and *oneiros* as synonyms for 'dream', based on a misunderstanding of the syntax of *Iliad* 2.56 (where *enhypnion* is in fact adverbial, 'during sleep'). He compounds this in the very next sentence by claiming that Homer is fond of pleonastic variation, giving *Iliad* 2.305 as an example (*amphi peri krēnēn*, 'round about a spring'), when in fact the two words that he regards as synonyms (*amphi* and *peri*) perform different grammatical functions (the first is adverbial, the second is a preposition).

None of this induces much confidence in Artemidorus' knowledge of Homer and Homeric language. Although he clearly had the kind of basic educational grounding in Homer that we should expect of any member of the literate Greek urban elite (albeit apparently largely confined to *Iliad* Book 2), there is little sign of a deep familiarity with the whole of the two epics. And as we shall see, the picture is broadly similar for the other acknowledged 'classics' of Greek literature.

Some Other Classics

After Homer, the poets who were most read in schools (at least in Greco-Roman Egypt, where most of our evidence is concentrated) were Hesiod, Euripides, and Menander. Artemidorus quotes all three by name, but the manner in which he does so hardly suggests a profound knowledge of their work. Menander and Euripides are each quoted twice by name, Hesiod only once. The two quotations from the comic poet Menander (*c.*344–292 BC) both concern rare bits of idiomatic vocabulary, as in the following passage, where Artemidorus is explaining why a dream of washing clothes signifies the exposure of secrets (2.4):

> The old authors used 'cleaning' (*plynein*) as a slang term for 'exposing', as Menander has it in one of his plays:
>   'If you foul-mouth my wife like this, I'll nail your dad
>   And take him to the cleaners—you and yours as well' [F433 Kassel-Austin]
> which stands for 'I'll expose him'. That is why it is malign for those fearful of exposure to dream of clothes being washed.

In fact, Artemidorus has misunderstood the meaning of the metaphor: the verb 'to clean' (*plynein*) here signifies not 'to expose' but 'to insult'. Whether Artemidorus knew this play (whatever it was) at first-hand is hard to say.

Both Menander and Euripides are unusually quotable writers—that is to say, both go in for snappy one-line aphorisms that make a neat or trite moral point. In antiquity, very many of these 'Wise Men Say' one-liners were assembled in large collections of *gnomai* ('maxims'). An ancient collection of over 850 one-line *gnomai* attributed to Menander (many of them in fact from Euripides and other writers) survives in our medieval manuscript tradition. Thousands of quotable *gnomai* of this kind also ended up in the fifth-century *Anthology* of Stobaeus, an enormous compilation of prose and verse aphorisms organized by theme, which presumably stands at the end of a long tradition of lost ancient 'Dictionaries of Greek Literary Quotations'.

At least one of Artemidorus' two quotations from Euripides is an aphorism of exactly this type. Artemidorus is talking about what it means to dream of different parts of one's house being on fire (2.10.3):

> Pillars burning in a clear flame without being destroyed signify that the dreamer's children will move on to a better, brighter life. But pillars collapsing in the fire signify the death of sons: as Euripides says, 'Male children are the pillars holding up the house' [*Iphigenia in Tauris*, 57].

How true, how true! But had Artemidorus actually read the *Iphigenia in Tauris* (not one of Euripides' better-known plays in antiquity)? This particular line turns up both in Stobaeus' *Anthology* (4.24.36, under the heading 'Male Children Better Than Female') and, misattributed, in the medieval collection of Menander's one-line *gnomai*. It is easier and more plausible to suppose that Artemidorus found this line in some Stobaeus-like collection of improving quotations.

It would be a tedious task to list all of the examples of 'aphoristic' quotations of this kind in Artemidorus. Suffice to say that his two quotations from the archaic poet Theognis (1.32.1; 1.66.1), his single quotations from the historian Xenophon (1.66.1) and the Hellenistic poet Callimachus (4.84.4), and both of his quotations from Pindar (2.9.5, discussed above; 4.2.3), are all of this aphoristic character. Pindar aside, all of these passages also turn up in Stobaeus' anthology, and in one instance (the quotation from Xenophon), Artemidorus abbreviates the original text in exactly the same way that Stobaeus does.

In a few cases, Artemidorus quotes literary aphorisms without knowing their original source. Early in the first book of the *Oneirocritica*, he is discussing why dreams of babies are generally inauspicious (1.15):

> To dream that one has or sees children who are no more than babies, if these children are imagined as one's own, is troublesome for both men and women. It signifies worry, grief, and anxiety over some important matters, as bringing up babies involves all this too. There is an old saying to that effect, which goes like this: 'A child is fear or grief to its father for ever.'

This 'old saying' is in fact the work of the obscure fifth-century elegist Evenus of Paros (F5 West); it is also quoted by Plutarch (*On Affection for Offspring* 497a4), who remarks that it is 'the only line of Evenus that is praised or remembered'. For Artemidorus, it was simply an anonymous bit of ancient popular wisdom. Similarly, he twice quotes, without attribution, the proverb 'to rule is to have the power of a god' (2.36.7; 2.69.1); we know, as Artemidorus did not, that this is in fact one of the innumerable aphorisms owed to the comic poet Menander (F201 Kassel-Austin).

One of the most revealing passages for Artemidorus' knowledge of Greek poetry is his discussion of dreams *about* poetry—that is to say, dreams in which the dreamer imagines that he or she, or another individual, quotes one or more lines of verse. Here is the relevant passage in its entirety, including no fewer than four direct quotations from different authors (4.59.3–4):

Dreams with something of a literary element to them are never seen by ordinary people (by which I mean the uneducated), but only by the intelligentsia and those who have had some education—and this is the clearest demonstration one could have that dreams are products of the mind, and do not come from any external source. When verses from epic or tragedy, epigrams, or any other quotations are heard spoken in one's sleep, those which encapsulate a complete thought independent of context are sufficient in themselves to provide the outcome. For example, someone dreamt that a trustworthy person quoted to him that line from Hesiod, 'Never a wrongful gain: such gains equate to disaster' [*Works and Days* 352]. The man attempted robbery, and was caught and punished.

But those quotations which do not comprise a self-sufficient thought refer interpretation to the whole subject-matter of the work in question. For example, a woman dreamt that her maidservant said to her, in that line of Euripides, 'Roast me, burn my flesh, take your fill of me' [*Syleus* F687]. This servant was subjected to the jealous rage of her mistress, and suffered no end of maltreatment. It made sense that the outcome for her was consistent with the plot of the play about Andromache. And then again a poor man dreamt that he spoke the line, 'And all I never expected has come to me at once' [Sophocles, F860 Radt]: he found a treasure-trove, and became rich. A woman dreamt that someone said to her, 'Patroclus lies dead, and they are fighting over his body: it is naked now, and Hector of the glinting helmet has his armour' [Homer, *Iliad* 18.20–1]. Her husband died when he was abroad, and his estate was claimed by the imperial treasury: the woman went to law and fought the case, to no avail, but died in the course of the lawsuit. You can see, then, that some literary references have revealed the outcome on their own without any additional dependence on the subject-matter of the works in question, while others have had outcomes which are related to the whole story told in those works.

The basic thought here is clear enough: if a quotation in a dream is 'aphoristic' (the examples from Hesiod and Sophocles), the dream should be interpreted in line with the content of the quotation; if it is non-aphoristic (the examples from Euripides and Homer), it should be interpreted in line with the overall plot of the text from which it comes. It is therefore easy to see why Artemidorus claims that such dreams are only dreamt by lovers of literature (though it cannot be said that the dreamers in the four examples given here—a robber, a slave-girl, a poor man, and an elite woman—look much like typical litterateurs).

It is hard to say whether these dreams are Artemidorus' own inventions, but the four quotations tell us a good deal about Artemidorus' cultural horizons. The first of them is the sole reference to Hesiod in the *Oneirocritica*; it comes as no surprise that Stobaeus also quotes this same Hesiodic aphorism (3.10.12, 'On Injustice'), and there is no reason to think that Artemidorus knew the *Works and Days* at first-hand. The third example is in fact a quotation from Sophocles—though Artemidorus appears to be ignorant of the fact—and it is again very likely that the line was in some way 'proverbial' (it is also quoted by Plutarch, *Convivial Questions* 732d). His fourth quotation (from Homer) shows a considerably greater familiarity with the source-text: the dream-outcome corresponds in a complex and sophisticated way with the plot of the *Iliad* (Patroclus dies at Troy = husband dies abroad; arms seized by Hector = property seized by Imperial Treasury; Achilles fights to recover his lover's arms = wife goes to court to recover husband's property; Hector (?or Achilles) dies = wife dies).

Most interesting of all is the quotation from Euripides. Artemidorus is clearly familiar with the basic plot of Euripides' *Andromache* (one of the best-known of Euripides' plays in antiquity), which centres on Hermione's jealousy towards her husband's slave Andromache; in one scene of the play, Hermione threatens to burn Andromache alive, and Andromache replies 'go ahead and roast me' (*Andromache* 258). However, the line quoted by Artemidorus in fact comes not from the *Andromache*, but from Euripides' lost satyr-play *Syleus* (F687, also quoted by Philo of Alexandria); the speaker is the hero Heracles. How has this peculiar confusion arisen? We can hardly assume that Artemidorus knew the *Syleus* at first-hand, and it is likely enough that the quotation comes from a collection of selected Euripidean aphorisms, with an absent or erroneous play-attribution. As for the *Andromache*, one wonders whether Artemidorus knew the play not in its original, canonical version, but from a simplified adaptation or summary, perhaps a prose digest of *Tales from Euripides* (known to have circulated widely in the Hellenistic and Roman imperial periods).

Overall, then, there is little reason to think that Artemidorus was widely read in the acknowledged 'classics' of Greek poetry after Homer (Hesiod, Theognis, Pindar, Euripides, Menander). His knowledge of their works appears to have been largely confined to the common popular stock of famous quotations and moral aphorisms. There is no sign that he was acquainted with Aeschylus, Sophocles, or Aristophanes; Herodotus and Thucydides are absent; and even his knowledge of Homer seems to reflect the basic school curriculum, rather than wide independent reading.

Further Off the Beaten Track

In the light of Artemidorus' limited knowledge of the 'classics' of Greek literature, it is all the more striking to find him referring in passing to a handful of literary and technical authors of (at least to us) fantastic obscurity: Evenus of Paros, Archelaus of Alexandria, Heraclides Ponticus. But once again, things may not be quite what they seem.

Much of the early part of Book 2 of the *Oneirocritica* (2.11–22) is dedicated to a spectacular menagerie of animal-dreams (Chapter 6). (Pity the poor translator who has to identify all sixty distinct species of sea-fish, molluscs and crustaceans mentioned in 2.14.) Given Artemidorus' particular interest in the animal kingdom, it is perhaps not surprising that he cites by name five different authors of technical works on animals. When discussing dreams about venomous snakes, he remarks (2.13.5),

> The snakes called *sēps, dipsas*, and *diphas*, the so-called chameleon, and all the other venomous reptiles listed by Nicander signify noth-
> ing good.

Nicander of Colophon's *Theriaca* is a 958-line didactic poem on venomous animals, still extant today (though I cannot say I have read it myself). It is possible that Artemidorus consulted it at first-hand, though he may equally well have known the poem only by repute: it was widely used by technical authors in the early imperial period, including Pliny the Elder, Galen, and Aelian.

More important are two passages where he refers to extensive prose works on animal biology. At 2.14.3, in the course of his discussion of salt-water fish, Artemidorus remarks,

> The red mullet is auspicious for childless women, because it spawns three times—hence the appropriate name it bears (*triglē*), as noted both by Aristotle in his treatise *On Animals* [5.9 (543a5)] and by Aristophanes in his *Epitome* of Aristotle.

And again at 4.22.3, while discussing cures derived from incubation-dreams:

> Many of these people [i.e. writers on incubation-cures] have also misappropriated from Aristotle's treatise on animals and from Archelaus and Xenocrates of Aphrodisias information about what cures any animal and what any animal fears or particularly likes, and cobbled that up into their own prescriptions and treatments.

Aristotle's zoological works, above all his enormous *History of Animals*, were very widely read in antiquity, most often in the abridged version produced by the great Hellenistic scholar Aristophanes of Byzantium (*c.*257–180 BC). Here, at least, we are on firm ground: the parallels between Artemidorus' discussions of animals and Aristotle's zoological works are sufficiently numerous as to suggest that he made extensive direct use of at least Aristophanes' abridgement (as 2.14.3 implies). We do not know enough about the lost works of Archelaus of Alexandria (third century BC, author of works *On Strange Creatures* in both prose and verse) or Xenocrates of Aphrodisias (mid-first century AD, author of a medical work *On Useful Things from Living Beings*) to have any idea whether Artemidorus consulted them directly; quite possibly, as with Nicander, these books were known to him only by reputation.

A more curious problem is posed by 4.63, where Artemidorus launches an attack against writers on dream-interpretation who invent elaborate riddling dreams modelled on obscure bits of Greek poetry and mythography. He gives two examples of absurd literary 'riddles' of this kind. Here is the first:

> A man who had lost a slave dreamt that someone said to him, 'Your man is with the non-combatants': the slave was found in Thebes, because the Thebans were the only Boeotians not to join the military expedition to Troy.

Whether or not the Thebans participated in the Trojan War depends on an abstruse topographical ambiguity in Homer's *Catalogue of Ships* (*Iliad* 2.505): Homer does not mention the Thebans per se in his list of Achaean contingents who came to Troy, but only a place called Hypothebes ('Under-Thebes'), which some ancient scholars interpreted as the lower city of Thebes itself, others as the separate town of Potniae (Strabo, *Geography* 9.2.32). Once we recall that *Iliad* Book 2 was Artemidorus' own favourite part of the *Iliad*, the suspicion naturally arises that Artemidorus has concocted this 'riddle-dream' himself, on the basis of an obscure literary puzzle that he recalled from his school-days.

Artemidorus strongly warns off the prospective dream-interpreter—that is to say, in Books 4 and 5, his son Artemidorus—from indulging in this kind of over-ingenious nonsense. But, he says, if you do wish to make yourself a specialist in literary riddles, it is easy to get hold of the relevant primary materials:

> Should you wish, it is easy enough for you to bone up on all this, so you can be well placed to answer these people. There are many recondite and out-of-the-way legends to be found in the *Alexandra* of Lycophron, the *Discourses* of Heraclides of Pontus, the *Elegies* of Parthenius, and in many other authors.

These are not the kinds of authors we expect to find in the pages of the *Oneirocritica*. Lycophron's *Alexandra* is still extant today: it is a 1474-line Greek poem, probably of the second century BC, in which Cassandra delivers a series of prophecies in spectacularly obscure metaphorical language. The *Conversations* of Heraclides the Younger (mid-first century AD) was a three-book poem in Sapphic hendecasyllables, likewise notorious for its obscurity. A few fragments survive of the verse elegies of

Parthenius of Nicaea (mid-first century BC), featuring much unorthodox treatment of mythological themes, complete with novel etymologies.

Did Artemidorus have access to copies of these rare and somewhat esoteric books? The phrasing of his recommendation to his son ('it will be easy for you...') does suggest that he knew of specific copies of these texts, presumably at Ephesus, and (more importantly) that he knew what kind of stuff was to be found in them. That is not to say that Artemidorus had read them himself. There is no sign elsewhere in the *Oneirocritica* that he was familiar with Lycophron's *Alexandra*, and his contemptuous dismissal of this sort of playful pseudo-scholarship shows a lack of sympathy with the genre. But this passage is a rare indication that Artemidorus possessed at least bibliographic knowledge that was a little out of the ordinary.

At first glance, a similar impression of deep and unexpected book-learning is left by the final passage I wish to discuss, an unusually long and complex dream-narrative from very early in the *Oneirocritica*. Artemidorus wishes to illustrate how an elaborate series of events in a dream may in fact symbolize a single, rather simple outcome (1.4.5):

Someone dreamt that Charon was playing draughts with some other man, and he, the dreamer, was prompting this man. The result was that Charon lost the game, flew into a rage, and went after the dreamer, who turned and ran, reached an inn called 'The Camel', hurried into a room and locked the doors. So the demon Charon left him and was gone, but grass began to grow on one of the dreamer's thighs. All of these details pointed to just one resulting event. The house in which the man was living fell down, and beams collapsing on him crushed and broke his thigh. The fact is that Charon playing draughts presaged something to do with death, but his failure to catch the man showed that he would not die, but there would be problems for his legs because of the pursuit. 'The Camel' as the name of the inn indicated that he would break his thigh, as the animal called a camel can bend its thighs in the middle to lower its long legs—and that is the etymology of 'camel' (*kamelos*), as if from *kammeros* ('thigh-bender'), as Evenus says in his *Erotica* addressed to Eunomus. And the grass growing on his thigh showed that he would no longer have the use of it, as grass tends to grow on land which is left fallow.

Evenus was most certainly not a household name in Artemidorus' day—far from it. (It is significant that this is one of very few quotations in the *Oneirocritica* where Artemidorus gives the name of the book, as well as the author, in full.) It is not even certain whether this Evenus is the same man as the fifth-century poet Evenus of Paros whom Artemidorus quotes (without attribution) at 1.15, or whether he is instead a later and even more obscure homonym.

But there are in fact strong reasons to think that this entire dream and its interpretation (including the learned reference to Evenus' spurious etymology of 'camel') has been lifted by Artemidorus from another work altogether. The passage includes two examples of the old dual number (used for pairs of things), which had long ago disappeared from the spoken Greek language: grass is said to grow on 'one of the dreamer's (two) thighs' (*toin mēroin*), and the camel bends its thighs 'to lower its (two) long legs' (*toin skeloin*). The dual form appears nowhere else in the *Oneirocritica*. It was, however, widely used by 'Atticizing' literary authors of the second century AD, who attempted to revive those distinctive features of the classical Athenian dialect which had disappeared in later Greek.

The combination of the obscure literary reference (Evenus on etymology) and the anomalous grammatical form are, for me, decisive: this passage is not original to Artemidorus, but is a paraphrase of a dream-narrative that he found in an earlier author. Who that author might have been, I cannot say.

Artemidorus and his Books

Artemidorus was not a bookish man. He knew some Homer, but probably no more than the average literate member of the Greek provincial elite of his day—he shows no extensive knowledge of the *Odyssey*, and he knew the standard 'school-book' of the *Iliad* (Book 2) far better than the rest of the poem. His cultural horizons encompassed the standard literary classics of his day: he seems to have known some Menander at first-hand, knew the plot of at least one Euripides play (the *Andromache*), and could quote famous lines and aphorisms from Hesiod, Theognis, Pindar, and Callimachus. Although he may not have read more obscure works such as Nicander's *Theriaca*, Lycophron's *Alexandra* or Parthenius' *Elegies*, he was at least aware of their existence and general literary character. Technical prose literature was more to his taste: he had clearly read widely in earlier books of dream-interpretation, and was fond of Aristotle's zoological works (which he probably knew through the abridgement of Aristophanes of Byzantium).

Books as physical objects are not prominent in Artemidorus' dream-world. At 2.45 he provides us with a notably brief discussion of the dream-symbolism of books:

> A book-roll signifies the life of the dreamer (people make their progress through a book as they do through their life), and also the remembrance of things past, as past events have been written down in books. To dream of eating books is beneficial for teachers and sophists and all who make their living from discourse or books. For all others it foretells sudden death.

The idea of a book-roll as a symbol of one's life recurs in a short dream-narrative in Book 5 (5.28: plastering over one's books with clay signifies serious illness), and at 2.49.3 he assumes that men of letters will leave 'works containing their wisdom' behind them as memorials. But that is pretty much it; and, as we have seen, in his discussion of dreams about works of literature (4.59), Artemidorus leaves the impression of being somewhat out of his depth.

There is no modern study of Artemidorus' own use of the Greek language. He makes no grand claims for his own literary abilities, as he rather coyly emphasizes to Cassius Maximus in the preface to Book 2:

> I would ask you to concentrate on the logical sequence of the material and the accuracy of my interpretations (the only aspect in which I take some pride), and not to make any stylistic comparison with your own writings. Rather, the extent of my power to give expression to my thoughts should be considered analogous to that of an oil-lamp as a substitute for the sun when people need light in darkness.

This is fair enough. His prose is formulaic and utilitarian, and shows little rhetorical or literary polish. At times, he uses Greek words and phrases that would have raised the eyebrows of a cultured Greek litterateur of the period. For example, Artemidorus consistently uses the verb *hiptasthai* for 'to fly', in place of the normal Greek *petesthai*. This was a notorious solecism, firmly castigated by the linguistic purist Lucian (*The Solecist*, 7; *Lexiphanes*, 25); it probably belongs to ordinary day-to-day usage in second-century Asia Minor (like the English 'knackered' for tired, or 'grub' for food). Similarly, when Artemidorus is listing Greek words whose component letters add up to 100 when treated as numerals ('isopsephism'), he includes the Greek word *angelia* ('message', 3.34.2). The 'standard' Greek spelling of this word would be *aggelia* (whose component numerals do not add up to 100). Artemidorus' rendering of *-gg-* as *-ng-* would have horrified an orthographic purist, but reflects the way the word was actually pronounced in his own day (this spelling is very common in inscriptions from Roman Asia Minor). Another dream-interpretation that depends on contemporary pronunciation appears at 5.15:

> A man dreamt that he had an iron penis. He fathered a son by whom he was killed. Iron is destroyed by the rust of its own generation.

In the spoken Greek of Artemidorus' day, the word for 'son' (*hyios*) was pronounced the same as the word for 'rust' (*ios*).

In short, in terms of his literary culture, Artemidorus is a rare and precious figure among ancient authors: an ordinary, representative member of the literate municipal *bourgeoisie* in the cities of the Greek East. He had studied some Homer with a *grammaticus* in his teens, and still had a fair bit of *Iliad* Book 2 by heart. He knew no Latin (so far as we can tell: see Chapter 12); he had dabbled in the 'classic' Greek poets, and could whip out some apposite (if not especially abstruse) quotes from Euripides, Hesiod, or Pindar when the occasion arose. Sturdy and respectable members of the small-town middle classes like Artemidorus do not normally end up writing books; and for this reason, as for so many others, the *Oneirocritica* is a true jewel among ancient texts.

9

The Gods

'Let us begin with Zeus', says the Hellenistic poet Aratus at the start of his *Phaenomena* (a didactic poem on astronomy and weather-signs). Artemidorus does not. In the vast Artemidoran universe of things about which one might be expected to dream, the gods do not occupy an especially privileged place; his main catalogue of dreams about gods appears late in Book 2 of the *Oneirocritica* (2.33–40), supplemented by a more general discussion towards the end of Book 4 (4.71–79). Artemidorus is aware that this is an unconventional choice. As he says early in Book 1, when laying out the structure of the first two books of the *Oneirocritica*, 'We shall not follow the old authorities in beginning with the gods, however impious that might seem to some, but with regard to the natural sequence of things we shall begin first with birth' (1.10.1).

The relative marginality of the gods in the dream-world of the *Oneirocritica* certainly does not mean that Artemidorus was any kind of religious sceptic. It is rather that he did not see dreams about the gods as categorically different in kind from dreams about grasshoppers or knucklebones. As we saw in Chapter 3, Artemidorus did not believe that predictive dreams were sent by the gods, and he is studiously vague about the origins of dreams solicited from particular deities (more on this below). Since dreams about the gods originate in the same internal anthropogenic processes as dreams about anything else, there is no reason to assign a special status to such dreams: they just follow the ordinary rules.

The kinds of interactions with the gods dreamt about by Artemidorus' clients are often remarkably intimate. Artemidorus informs us, among other things, of the significance of chatting with the gods (1.2.9), dining with a god (1.5.4), having sex with a god (1.80.3), sharing a god's experiences (2.37.6), entertaining a god (3.14.1), wearing a god's outfit

(3.14.2), and playing ball with a god (4.69). All of this beautifully illustrates the close and even affectionate relationships that ordinary Greeks and Romans felt themselves to have with their deities. When the Christian martyr Perpetua—an exact contemporary of Artemidorus—dreamt of 'nattering' (*fabulari*) with the Christian God, she is simply reflecting normal assumptions about the kinds of contact people could expect to have with the divine.

Artemidorus' own personal attitude towards the gods is hard to judge. When gods speak in a dream, he says, one should always believe them, 'because to lie is foreign to a god's nature' (2.69.1); if they speak in riddles, that is 'because they are wiser than us' (4.71.2). He believes that there is such a thing as a 'true prophet' (3.20), and 'godlessness and impiety' are strongly negative characteristics among both animals and people (2.46, 5.4). In the final lines of Book 2, Artemidorus does claim that it was Apollo Mystes, patron deity of Daldis, who inspired him to write the *Oneirocritica* (2.70.13):

A god is the supervisor and guarantor of all that I write, and this is Apollo, the god of my own native land, at whose persuasion I came to undertake this work. He has urged me to it many times before, but especially now that I have made your acquaintance, Maximus, he has manifestly insisted and virtually commanded me to write this treatise. So it is no wonder that Apollo of Daldis, in our country known by the traditional epithet Mystes, should have given me this commission with your quality and wisdom in mind.

Nonetheless, this is the only point in the entire five-book *Oneirocritica* where Artemidorus invokes divine inspiration in this way, and we may suspect that these lines are more of a literary flourish than a genuine reflection of Artemidorus' own beliefs. At the start of Book 4, when Artemidorus reflects on the composition of his original two-book *Oneirocritica*, he says nothing about Apollo, but refers only to the prompting of his own 'guardian spirit' (*daimōn*) (4.Pref.1). There is no reason to think that Artemidorus had a developed theological conception of what precisely this *daimon* might be (some kind of personal destiny or guiding-spirit: cf. 1.16.1, 5.43). Artemidorus was no religious sceptic; but nor, to all appearances, was he a habitual god-botherer.

The Dream-Pantheon

Artemidorus' pantheon of gods about whom one might dream is at first sight a fairly conventional one, consisting of the named gods of Greek myth (Zeus, Hera, Artemis); natural forces, some of them personified (Achelous, the tutelary deity of fresh water), others not (Stars, Clouds, Winds); and personifications of abstract concepts or qualities (Peitho, 'persuasion'; Pronoia, 'providence'). But I should say at once that this is not how Artemidorus himself chooses to organize his list of gods. His catalogue is prefaced with what at first sight looks like a promisingly sophisticated double classificatory system (2.34.1):

> Of the gods, some are intelligible (perceived by the mind) and others sensible (perceived by the senses). Most of the gods are in the intelligible category, and only a small number in the sensible. What follows will give more precise detail. And we speak of some of the gods as Olympian (also called ethereal), some as celestial, some as terrestrial, some as marine or fluvial, some as chthonic, and some as outlying.

The 'sensible' gods consist of stars, clouds, rivers, and suchlike (directly perceptible by the senses); 'intelligible' gods are those like Zeus or Heracles, who can only be perceived in visions or in the form of painted or sculpted representations. Cutting across this twofold classification is a separate sixfold spatial division into the ethereal, celestial, terrestrial, marine/fluvial, subterranean, and encircling: so the Sea is a sensible marine god, Pluto is an intelligible chthonic god, and so on. This way of classifying the gods is well paralleled in contemporary middle Platonism. Maximus of Tyre, the addressee of Books 1–3 of the *Oneirocritica*, similarly distinguishes between 'sensible' and 'intelligible' gods in his extant philosophical orations, and it is possible that Artemidorus has deliberately tailored his account here to suit Maximus' intellectual interests.

Nonetheless, it cannot be said that Artemidorus applies this schema with any great conviction or consistency. When he tries to generalize about entire categories of gods, the results are frankly feeble. 'A dream-vision of the Olympians', he says, 'is advantageous for rich and powerful men and women, of the celestial gods for those of moderate means, and of the terrestrial gods for the poor' (2.34.3). This attempt to fit the spatial classification of the gods (highest, middle, lower) to a social hierarchy (rich, middling, poor) has patently been made up on the spot, and is repeatedly contradicted in his detailed analysis of particular gods: the terrestrial gods Hermes and Hestia, for example, are primarily auspicious for the rich. 'None of the gods who are perceived by the senses', he claims later on, 'is beneficial for anyone who is poor' (4.77.1). Once again, this bears very little relation to his actual analysis of sensible gods: Helios, for example, is perfectly auspicious for the poor. Artemidorus' 'philosoph-ical' classification of the gods does not show him at his best: it gives a thin veneer of scientific credibility to a discussion which remains, as always, almost entirely empirical and analogic.

Most of the gods who appear in Artemidorus' catalogue are standard figures of Greek myth and ritual (Zeus, Apollo, Dionysus etc.), but he does include some deities of very marginal significance in both Greek thought and cult practice. For example, the goddesses Aristoboule ('best counsel') and Eunomia ('lawful order'), who are said to signify 'the same as Nemesis' (2.37.15), are both real rarities: Aristoboule is only attested at Rhodes and Athens (where she was identified with Artemis), and a cult of Eunomia is known only from Perge in Pamphylia. It is difficult to believe that the space dedicated to particular deities reflects the frequency with which people dreamed about them in real life. Zeus is knocked off with remarkable brevity (2.35.1: basically good, espe-cially for the rich), and Hera merits only a single phrase (2.35.2: same as Zeus, but for women), while Helios-dreams receive several pages of detailed analysis.

There are some surprising absences from Artemidorus' pantheon. Roman emperors and the personified goddess Roma, who received formal worship both at the provincial level and in the individual cities of the Greek world, are perhaps the most striking absentees; indeed, aside from a single oblique passing reference (4.31: a man becomes the revenue-collector of an imperial temple), the *Oneirocritica* is completely silent on the imperial cult. 'It would be interesting', wrote Simon Price in his classic study of the Roman imperial cult in Asia Minor, 'to be able to ask a Greek to list a number of gods. Would the emperor be included in any such list?' *Oneirocritica* 2.34–39 is pretty close to being just such a list, and the emperor and Roma are indeed absent.

There are other significant 'missing persons' in Artemidorus' register of gods. No doubt Artemidorus would have turned his nose up at idiosyncratic figures like the snake-god Glycon, whose cult in Asia Minor was anyway largely restricted to Paphlagonia and Bithynia; the cult of Mithras was never widespread in Asia Minor, and Jews and Christians (whose numbers in Asia Minor are hard to judge in this period) were presumably not a regular part of Artemidorus' clientele. But it is harder to account for the complete absence of the Anatolian moon-god Meis, one of the two or three most popular deities in Artemidorus' native Lydia, whose cult was quite exceptionally widespread throughout western Asia Minor in this period. The only moon-deity recognized by Artemidorus is the female goddess Selene (2.36.7–9), whose cult is exceptionally rare in Roman Asia Minor. Scarcely less prominent than Meis in the pantheon of western Asia Minor (particularly in rural Lydia) was the Anatolian goddess Anaeitis or 'Great Mother', often identified with Artemis by her worshippers. She too is absent from the *Oneirocritica*: Artemidorus' brief discussion of the 'so-called Dindymaean Mother of the Gods' (2.39.4) treats her solely as a minor goddess of the underworld.

Given the presence of obscure figures like Pronoia and Eunomia— whom most of Artemidorus' clientele would scarcely have heard of, let alone dreamed about—the absence from the *Oneirocritica* of immensely popular local deities like Meis, Anaeitis, and other widespread Anatolian gods (Cybele; Attis; Holy and Just) is something of a puzzle. It is possible that Artemidorus recognized two broad categories of god, the 'universal' and the 'local' (cf. 1.8.1, 4.4.1). We know that he aspired to write a book that would be useful for any cultivated Greek end-user, and this may have led him to include only those gods who were recognized (if not perhaps widely worshipped) throughout the Greek world. Anatolian deities like Meis or the Great Mother were just too local: the reader in Athens or Tyre would be baffled.

But this 'lowest common denominator' approach runs up against Artemidorus' willingness to discuss 'universal' deities in their specific local manifestations. So, for example, when analysing dreams about the goddess Artemis, he happily assigns a specific meaning to Anatolian cult-statues of the 'sedate' Artemis, 'for example the Artemis of Ephesus or Perge, or the Artemis called Eleuthera (the free) in Lycia' (2.35.3: see further below). The Ephesian Artemis was a very widely known cult-image, but the same cannot be said for her Pergaean or Lycian incarnations. Most of Artemidorus' readers would undoubtedly have been far more familiar with the iconography of Meis (floppy Phrygian bonnet, crescent moon behind his shoulders) than with that of the distinctly niche Artemis Eleuthera.

Seeing the Gods

Artemidorus determines the meaning of a god in a dream in two ways: by the god's intrinsic characteristics and sphere of authority, and by his or her particular visual appearance in the dream. The first line of interpretation is relatively unproblematic, since Artemidorus generally follows standard Greek opinions on the gods' characters. So a dream-epiphany of Athena is auspicious for artisans, because she is the patron goddess of crafts; she is auspicious for philosophers, because she was born from the brain of Zeus and is the embodiment of intelligence; and she is inauspicious for prostitutes and adulteresses, because she is a virgin goddess (2.35.5).

Things get more complicated when Artemidorus comes to discuss the particular appearances of gods in dreams. By definition, we do not know what the 'intelligible' gods really look like: if we did, they would be 'sensible' gods. As a result, when we see a god in a dream, we inevitably tend to see him or her in the form familiar to us from cult statues, although we have no way of knowing whether this form is the 'true' appearance of the god.

As a result, Artemidorus is unable to draw a clear distinction between dreams about gods and dreams about statues of gods: 'statues of the gods have the same significance as the gods themselves' (2.39.9). That is not to say that we cannot tell the difference between a dream about Zeus and a dream about a statue of Zeus. A statue of Zeus will visibly be made of some non-fleshly material (gold, stone, terracotta), the more durable the better (2.39.9). A statue of Zeus, unlike Zeus himself, will tend not to move; moving statues are bad news (2.33.4). But the basic significance of the dream is the same whether we see the god 'in the flesh' or 'in marble', as Artemidorus explicitly states in his discussion of dreams about the goddess Artemis (2.35.3):

It makes no difference whether we see the goddess herself as we have imagined her or a statue of her. The same interpretation applies whether the gods appear in our dreams in the flesh or as statues made out of whatever material. But both the good and the bad outcomes signified have more immediate effect if the gods themselves are seen rather than their statues.

A large part of Artemidorus' account of dreams about gods in Book 2 is therefore devoted to the various cult-images that his clientele would have seen in their day-to-day lives. Dreams about Hecate will, he assumes, usually take the form of 'the three-faced Hecate standing on a plinth' (2.37.1), since this was the most common form of cult-image of Hecate (often erected at crossroads). Likewise, dreams of the god Hermes will in practice tend to be dreams of the monument known to us as a 'herm', a rectangular pillar with a bust of Hermes and erect phallus, typically set up in libraries and gymnasia. The herm may either appear as 'a square-shaped image of Hermes with a wedge-like beard' or 'a square-shaped Hermes with no beard' (2.37.9), since these were the two kinds of herm most commonly seen in Artemidorus' own day.

Artemidorus takes it for granted that dreamers will be able to distinguish between the most widespread statue-types of the better-known Olympian gods. His discussion of dreams about Artemis assumes an impressively broad knowledge of the goddess' iconography (2.35.3):

> She is especially advantageous for hunters as Artemis Agrotera (the huntress), and for fishermen as Artemis Limnatis (goddess of lakes)...
> She is always more beneficial to any sort of enterprise as Artemis Agrotera or Elaphēbolos (the deer-shooter) than when depicted in any other guise: but for those who have chosen a more austere mode of life, the sedate images of Artemis are more auspicious, for example the Artemis of Ephesus or Perge, or the Artemis called Eleuthera (the free) in Lycia.

The 'sedate' cult-images of Artemis Ephesia and Artemis Pergaea are stiff, sober, fully frontal statues, whose motionlessness is contrasted with the dynamic Greek cult-images of Artemis the huntress. Fig. 9.1 shows the reverse types of two coins of Perge, depicting Artemis in these two

Fig. 9.1. (Left) Tetradrachm of Perge (third century BC). AR 15.78g, 30mm. ANS 1967.152.482. (Right) Cistophorus of Trajan (AD 98), RPC III 1310. AR 10.22g, 24mm. ANS 1944.100.44674.

Photos courtesy of the American Numismatic Society.

very different aspects, 'dynamic' and 'sedate'. Similarly, Aphrodite means different things depending on whether she appears as Aphrodite Pandemos ('vulgar'), Aphrodite Ourania ('heavenly'), Aphrodite Pelagia ('of the sea'), or Aphrodite *Anadyomenē* ('rising up out of the sea') (2.37.11–12). The 'heavenly' and 'vulgar' Aphrodite were the two chief aspects under which the goddess was worshipped in the ancient Greek world. Pausanias describes the different cult-images of Aphrodite Ourania and Pandemos at Elis in the Peloponnese: heavenly Aphrodite rests her foot on a tortoise, evoking modesty and privacy, while vulgar Aphrodite is mounted on a he-goat (*Description of Greece* 6.25.1). By contrast, Aphrodite 'of the sea' and Aphrodite 'rising up out of the sea' were not (it seems) distinct cultic aspects of the goddess, but compositional types that informed many different visual representations of Aphrodite, including some cult-statues. Dreaming of Aphrodite Anadyomenē means different things, depending on whether the goddess' lower body is covered or not (2.37.12):

> This Aphrodite is considered always auspicious when she appears with her lower body covered up to her waist, because she then has her breasts, which are the most nourishing parts of her, naked and displayed. But if she appears totally naked, she is auspicious only for prostitutes and signifies good custom for them: for all else she signifies disgrace.

Finally, a few of the gods discussed in the *Oneirocritica* appear in dreams in both 'sensible' and 'intelligible' forms. The clearest example is the sun-god Helios, who can be seen either in his 'sensible' form (the sun itself) or in his 'intelligible' form (the anthropomorphic god Helios). When perceived in his traditional anthropomorphic guise as a charioteer, Helios has a discrete set of meanings based on that particular iconography ('auspicious for athletes, for those setting out on travel abroad, and for charioteers: but for the sick it is certainly dangerous, and fatal': 2.36.5).

A more surprising category-crossing god is the healing deity Asclepius: Artemidorus is uncertain whether to classify him as 'intelligible' or 'sensible' (2.34.2). At first sight, this hesitation is rather curious, since we would tend to classify Asclepius as a straightforwardly 'intelligible' deity, who cannot be directly perceived in real life. I assume that the dual character of Asclepius in the *Oneirocritica* reflects the regularity with which people 'saw' Asclepius in therapeutic dreams at healing sanctuaries (see further below). As an anthropomorphic deity like Athena or Artemis, he could in principle be known only by thought, but he was in practice 'perceived' with unusual consistency and regularity.

Requesting Dreams from the Gods

As we saw in Chapter 3, Artemidorus firmly believes that dreams arise from a process internal to the dreamer: 'dreams are products (*erga*) of the mind (*psychē*), and do not come from any external source' (4.59.3). Artemidorus is well aware that this is an idiosyncratic position. He is, for example, mindful of the fact that in ordinary Greek usage, dreams that come unexpectedly are called 'god-sent' (*theopempta*): but he is careful to emphasize that he does not necessarily endorse divine causation for such dreams (1.6, cf. 4.3, 4.63.1):

Dreams which visit people who have no particular worries, and foretell some future event, good or bad, are called 'god-sent'. I am not now concerned to join Aristotle in the debate whether the cause of dreaming is something outside us, originating from god, or there is some internal causation working on our mind and creating purely natural events in it. Rather, the term 'god-sent' here has the usual application we give it to all things unexpected.

This studied neutrality becomes particularly important when Artemidorus has cause to discuss 'solicited dreams', that is to say, dreams that arise 'when people ask a god for some dream-vision relevant to their immediate concerns' (4.2.11). Artemidorus is visibly uncomfortable discussing dream-requests of this kind, and his position on the status of the resulting dreams is a rather complex one. In Book 1, he warns the dreamer that *if* the dream that results from a request of this kind corresponds very directly to your immediate problem, then it is certainly a non-predictive *enhypnion*, reflecting only the dreamer's immediate physiological or mental condition (1.6):

> We must recognize that what is manifested to people who are worried about something and have asked the gods for a dream does not come with any correspondence to their worries or signify anything about the immediate issues, since dreams corresponding to what is on one's mind are non-significant and to be classed as *enhypnia*, as explained earlier.

This does not rule out the possibility that a 'solicited dream' may in fact be a true, predictive *oneiros*; but it should only be considered as such if the dream-content does *not* correspond directly to your immediate concerns (i.e. is allegorical in form). In his longer account of 'solicited dreams' in Book 4, Artemidorus draws out some of the consequences of this position (4.2.11–12). In requesting a dream from the god, you must not resort to any quasi-magical practices: 'you should not offer the smoke of incense or use any mystic names'. Nor should you put 'impertinently precise questions' to the gods ('What ought I to do to heal my eye-condition?'), and you must above all avoid 'dictating to the gods' by specifying the particular dream-content you wish to see ('If yes, let me see the fruit of Demeter, but if no, the fruit of Dionysus'). This last stipulation is clearly directed at magical dream-invocations (rightly despised by Artemidorus), which do indeed often take exactly this form. Here, for example, is a typical dream-invocation from a third- or fourth-century AD compilation of magical spells (PGM VII.250–4):

Request for a dream oracle, a request which is always used. Formula to be spoken to the day lamp: 'NAIENCHRĒ NAIENCHRĒ, mother of fire and water, you are the one who rises before, ARCHENTECHTHA; reveal to me concerning such-and-such a matter. If yes, show me a plant and water, but if no, fire and iron; immediately, immediately, quickly, quickly.'

The upshot is that if you request a dream from a god in an appropriately open-ended way (no specific questions, no stipulations about content) and receive a self-evidently allegorical dream which does not correspond in a direct and obvious way to your problem, Artemidorus is quite happy to accept that the resulting dream is a genuine predictive *oneiros*, and you can quite reasonably offer sacrifice and give thanks to the god. But he is still very careful to leave it open whether such dreams do in fact come from a god, or whether they arise from your own mind like any other predictive dream: 'The god—*or whatever else is the cause of dreaming*—presents to the dreamer's mind, which is itself prophetic by nature, dreams which point to some future outcome'; 'people should by all means pray to the gods for a dream about what worries them: but what prediction should be made must be left to the god himself *or their own prophetic mind*' (4.2.12—my emphasis, in both cases). In short, 'solicited dreams' are not fundamentally different from any other kind of dream. If you want to see them as the result of divine intervention, that is, in context, understandable; Artemidorus prefers to leave the question open.

In Book 5, Artemidorus gives a few examples of 'solicited dreams'. As we would expect, in no case does he explicitly say that the dream was in fact sent by the god. Here, for instance, is a dream that results from a request to the healing-god Asclepius (5.89):

A man who had a stomach disorder and wanted a prescription from Asclepius dreamt that he entered the god's temple and the god held out the fingers of his right hand and invited him to eat them. The man ate five dates and was cured. The top-quality fruits of the date-palm are called 'fingers'.

For what it is worth, this is very likely to be a *bona fide* dream reported to Artemidorus by a devotee of Asclepius: in the mid-second century AD, the orator Aelius Aristides also experienced a dream in which the god Asclepius transmitted a message to him by movements of his fingers (*Sacred Tales* 2.18). But was Asclepius in fact the real source of the date-fingers dream? Artemidorus does not say so; for him, that the dream has genuine predictive power is indicated purely and solely by its allegorical character (dates = fingers).

Another dream recorded in Book 5 nicely illustrates Artemidorus' dictum that one should not specify particular dream-symbols when soliciting a dream from a god (5.92, cf. 4.2.12):

A man who was sick prayed to Serapis, asking the god to wave his right hand at him in a dream if he was going to recover, and his left hand if not. And indeed he did dream that he entered the temple of Serapis, and Cerberus waved his right paw at him. He died on the following day, and that made sense: by raising his right paw Cerberus, considered to be the embodiment of death, was indicating his readiness to welcome the man.

And a further dream is apparently meant to illustrate the danger of asking 'impertinently precise questions' to the god (5.94, cf. 4.2.11):

A man who was due to have surgery on his scrotum prayed to Serapis about the operation and dreamt that the god told him. 'Go ahead and have the operation: the surgery will cure you.' He died: like a man cured, he was to have no more pain. And it made sense that this was how it turned out for him, because Serapis is not one of the Olympian or ethereal gods, but a chthonic god.

It is no coincidence that all three of these dreams are directed to the gods Asclepius and Serapis. Private magical practices aside, the main context in which individuals requested dreams from the gods in the Greco-Roman world was at great 'incubation sanctuaries' such as the Asclepieum at Pergamum and the Serapeum at Alexandria. Incubation was a special form of divination, usually employed by people suffering from physical ailments, that involved sleeping in the sanctuary of a healing god such as Asclepius. Having performed certain preliminary rituals (usually including a fee to the cult officials), the individual would request a dream from the god. The resulting dream would typically provide therapeutic advice for the sufferer (which would then be interpreted and implemented by the sanctuary personnel), or occasionally a miraculous overnight cure.

Artemidorus' attitude towards these healing sanctuaries was ambivalent. Inasmuch as they encouraged people to believe in the predictive powers of dreams, they were clearly a good thing. But he was, of course, professionally committed to the idea that useful predictive dreams did not require elaborate rituals at a healing sanctuary or the intervention of specialized religious personnel. There is no sign that he had visited the Serapeum at Alexandria, but the Asclepieum at Pergamum—at the height of its popularity in the second and early third centuries AD— was clearly well known to him. Many of his references to these sanctuaries and their dream-cures have an unmistakably waspish tone. The most striking example comes in Book 4, where Artemidorus gives a long and polemical account of 'therapeutic' dreams alleged to derive from the gods. He begins by acknowledging, reasonably enough, that there is nothing intrinsically implausible about the idea that genuine cures might be encoded in (some) therapeutic dreams (4.22.1):

> As for divine prescriptions in dreams, it would be idle to question the fact that gods do prescribe cures for people. Many have been cured by prescriptions received at Pergamum and Alexandria and elsewhere: and there are those who say that the art of medicine actually originated from such prescriptions.

But Artemidorus then immediately launches into a ferocious attack on a group of unnamed writers who, he claims, fabricate unnecessarily elaborate therapeutic dreams (4.22.2–3):

> But I think it clear enough to those with even a modicum of intelligence that the dream-prescriptions recorded by some writers are a farrago of ridiculous nonsense—these are not the records of actual dreams, but fancies of their own invention. When one of them says that 'Nereid soup' has been given as a prescription to some people in winter, I think he tossed up between 'clams' and 'mussels' as the answer to the riddle and came down in favour of clams. Other such riddles they invent are

'the brain of a < . . . >' for a cock, 'biting Indians' for pepper (because pepper is black and it bites), 'virgin's milk' for a dose of salts, 'blood of the stars' for dew, 'a Cretan sheep' for a Cydonian apple, and other stuff like that. No need for me to go on: we should not let exposure of other people's nonsense divert us from our main subject, as quoting just a few examples is enough to nail this sort of rubbish . . . A contemporary of mine is guilty of fabricating such prescriptions and treatments, and has taken that to notable excess in the third book of his treatise.

The unnamed 'contemporary' is probably Geminus of Tyre, cited in Book 2 as the author of a three-book compilation of prescriptions and cures offered by Serapis at Alexandria (2.44.3). Artemidorus' sudden vehemence here is surprising, particularly since these examples of 'ridiculous nonsense' are really no more abstruse or implausible than the elaborate puns and riddles that he often employs in his own dream-interpretation: 'biting Indians' for 'pepper' is just the kind of thing that Artemidorus normally relishes.

So why does Artemidorus come down so hard on Geminus and other compilers of incubation-dreams? I suspect he is engaging in a bit of polemic against the claims of the great incubation sanctuaries and their publicists to a recondite 'religious' science of dream-interpretation. Pay no attention, he says, to the voodoo of Geminus and other quacks—there is really nothing special about the dream-interpretation and medical treatment available at Pergamum or Alexandria (4.22.4–5):

But you will find that the gods' prescriptions are in fact straightforward and not at all enigmatic. They use the same terms as we do in prescribing ointments, poultices, food, or drink, and when they do send an allegorical dream the riddle in it is quite transparent. For example, a woman who had an inflammation of the breast dreamt that she was suckled by a sheep. She was cured by the application of a poultice compounded of plantain, because the name of the plant is a compound (*arno-glosson*), and explains both the tongue of the lamb in her dream and the herb itself, whose name literally means 'lamb's-tongue'. And if you look closely at any of these cures by divine prescription which you come across, whether you make the interpretation yourself or hear of their fulfilment at someone else's interpretation, you will find that they are completely consistent with medical practice and do not stray outside the science of medicine.

In short: there is nothing unusual or technical about incubation dreams. They follow the same symbolic rules as ordinary predictive dreams, and the therapies that they prescribe are the kinds of common or garden treatments that any competent pharmacist could come up with. You might as well save your money and consult Artemidorus instead.

10
Festivals and Games

Greek agonistic culture and public spectacles are remarkably prominent in the world of the *Oneirocritica*. Athletes and actors are among the most visible of all social groups and professions, as hypothetical categories of dreamers (mostly in Books 1–3: 'for an athlete, to dream of *x* is auspicious'), as specific historical individuals (mostly in Books 4–5: 'I know an athlete who dreamt of *x*'), and as people whom others are expected to dream of ('A man dreamt that he became an athlete'). This undoubtedly reflects the enormous popularity of theatre-performances, athletic contests, and gladiatorial shows in the Greek East. Indeed, as has long been recognized, Artemidorus' lifetime (spanning the late second and early third centuries AD) saw a dramatic expansion in the popularity and prominence of agonistic culture across the Greek-speaking world: new contests and festivals were founded, there was a late boom in theatre-building, and even Greek civic bronze coins become increasingly dominated by agonistic imagery.

The prevalence of Greek athletics and athlete-dreams in the *Oneirocritica* is in fact so extreme that we can reasonably use it to reconstruct a crucial aspect of Artemidorus' own life and work. His geography of the Roman empire is almost exclusively an 'athletic geography'—that is to say, his personal experience of the world outside western Asia Minor seems to be completely confined to the great international athletic festivals at Rome, Olympia, Nemea, and elsewhere. Public spectacles, whether theatrical, athletic, or gladiatorial, were a central aspect of Greek culture in the Roman period; but equally importantly for us, they were also one of the key institutional contexts in which oneirocriticism was practised. I do not doubt for a moment that Artemidorus had his regular stall at the Olympic Games, apparently not far from the athletes' village ('Athletes! Get Your Performance-Anxiety Dreams Interpreted Here'), alongside the jugglers, tightrope-walkers, and conjurors bamboozling the punters with the old three-cup trick

(1.76.5, 3.55). To judge from the *Oneirocritica*, very many of the competitors chose to make use of his services.

Days at the Theatre

It is unambiguously the theatrical culture of Artemidorus' own day, not that of the Classical and Hellenistic Greek world, which emerges so vividly from the pages of the *Oneirocritica*. The various troupes of itinerant actors, dancers, and musicians that performed at festivals across the Greek East are now organized into a single empire-wide guild of 'Artists of Dionysus' (1.18, and frequently). These theatre-people have a distinctive appearance, with long hair (1.18) and multi-coloured or purple clothes (2.3.4). Comic and tragic competitions are still going strong (1.56.4–5, 4.33.2, 4.37), as are choral performances (1.56.6, 5.81), but they now jostle for prominence with other genres, some of relatively recent popularity. Pantomime or 'tragic dance' is a particularly notable example (1.76.4):

> To dream that one is dancing in the theatre, complete with mask and costume, and winning fame and plaudits, signifies for a poor man that he will become rich, but that wealth will not last into his old age: the dancer portrays royal characters and has a large supporting cast, but when the play is over he is left on his own.

As Artemidorus' description implies, the pantomime was a form of interpretative dance theatre, wildly popular in the Roman period, in which a tragic myth was represented in mime by a masked dancer, accompanied by musicians and a chorus. It appears to be this form of dance theatre that Artemidorus has in mind when he refers, as he often does, to 'those who mount on the podium' (2.3.4–5, 2.30.4, 2.37.11, 2.69.3, 3.4); pantomime dancers seem to have performed from a raised platform in the middle of the orchestra, rather than the stage. Acrobats, mimes, and clowns appear in passing (1.76.5), the last distinguished by their shaved heads and ridiculous dress (1.22.1, 3.24). A surgeon called Apollonides dreamt that he became a member of the 'Homeristai' or 'Homeric players', actors who performed scenes from Homer in full costume with appropriate props, who had an enormous vogue in the Greek world of the Roman imperial period (4.2.9; Achilles Tatius, *Leucippe and Clitophon* 3.20; see also Chapter 9).

For Artemidorus, the most important symbolic connotation of the theatre was mass public visibility. Here, more than any other of the public spaces of the Greek city, was where the urban masses gathered to see and be seen. It is true that the theatre is only one of several public spaces where crowds are said to gather, along with the marketplace (*agora*), streets, suburbs, temple precincts, and promenades (3.62); but the real-life dreams recorded by Artemidorus show very clearly that it was the theatre, not the marketplace or any of these other spaces, that tended to jump into people's minds as the archetypical place for being observed by others, for good or ill.

The moment of maximum excitement and social anxiety appears to have been the minutes before the performance started, while the crowds were taking their seats in the theatre, scanning the rows around them. Who is that? Who is he with? What is he wearing? Artemidorus records the dream of a young man from Paphos, 'who applied make-up to his face as women do, and then took his seat in the theatre'; the result was that he was caught in adultery and disgraced (4.41.1). As presented by Artemidorus, the dream is predictive, but it takes little effort to read this as a classic anxiety-dream. The man knows he is engaged in an affair which will (if revealed) lead to public disgrace; this anxiety takes the symbolic form of taking his seat in the theatre with his adultery quite literally painted all over his face. A rather similar dream appears a few chapters further on (4.44.2):

A man dreamt that he urinated in the middle of the theatre as the crowd were taking their seats. No wonder, then, that in real life he committed a criminal offence: he showed contempt for the rule of law just as in his dream he had shown contempt for the theatre audience.

Artemidorus classifies this as a dream about the dangers of showing contempt, but once again, it is hard not to see this as a straightforward guilt-dream, with public urination at this moment of supreme visibility reflecting the man's fear of exposure.

For the more assertive members of the *polis*-community, the watchful eyes of the theatre-crowd could bring positive connotations of public recognition and esteem. Artemidorus describes the case of a man who dreamt 'that an eagle ripped out his innards with its talons, carried them through the city to the theatre, which had a full crowd, and displayed them to the spectators' (5.57). A year later, the man had a son, who went on to become a prominent member of the civic elite. The eagle signified the year, since the Greek word for eagle (*aetos*) can be broken down into 'one' (*a*) and 'year' (*etos*) (cf. 2.20.4), and the man's innards signified his child. Therefore, says Artemidorus, the presentation of the man's guts to the spectators in a packed theatre signified 'the distinction and fame which the son would achieve'.

The theatre-crowd is designated by Artemidorus with the word *ochlos*, a rather negative Greek term with similar connotations to the English 'rabble' (2.30.4, 3.62, 4.44.2, 5.57: see Chapter 7). Theatre-actors and musicians are conceived by Artemidorus as belonging to a larger category of 'those who make their living from crowds' (1.64.4, 2.30.4), a category which also encompasses orators and politicians. There is a pleasing logic to the idea that the goddess whom it is most auspicious for an actor or musician to see in a dream is Aphrodite Pandemos (the 'vulgar' Aphrodite, or more literally Aphrodite 'of the whole people'), since it is from the 'whole people' that actors and pantomime artists get their living (2.37.11: also auspicious for innkeepers, prostitutes, and others).

The *ochlos* in the *Oneirocritica* is an unpredictable and slightly threatening thing, symbolically associated with anything teeming or disorderly: frogs (2.15), ants (3.6), the sea (3.16.2: 'like a crowd because it observes no sort of discipline'), a mob of stone-throwers (3.48), even a dung-heap (3.52). The dreams of theatrical performers are predictably dominated by hopes of the crowd's approval and fear of its disapproval. To dream of making public donations is, we are told, 'auspicious for actors and pantomime artists and all who present themselves in performance before a crowd, as it signifies huge appreciation on the part of the crowds—those who make civic donations win applause' (2.30.4; compare 1.76.4, for the 'fame and plaudits' won by successful pantomime artists).

Artemidorus gives two concrete examples of performers' dreams which focus on their relationship with the theatre-crowd. The first comes in the course of his discussion of baths and bath-houses, where he tells us that to find no water in the pools of a bath-house is inauspicious for those who make their living from a crowd (1.64.4):

> I know of a professional performer on the lyre who was about to compete in the sacred Hadrianic games in Smyrna, and dreamt that he was going to take a bath but found no water in the bath-house. What happened was that he was caught attempting to rig the contest, and was fined and thrown out of the games. This was what the dream signified for him, that he would not find what he was looking for, with the bath-house symbolizing the auditorium.

An empty bath-house, an empty auditorium: what could be worse for a performer? The second example relates to a tragic actor about to compete at the Capitolia games at Rome, held once every four years, and one of the great athletic and musical festivals of the Roman world (4.33.2):

> Heraclides of Thyatira was a candidate in the tragedy competition at Rome, and dreamt that he butchered the audience and the judges. He lost. People might kill enemies, but not friends. So in a way the dream was telling him that the audience and the judges would be hostile to him: and in any case they were hardly going to cast their votes for him with their throats cut.

As Danièle Auger has pointed out, Artemidorus has in fact missed a trick in interpreting this dream. It seems to be modelled on a famous tragic myth that Heraclides, as a professional tragic actor, must have known well. In Sophocles' *Ajax*, the eponymous hero has just been defeated by Odysseus in a contest for the arms of Achilles; enraged and humiliated, Ajax attempts to slaughter the Greeks who had voted en masse for his rival. Heraclides' dream thus predicts both his defeat at the Capitolia and his fury at the audience for favouring a rival actor, symbolically modelled on a closely analogous scenario in Greek tragedy (Ajax's murderous rage at the Greeks for favouring Odysseus).

The other major theme of theatre-dreams in Artemidorus is, predictably, deceit, since theatrical performance is by definition a kind of 'pretence' (1.56.6, 1.76.5). 'Telling lies brings no advantage except for pantomime artists, beggars, and habitual liars' (3.4). At the end of his chapter on trustworthy people, after listing many categories of person worthy of trust (gods, priests, kings and magistrates, parents and teachers, etc.), it is actors who come to mind first as quintessentially untrustworthy: 'Actors and pantomime performers of their very nature should not be believed by anyone, because of their play-acting' (2.69.3). This should not, of course, be taken as casting any aspersions on the morals of actors and performers outside of their working life. On the contrary, it is clear that actors, musicians, and other theatrical professionals made up a significant and valuable element of Artemidorus' clientele. In Books 1 and 2 of the *Oneirocritica*, the 'Artists of Dionysus' are a strikingly common category of dreamer (1.18, 1.67.3, 1.77.8, 2.3.4, 2.37.2, 2.37.7), and we may suspect that some of Artemidorus' dream-interpretations have been gently tweaked to meet the specific aspirations of this constituency (2.3.5):

> A dream of wearing women's clothes is favourable only for unmarried men and performers in the pantomime. The former will marry such like-minded wives that they can imagine themselves dressing alike, and the latter will win important engagements and large fees because they regularly wear women's clothes for the roles they play.

Important engagements and large fees—just what a freelance pantomime artist dreams of.

A World of Athletes

Greek athletics are one of the central themes of Artemidorus' waking world. A very great number of dreams in the *Oneirocritica* are dreamt by athletes, both as a hypothetical category of dreamer (mainly in Books 1–3) and as real individual dreamers (mostly in Books 4 and 5). Athletes appear as a class of dreamer around twenty times in Books 1 and 2 of the *Oneirocritica*, and no fewer than twelve of the ninety-five dreams in Book 5 involve professional athletes. Several professional athletes are mentioned by name: the pancratiast Menippus of Magnesia, the two sons of Zoilus, the Syrian wrestler Leonas, Menander of Smyrna (4.42.2, 4.52, 4.82.1). We should assume that most of these athletes were members of the civic upper crust: these were not events for the poor. The sole attested Olympic-victor from Artemidorus' native town of Daldis, one Marcus Aurelius Pius, was also a member of the town-council and a mint-magistrate at Daldis (*TAM* V 3, 1511).

In Book 1 of the *Oneirocritica*, Artemidorus describes the major events in Greek athletic contests and their symbolic connotations in exceptionally rich and loving detail (1.56.7–1.63). All of the main events are there: horse- and chariot-races, the pentathlon (broken down into its five elements), the stade-race (*haplous dromos*), the double-stade race (*diaulos*), the long race (*dolichos*), wrestling, boxing, the pancratium (no-holds-barred fighting with bare fists), and the race in armour. The 'heavy events' (*ta barea*), wrestling, boxing, and the pancratium, appear as a distinct athletic subcategory (1.26.3, 1.56.8; Philostratus, *Gymnasticus* 3); versatile athletes might compete in more than one of these heavy events (5.48), just as a skilled runner might enter for more than one foot-race (5.55).

Elsewhere in the *Oneirocritica*, for reasons not wholly clear to me, certain events are very much more prominent than others. The various equestrian events are given only a very cursory analysis in Book 1 (1.56.7–9), and then do not recur again; the pentathlon, boxing, and race in armour also appear only in the general synopsis of athletic events in Book 1. By contrast, particularly in Books 4 and 5, Artemidorus records significant numbers of dreams seen by runners (6), pancratiasts (5), and, above all, wrestlers (7). Why these events should be so relatively over-represented in the *Oneirocritica* is not obvious; were equestrian specialists less likely than runners and heavy athletes to consult dream-interpreters?

Artemidorus himself was clearly something of a connoisseur of Greek athletics. He regularly uses the verb *leipein* ('leave') in the passive to designate losing an athletic event (e.g. 5.55); this is a technical bit of sports jargon, meaning something like 'be left behind/left standing', often used in contemporary inscriptions relating to athletic success or failure (e.g. an athlete can boast of 'never been left standing'). At times, Arte-midorus reveals a highly specialized knowledge of heavy athletic tech-niques (1.60.1):

I know of someone who dreamt that he was in a wrestling match and used his fingers in the so-called 'two-on-one' hold to throw his opponent:

what happened was that he won his lawsuit after getting hold of some letters written by his adversary.

The basic logic of the dream is clear enough, but exactly what this wrestling-hold might have been is as obscure to us today as the concept of 'reverse swing' will be to the future historian of cricket.

In the prefaces to Books 1 and 5 of the *Oneirocritica*, Artemidorus claims to have collected dreams in the course of visits to festivals in 'Asia' (that is to say, his native province of Asia in modern Turkey, not the continent of Asia), Greece, Italy, and 'the largest and most populous of the islands' (1.Pref.4, 5.Pref.2). His geographical knowledge of these various regions (particularly Greece and Italy) is to a quite remarkable extent an 'athletic geography'. In Italy, he records dreams associated with the Capitolia games at Rome (4.33.2, 4.42.2, 4.82.1) and the Eusebeian games at Puteoli (1.26.3); no other places in Italy are mentioned anywhere in the *Oneirocritica*. The Aegean islands are represented only (obliquely) by Rhodes, where white poplar was used for victory-wreaths at the athletic festival of the Tlapolemeia (2.25.3, 5.74).

In Greece, Artemidorus records nine dreams associated with the Olympic games in the western Peloponnese (1.59, 2.30.5, 4.42.2, 4.52, 4.82.1, 5.48, 5.55, 5.75, 5.76). The only other place in the western or southern Peloponnese mentioned by Artemidorus is Cyllene, the main port for Olympia, which he claims to have visited in person (1.45.1); the other major cities of the region (Sparta, Messene, the cities of Arcadia) are nowhere mentioned. In the north-east Peloponnese, we have dreams associated with the Nemean games (1.77.4, 5.7) and with the sanctuary of Poseidon at the Isthmus, the site of the Isthmian games (5.1, 5.41); it may have been here that he met a certain Chrysippus of Corinth (4.31). Athens, very remarkably, is almost totally absent from the *Oneirocritica* (see also Chapter 7), and is only mentioned in relation to a contest at Eleusis (1.8.2). Mainland Greece north of Attica is pretty much a blank, aside from an athletic contest at Thessalian Larisa (1.8.2); the Pythian games at Delphi may be obliquely referred to in an athlete's dream in which a spring symbolizes the games (the Castalian spring was one of the most famous landmarks at Delphi: 5.78).

It is difficult not to conclude that Artemidorus' travels outside of western Asia Minor were almost entirely confined to visits to major athletic festivals. We should presumably imagine Artemidorus as a professional service-provider to anxious athletes (and their parents: 4.52, 5.75–6), offering reassurance or discouragement to athletes plagued with vivid and alarming dreams on the nights before their big event. It is no surprise that, for Artemidorus, to become an athlete means to 'travel the world coming into contact with all sorts of men and different races' (5.74).

Dreams of Victory

Inevitably, the chief focus of athletes' dreams was victory, and the prestige and fame that accompanied it. Athletic fame is as bright as a dazzling thunderbolt (2.9.5); failure is therefore like the darkness of night (4.42.2). For an Artemidoran athlete, 'it's the taking part that counts' was simply not part of his conceptual world (cf. Pindar, *Pythian* 8, 81–7).

The chief dream-symbol of athletic success in the *Oneirocritica* is of course the victory-wreath (*stephanos*). I say 'of course', but in fact the near-exclusive emphasis on the wreath as a symbol of victory tells us something important about the kinds of athletic victory that were particularly valued in Artemidorus' world. Not all athletic contests had wreaths as the main prizes: many minor local competitions offered money-prizes ('thematic' or 'argyritic' games). It was only the great Panhellenic contests (at Olympia, Nemea, etc.) that were recognized as 'stephanitic' or crowned games. Contests of this kind were known as 'sacred games', and victors in these competitions (restricted to free men: 1.62) were 'sacred victors' (*hieronikai*, 1.56.9). It is worth emphasizing that athletes in Artemidorus never dream of getting rich as a result of winning a money-prize; indeed, no direct association seems ever to be drawn between athletic victory and wealth. The only kind of athletic success that mattered was the success which brought the symbolic prestige of a victory-wreath.

The vegetal wreaths presented to victorious athletes at sacred games were made of various different plants, depending on the contest: marsh-celery at the Nemea (1.77.4, 5.7), white poplar at the Halieia on Rhodes (2.25.3, 5.74), elsewhere olive, palm, oak, and laurel (1.77.5). The plants themselves became closely associated with agonistic success: dreaming of a poplar tree signifies that your son will become a successful athlete (5.74), and for a man involved in a law-suit over ownership of a patch of marshland, dreaming of competing at the Nemean games foretells victory in his law-suit, because celery grows in marshes (5.7).

Dreaming of a wreath is almost invariably auspicious for an athlete, since it connotes victory, fame, and simply having people talk about you (1.77.5). Having many heads is also favourable, because the number of heads you have reflects how many victory wreaths you will win (1.35.9). Conversely, when a dream features a wreath being worn on the wrong part of the body, the dream predicts failure (or worse) for an athlete. A certain Zoilus, the father of two boy-athletes about to compete in the Olympic games, dreamt that his two sons had wreaths of olive and wild olive around their ankles; the two boys both died before they could compete (4.52). Similar symbolism is found in the dream of a boy-athlete at Olympia (5.55):

> A runner who had won the crown in the boys' stade-race at Olympia, and was about to compete in another event, dreamt that he was using the Olympic crown like a basin to wash his feet. He lost that second race and was forced to make an inglorious exit from the racecourse: the reason was his sullying of that earlier crown.

Here of course it is not a simple wreath that is at issue (one could hardly use a wreath as a basin), but rather the large showy cylindrical prize-crowns that victors received at many athletic contests. These spectacular objects, apparently made of light openwork metal, first appear on coins and in sculpture during the reign of Commodus, and so were presumably a relative novelty in Artemidorus' day.

Various other forms of honour deriving from athletic victory are evoked from time to time in the *Oneirocritica*. Major international athletic competitions were called *eiselastikoi*, literally 'driving-in' festivals, because victorious athletes in these contests were granted the right of making a triumphant re-entrance into their native city in a chariot (Vitruvius, *On Architecture* 9, Preface). It is, therefore, good news when an athlete dreams of a four-horse chariot, riding a chariot into a city, or of seeing the Sun-god in the form of a charioteer (1.56.8–9, 2.36.5). Since a victorious athlete can expect to have a bronze statue of himself erected in his native city, it is highly auspicious for an athlete to dream that he is transformed into bronze (1.50.5). Such statues were always accompanied by honorific inscriptions, and so it is good for an athlete to dream of dying and being buried, since the dead can also expect to receive an inscription (5.76, cf. 4.82.1). For an expectant mother, it is good to dream of giving birth to an eagle, so long as her son is of at least moderate means (poor men did not become athletes): her son will receive the honour of being presented to the emperor in the wake of his athletic victories (2.20.3). (How common this last distinction was in real life, we do not know.)

Athletic Anxieties

With the stakes of victory so high, it is hardly surprising that athletes and their families were a highly strung lot. A striking number of dreams in the *Oneirocritica* relate to boy-athletes, that is to say, athletes who competed in the age-class of *paides* ('boys'); three of these are dreams seen by their fretful fathers, worrying about their sons' prospects at the Olympic games (4.52, 5.75, 5.76). Athletic contests at Olympia were divided into two age-classes, boys and adults; other contests also included a third intermediate class of *ageneioi*, 'beardless youths' (not attested in the *Oneirocritica*). The cut-off point for boys seems to have fallen around the age of 17. Candidates for the youngest age-class underwent a pre-selection process (*enkrisis*) to determine whether they were still of an eligible age (Xenophon, *Hellenica* 4.1.40). Naturally it was in the interests of such boy-athletes to push as close to the age-limit as possible, so the process of age-examination must have been a point of particularly intense anxiety, particularly for athletes who had come from far-off parts of the Greek world: would their long journey (and arduous training) all have been wasted?

The most explicit instance of selection-anxiety (and, indeed, one of the clearest examples of an 'anxiety-dream' in the *Oneirocritica*) comes early in Book 5 (5.13):

> A junior wrestler who was anxious about the pre-selection for the games dreamt that the adjudicator was Asclepius, and that as he paraded for review with the other juniors he was disqualified by the god. And in fact

he died before the games started. The god had disbarred him not from the games but from life itself, the more usual question on which he is thought to adjudicate.

It is not hard to see similar anxieties underlying other dreams involving the *enkrisis*. It is, says Artemidorus, inauspicious for a boy-athlete to dream of defeating an adult man in the wrestling: 'it signifies that he will not qualify for selection in the junior category' (1.60.3). Likewise, it is inauspicious for a boy-athlete approaching his *enkrisis* to dream of becoming an ephebe (a formal age-class of boys in their late teens), 'as it foretells that he will be disqualified for being over the age-limit—it will not be long before the ephebe becomes a man' (1.54.3). Artemidorus even includes a whole chapter on dreams about passing or failing the *enkrisis* (1.59); he claims to have met a man who dreamt of failing the *enkrisis* at the Olympic games, and was condemned to hard labour in the mines, a nice indication of how traumatic failure in the selection-process must have been.

Another cluster of athlete-dreams is focused around the formidable figures of the athletic judges (called at Olympia the Hellanodikai, 'judges of the Greeks'). Artemidorus knows of a man 'who was on his way to compete in the Olympic games and dreamt that the Hellanodikai were handing out loaves of bread to the athletes, but had nothing left to give him because he had arrived late'; the athlete died before arriving to register at Olympia, because donatives are not conferred on the dead (2.30.5). In the first section of this chapter, we met the tragic actor Heraclides of Thyatira, who dreamed of slaughtering the judges at the Capitolia games at Rome (4.33.2). Conversely, the father of a boy-wrestler dreamt that his son was slaughtered by the Hellanodikai and buried in the stadium at Olympia (5.76); this turned out in fact to be an auspicious dream, because 'the dead, like victorious athletes, have reached the finishing line' (2.49.3; cf. 4.82.1).

The reason why the judge was such a fearsome figure to the athlete was his ability to swing close contests in favour of one or other competitor. In Book 5, Artemidorus includes the poignant story of a runner, probably at the Pythian games, who was robbed of the victory-wreath (or so he claimed) because of the judge's bias in favour of a rival (5.78):

He tied in a race with another competitor, and although he had the marginal advantage he was obliged to run again. For the second time it was a tied finish at the line with his competitor, so there was a third race. This time he had a significant advantage, but he was denied the crown because the referee was biased in favour of his competitor.

Draws seem to have been fairly common in Greek athletics, particularly in wrestling contests. It is striking that in all our attested examples of wrestling-draws (known mostly from honorific inscriptions for athletes, particularly from Balboura in Lycia), one of the joint-winners is always a well-connected member of the civic elite; this strongly suggests that bouts may regularly have been stopped by the judge at the moment when the less aristocratic athlete was about to win. One wonders whether a disparity of status between the two runners might account for the judge's biased decision in the Pythian foot-race.

For some, the temptation to bend the rules was overwhelming. We have already met the professional lyre-player who was caught attempting to rig the contest at the sacred Hadrianic games at Smyrna (1.64.4). The most detailed account of athletic cheating comes in the context of a remarkable dream set at the Capitolia games at Rome, the significance of which rests on the association between death and athletic victory (4.82.1):

The Syrian wrestler Leonas was about to compete in the games at Rome when he dreamt that he had died and was being carried out for burial, but a trainer came on the scene and was angry at the undertakers for being so quick and officious to carry him out, saying that he could come back to life. Then the trainer applied warm olive oil and wool to his chest and brought him back to life. Leonas had a good day at the games and distinguished himself in the wrestling, but when he was set to go for the crown he was prevented by the trainer, who had previously fixed the way that the crowning bout would work: he had been bribed to disbar Leonas from going on to compete for the wrestling crown.

Outright corruption of this kind, especially the 'throwing' of wrestling-bouts for money, was a major problem at international athletic festivals in the Roman imperial period (Pausanias 5.21). In his *Gymnasticus*, the early third-century author Philostratus specifically refers to corrupt athletic trainers 'trafficking in the virtue of the athletes' for their own profit: 'for they turn up at training sessions with money, and they make loans to the athletes at levels of interest higher than those normal among seagoing merchants, and they pay no attention to the reputation of the athletes but instead act as their advisors in buying and selling, out of a concern for their own profit, which they secure either by giving loans to those who want to make purchases or by taking repayments from those who have made sales' (*Gymnasticus* 45).

The Athletic Body

As a slave receives benefits from his master, says Artemidorus, so a private citizen receives them from a civic magistrate, a soldier from the emperor, and an athlete from his well-conditioned body (2.12.6). The analogy is a startling one. The first three examples are straightforward relationships of patronage and subordination, but in the case of the athlete, it is not an external figure, but rather the toned perfection (*euhexia*) of his body that he depends on for his success in life.

As we would expect, athletes seem often to have had anxiety-dreams focused on the parts of their bodies on which their athletic success particularly depended. A heavy athlete who was about to compete at the Olympic games in both the wrestling and the pancratium dreamt that both his hands had turned into gold; he lost in both his events, finding his hands 'as useless and inflexible as if they were made of gold' (5.48). Another pancratiast, Menippus of Magnesia, had an inauspicious dream shortly before the Capitolia at Rome (fighting at night), with the result that he injured his hand in real life and had to withdraw (4.42.2). For runners, the crucial limbs were their legs and feet. It is auspicious, for fairly obvious reasons, for sprinters to dream that their feet are on fire (1.48.5). We have already met the victorious Olympic boy-runner who, shortly before running in a second event, dreamed that he washed his feet in his first victory-crown, and lost his race (5.55). For a runner to dream of driving a four-horse chariot is inauspicious, says Artemidorus, 'as it is telling them that they are not good enough on their own legs' (1.56.8).

The association of athletic success with strength and masculinity meant that athletes' body-dreams often involve transformation into a stereotypically weaker body-type. For an athlete to dream of breast-feeding foretells sickness, 'as it is the bodies of the weaker sex that have milk' (1.16.2); similarly, a pancratiast—competitor in the most 'masculine' of all athletic events—dreamt he was breast-feeding his own baby, lost his bout, and gave up the sport, because 'his dream had shown him undertaking a woman's role rather than a man's' (5.45: see also Chapter 4). Dreams of becoming a baby are bad for athletes, since 'babies do not walk or run, and cannot defeat anyone, when they cannot even walk' (1.13.3). If a grown man dreams of wrestling with a boy, and he is defeated, he will suffer ridicule and sickness: 'ridicule because of the outcome, and sickness because he has succumbed to a weaker constitution' (1.60.3).

Two dreams in Book 5 of the *Oneirocritica* relate in more specific ways to beliefs about how best to cultivate the body for athletic success. The first is fairly self-explanatory (5.79):

A runner who was about to compete in the sacred games dreamt that he took a broom and cleared out a channel which was clogged with excrement and mud, then washed it through with a great deal of water, to leave it free-flowing and clean. On the next day, despite the imminence of the games, he gave himself an enema and removed the faecal matter from his intestines: this made him light and quick on his feet, and he won the crown.

The second is somewhat more interesting, as reflecting a set of highly culture-specific beliefs about sexual abstinence and bodily strength (5.95):

An athlete dreamt that he cut off his penis, bound his head, and won the crown. He became a victor in the sacred games and acquired quite a reputation. As long as he remained chaste, he had a brilliantly distinguished athletic career, but once he succumbed to sexual indulgence it came to an inglorious end.

Semen was regarded as a major source of bodily strength, and hence ancient athletes were recommended to refrain from sex (Philostratus,

Gymnasticus 52). When Artemidorus' older contemporary Galen suggests that Olympic athletes would castrate themselves if they thought they could do so without loss of vitality, we need not take him literally at his word: this is a kind of *reductio ad absurdum* to illustrate how seriously athletes took the need for sexual abstinence (*On Semen* 1.8). The athlete's castration-dream in the *Oneirocritica* fits perfectly into this mode of thinking.

Gladiators

Gladiatorial combats were unknown in the Classical and Hellenistic Greek world, but became an exceptionally popular form of public entertainment in the Greek East during the Roman imperial period. In his account of gladiator-dreams at 2.32, Artemidorus casually assumes that his readers will be familiar with nine different types of gladiator (the *thraex, secutor, retiarius, essedarius, provocator, arbelas,* and others), all of whom carry slightly different symbolic connotations. The so-called *arbelas,* a gladiator who fought with a small semi-circular knife resembling that of a leather-worker, is in fact unattested elsewhere, although he is depicted on a handful of gladiatorial funerary reliefs from western Asia Minor and elsewhere. In some instances, the basis of the analogy between a type of gladiator and his symbolic meaning is deeply obscure, and must rest on popular associations of particular gladiator-types that are now lost to us: why does a *provocator,* a gladiator in full legionary armour, signify a wife who will be 'beautiful and charming, but also flirtatious and randy'? At any rate, the sheer richness and variety of gladiatorial symbolism nicely illustrates the intense interest that Artemidorus and his clients clearly took in the various modes of gladiatorial combat.

The image of the gladiator in the *Oneirocritica* offers both similarities and contrasts to the image of the successful athlete. Since success in both professions depends on intense physical training, gladiators and athletes can be grouped together as classes of person for whom dreams of breast-feeding are profoundly inauspicious (1.16.2). But the social status of gladiators was immeasurably lower than that of athletes: gladiators typically (though not always: 5.58) entered the profession as condemned criminals (4.65.2). Tellingly, gladiators nowhere appear as a real or even hypothetical class of dreamer in the *Oneirocritica*; practising gladiators were not among Artemidorus' clientele. (Book 5 includes a dream that foretells that a man will later become a gladiator, but that is a rather different matter: 5.58.)

The primary connotations of gladiator-dreams for Artemidorus are predictable enough: violence, conflict, terror, and death. 'To dream of being a gladiator signifies getting involved in a lawsuit or having some other dispute or fight on one's hands' (2.32.1). If you carry 'defensive' weapons (e.g. the net and trident of the light-armed *retiarius*), you will be the defendant in the law-suit; if 'offensive' weapons (e.g. the legionary sword of the *secutor*), the prosecutor. Dreams of the gods Deimos ('Terror'), Phobos ('Fear'), and Ares are auspicious for gladiators, as also for generals, soldiers, bandits, and gamblers. A long dream recorded in Book 5 vividly evokes the lifestyle of the gladiator, accompanied by social dishonour, savagery, and constant danger (5.58):

> A man dreamt that some people lifted him up and carried him about in a sarcophagus full of human blood, and that he ate the blood where it had congealed; then his mother met him and said, 'My child, you have brought dishonour on me'; and then he dreamt that the people carrying him set him down and he returned home. He signed up as a gladiator and over many years fought fights to the finish. His eating of that human blood in his dream signified the god-forsaken savagery of the livelihood he earned from human bloodshed; his mother's protest foretold a dishonourable way of life; and the carrying about in the sarcophagus signified the constant danger which would always attend him—the contents of a sarcophagus are inevitably consumed to nothing. And he would probably have died as a gladiator, if he had not been set down in his dream and gone back home: late in the day some people urged him to abandon his gladiatorial career, and he did so.

However, gladiator-dreams also evoke a completely different set of associations, founded on gladiators' proverbial sexual attractiveness to women (Juvenal, *Satire* 6.103–13). Early in Book 1, Artemidorus tells us that for a bachelor to dream of fighting as a gladiator is auspicious, because it foretells marriage (1.5.5). The same idea runs throughout Artemidorus' long account of gladiator-dreams in Book 2: dreaming of gladiators often foretells 'marriage to a wife who corresponds in an analogous way to the type of weapons the dreamer imagines himself using or to the type of opponent he sees himself fighting' (2.32.2). Dreaming of the nimble *retiarius*, 'poorly' armed but moving swiftly and 'promiscuously' around the arena, means that you will marry a wife who is similarly poor and promiscuous. If someone dreams of fighting against a Thracian (*thraex*), a gladiator armed with greaves, a helmet with visor, a short curved sword and a small shield, 'he will acquire a wife who is rich but devious and keen to come first—rich because the Thracian has full armour, devious because his scimitar is not a straight sword, and keen to come first because he is the one who advances to the attack' (2.32.3).

The Artemidoran pictures of the athlete and gladiator, the two arche-typical 'culture-heroes' of the Greek East in the Roman imperial period, thus stand rather nicely in counterpoint to one another. The victorious athlete is a figure of public honour and prestige, closely associated with the Greek citizen elite, bright like a thunderbolt and glorious like the Sun-god; but he is not a strongly sexualized figure (you want to be an athlete, not sleep with an athlete). The gladiator, by contrast, is a figure of profound public dishonour, slavish, 'blood-eating', associated with strife and conflict; but unlike the athlete, he is invested with strong sexual desirability. For Artemidorus' clientele, as for us, the athlete and the gladiator were eminently good to think with.

11
Status and Values

As we saw in Chapter 3, Artemidorus assumes throughout the *Oneirocritica* that the meaning of a predictive dream is determined not by the dreamer's individual life-history, but by their position within society and the human life-cycle, as defined by wealth (rich or poor), legal status (slave or free), gender (male or female), profession (artisan, athlete, farmer), age, marital status, and health. The dreamer's personal habits and predilections can also affect the meaning of a dream, but usually in a very straightforward and transparent way (1.75):

> To apply perfume is auspicious for all women except adulteresses: but for men it will be a cause of disgrace, unless it is their habit (*ethos*) to do so.

This emphasis on social status (broadly understood) as the key determinant of a dream's meaning makes the *Oneirocritica* a precious tool for understanding class dynamics and status-assumptions in Greco-Roman society. On one level, Artemidorus' narratives of dream-outcomes clearly show that inherited social status was not fully determinate in the Roman provinces of the late second century AD: poor people become rich, free persons fall into slavery, and children can take up different professions from their parents (5.74). But Artemidorus' whole system of interpretation assumes that the dream-interpreter can 'place' a client with absolute clarity and certainty on a spectrum of overlapping statuses, and that this placement will be the primary determinant of the meaning of his or her dream. 'You should interpret all vomiting, whether of blood, food, or phlegm, as indicating benefit for the poor and harm for the rich' (4.26.1). One law for the rich, one for the poor.

Rich and Poor

When Artemidorus classifies free persons in terms of their material wealth, he normally recognizes two categories only: the poor and the rich. The poor are somewhat better represented than the rich as a class of dreamer: some fifty-three dream-meanings are said to apply to the rich, compared to seventy-two for the poor (and eighty-nine for slaves, who are always distinguished from the free poor). I claim no grand statistical significance for these numbers: but, at the very least, they do suggest that Artemidorus' clientele was a very socially mixed one.

Wealth is very firmly associated with (political) power: the 'rich' (*plousioi, euporoi*) are often explicitly paired with the 'powerful' (*mega dynamenoi*), for whom auspicious dreams very often signify public office of some kind (e.g. 1.17, and eight further examples in Books 2 and 3: see further Chapter 7). The rich are often casually grouped with or compared to kings (2.20.2, 2.35.1) or even the gods (3.13–14, 4.49). Greater wealth is associated with superior age (1.78.6, 2.25.2); wealth can even be treated as a gendered phenomenon, such that it is auspicious for a poor man to dream of being transformed into a woman (he will have someone to nurture him, as a woman does), but malign for a rich man (women tend to stay at home, so he will not be appointed to public office) (1.50.3). For a woman, wealth and beauty are casually associated in a way that indicates that Artemidorus sees the two as intrinsically linked (2.25.2, 2.31.1, 2.32.3).

Artemidorus' category of the 'poor' (*penētes*) encompasses not just the truly indigent, but any free person who is not a member of the civic elite: for example, he unhesitatingly ranks artisans among the 'poor' (1.13.1). As 'poor' is to 'rich', so the 'private citizen/commoner' (*idiōtēs*) is to the 'magistrate' (*archōn*): the poor man is quintessentially a person who possesses no political power (2.37.16, 2.68.2), and it is inauspicious (because unrealistic) for a poor man to dream of becoming a civic magistrate (2.30.2). Accordingly, Artemidorus follows earlier dream-interpreters in assuming that the 'poor' man (also called the 'small man' or the 'commoner') will not have dreams about public business, but only about his own small-scale affairs (1.2.11):

> It is impossible that an insignificant man (*mikros*) should go beyond his capability and be granted a vision of momentous events. Since these

dreams too are personal and have outcomes for the dreamers themselves, it stands to reason that they will only be seen by kings, magistrates, or great men. These men have thought about public affairs, and can be granted a vision about them, as they are not like private citizens (*idiōtai*) with only minor responsibilities, but commanding figures, concerned with various matters pertaining to the common good.

The relationship between the 'rich and powerful' and the 'poor and powerless' is sometimes conceived as a contrast of 'big' and 'small' (e.g. 1.2.11, 4.84.4), but more often as a vertical hierarchy ('higher' and 'lower'). This is perhaps most explicit in Artemidorus' account of dreams about flying (2.68.1–2):

> The further one is above the earth, the greater one's elevation over those who walk below: and we regularly speak of more prosperous people as 'high-flyers'... To dream of winged flight is auspicious for all alike. After having this dream slaves will be freed, as all birds that fly have no master and no one above them; poor men (*penētes*) will earn a great deal of money, since money lifts men up just as their wings lift the birds; and for the rich (*plousioi*) and powerful (*mega dynamenoi*) the dream brings government office, because magistrates (*archontes*) are as high above commoners (*idiōtai*) as flying creatures are above those that can only creep along the ground.

Very occasionally Artemidorus employs a tripartite vertical division into the poor, the middling (*metrioi*), and the rich (4.84.4). We are told that 'a dream-vision of the Olympians is advantageous for rich and powerful men and women, of the celestial gods for those of moderate means, and of the terrestrial gods for the poor' (2.34.3). Someone of 'middling' background can, we are told, reasonably aspire to become a famous athlete (2.20.3), which suggests that Artemidorus is thinking of a lower stratum within the elite, rather than, say, craftsmen or shopkeepers.

The categories 'poor' and 'rich' are not impermeable ones: social mobility is a realistic possibility in the world of the *Oneirocritica* (4.7). Artemidorus consistently assumes that the poor, like slaves, will be unhappy with their station and wish to improve it (4.15.1): 'to dream of being poor', he says, 'is not advantageous to anyone' (4.18). A poor man can be 'taken in hand' by a rich man and become wealthy through his patronage (2.20.2, cf. 1.13.1), and Artemidorus sees nothing implausible in the idea that a poor man could end up acquiring his own household slaves (1.48.2, 3.17). A poor man can, in principle, end up having a rich daughter (presumably by marriage?) (1.78.9). Similarly, a poor man can become wealthy through an inheritance from his rich father (3.66.5); the scenario envisaged here is perhaps an illegitimate son who would not normally expect to inherit his father's wealth.

Still, 'social climbing' in the *Oneirocritica* always remains within realistic limits. For a mother of any class to dream of giving birth to an eagle signifies spectacular success for her son: in particular, if a poor mother has a dream of this kind, it indicates that her son will become a soldier in the Roman army, and may even end up 'leading an army' (2.20.3), that is to say, being promoted to the office of *primus pilus* (senior centurion of a legion). With only 60 *primi pili* in a standing army of 180,000 legionaries in the second century AD, this was a pipe-dream for most people; but Artemidorus' interpretation of the dream does still indicate that a poor man's chances for social advancement must have been better in the Roman army than in any other institution of provincial society.

The different lifestyles of rich and poor are vividly evoked in the *Oneirocritica*. The rich are assumed to live in a state of indulgent luxury (*tryphē*: e.g. 2.3.7, 2.37.14, 3.59.1); they are expected to bathe with a retinue of attendants, while the poor man bathes alone (1.64.3). Artemidorus assumes that the rich and poor eat different kinds of food: it is, he says, 'auspicious to dream of eating the type of bread to which one is accustomed—bran bread is suitable for the poor, and refined white bread for the rich' (1.69). Flavoured wines are also a strong indicator of social status: 'To drink mead, apple cider, honey liqueur, myrtle wine, or any other flavoured wine is auspicious for the wealthy, because these are luxury products, but it is harmful for the poor, because they do not otherwise turn to beverages of this sort except under prescription for some illness' (1.66.2). It is poignant to read that for a poor man, a really auspicious dream may simply foretell a regular and consistent supply of food (3.56.1, 4.16). It is good for a poor man to dream of small birds, not just because poor men are 'small', but because 'the small birds which eat seeds have a ready supply of food and never go short' (2.20.1).

Nonetheless, there is little sign that Artemidorus holds the poor in contempt. It is telling that the only instance of genuine disdain for the poor in the *Oneirocritica* comes in a summary of the views of certain unnamed 'early authorities' on dream-interpretation, who clearly took a much less sympathetic view of the lower social orders (2.9.3):

> As for a direct hit by a thunderbolt, the very early authorities made a distinction, saying that such a dream was auspicious for the poor, but bad for the rich. Their reasoning was as follows. Poor men are like those insignificant bits of wasteland where people chuck dung and any other rubbish, while the rich are like the reserved precincts of gods or men, the temples or shrines of gods, sacred groves, or any other sort of prestigious place. So just as thunderbolts bring fame to insignificant places (because of the altars that are established there and the festivals held when sacrifice is made at them), and render prosperous places deserted and taboo (because no one then wants to go anywhere near them), so this dream benefits the poor and harms the rich.

Artemidorus himself thinks this is quite wrong (2.9.5): the dream is beneficial for slaves, poor, and rich alike.

Slaves and Masters

As has long been recognized, Artemidorus is an exceptionally important source for the mentalities of both slave-owners and slaves in the high Roman imperial period. Slaves are a constant presence in the *Oneirocritica*, both as a hypothetical category of dreamer and—more interestingly—as 'real-life' dreamers (a total of eighty-nine dream-outcomes, real and hypothetical). By my count, Artemidorus includes twelve 'real-life' dreams attributed to slaves, and I see no good reason to doubt that slaves formed a small but significant part of his own clientele (1.78.7, 2.15, 4.Pref.9, 4.4.1, 4.24.3, 4.61, 4.64 (two dreams), 4.69, 5.23, 5.85, 5.91).

The mentality of the Greco-Roman slave-owner is perhaps most vividly evoked in Artemidorus' account of dreams about mice (3.28.1):

> A mouse signifies a household slave: it lives in our house, it shares our food, and it is a constant presence. So it is auspicious to dream of

having many mice in one's house kept happy and playful: they foretell much good cheer and the acquisition of more household slaves.

This is all very charming, and it is not hard to find other examples of dream-symbolism in the *Oneirocritica* that give a similarly harmonious impression of master–slave relationships: a man who dreamt that his slave had a fever fell sick himself, because 'the relation of his household slave to the dreamer is the same as that of his body to his soul' (4.30.3). But this cosy picture of happy symbiosis certainly does not reflect the slave's own experience of the relationship. Of course, we have no way of knowing for certain how 'real' the 'real-life' slave-dreams of the *Oneirocritica* actually are. But it is very striking how many of them casually assume relations of mutual tension, hatred, or physical violence between master and slave.

Being beaten or whipped is a very common dream-outcome for a slave. Artemidorus knew of a slave 'who dreamt that he was being masturbated by his master: he was tied to a post and soundly whipped—that was how his master had him erect' (1.78.7). Dreaming of beef is inauspicious for a slave, 'because straps and whips are made of oxhide' (1.70.1). It is bad for a slave to dream of dancing, because it symbolizes the writhing of his body during a hard beating (1.76.4), and olive-trees are malign for a slave 'because the tree is beaten to drop its fruit' (2.25.1). At least some slaves seem to have fully internalized this association between domestic authority and physical violence, to judge from the depressing case of the slave who dreamed of inflicting violence himself, and consequently won a promotion (2.15):

> I know of a household slave who dreamt that he was punching frogs, and he was put in charge of his master's house, with authority over the household staff—the pond signified the house, the frogs the domestics, and the punches the orders he gave them.

Artemidorus vividly evokes the hatred that slaves could feel for their masters. In the Preface to Book 4, he gives the example of a painter in Corinth, evidently of slave-status, who 'wanted to see his master buried'. Unfortunately, the slave's knowledge of the rules of allegorical dream-interpretation meant that his dreams, despite their apparently symbolic content, were not genuine predictive *oneiroi* but simply wish-fulfilment *enhypnia* (4.Pref.9):

He often dreamt of the roof of the house where he lived collapsing, and of his own beheading: but even so his master outlived him and is still alive to the present day. What was happening was that, given the man's ability to interpret this sort of symbolism in dreams, his mind was playing a rather esoteric trick on him: for any other dreamers these same visions would prophesy the death of their master.

Manumission dreams are predictably frequent in the *Oneirocritica* (thirty-two out of eighty-nine dream-outcomes) often taking the form of a slave dreaming of an activity only permitted to free persons: serving as a soldier (1.5.5), having a bronze portrait statue erected (1.50.5), becoming an ephebe (1.54.1), acting as a sacred trumpeter or herald (1.56.1–2), competing in sacred games (1.62.2), or wearing purple (2.3.4). Artemidorus records the dream of a slave-prostitute who imagined entering the temple-precinct of Artemis at Ephesus, and was subsequently manumitted, since the precinct was only open to married free women (4.4.1). He seems to have been particularly taken with the dream of a slave who dreamt that he had three penises (1.45.4 = 5.91, described by Artemidorus as 'a one-off occurrence'). The three penises symbolized the 'three names' that the slave would receive on obtaining his freedom: when the slave of a Roman citizen was manumitted, he took the *praenomen* and gentilician of his former owner in addition to his existing name. As we will see in Chapter 12, Artemidorus distinguishes carefully between Greek and Roman manumission practices: for example, wearing white is auspicious only for slaves of Greeks, since white garments were worn at Greek manumission-ceremonies (2.3.2).

Manumission-dreams can be fallacious, as in the melancholy case of a slave whose hopes were raised unduly by a dream about the stars (5.23). He dreamed of one star falling to earth, and another rising from the earth to the sky. His master died soon after (the falling star), and the slave fully expected to receive his freedom; but his master's son (the rising star) then appeared on the scene and 'forcibly' took him over as his own slave. The slave's expectations were natural enough, since death and manumission were closely linked in both dreams and real life (2.49.1). A slave who dreamt of being murdered by his master was subsequently freed by him (4.64); a freedman's dream of being manumitted a second time symbolized the death of his patron and former master (4.81).

A striking feature of the mentality of slave-owners in the *Oneirocritica* is that of anxiety over slaves' sexuality. A curious dream recorded by Artemidorus in Book 3 links this anxiety with the notion of the slave as the owner's alter ego (3.51):

> I know of someone who was lame in his right leg, and dreamt that his household slave was lame in the same leg and limped as he did. What happened was that he caught the slave on top of the mistress with whom he himself was smitten: and so this is what the dream was telling him, that the slave would share his own failing.

From the slave's perspective, dreaming of sex with his mistress is auspicious, since it foretells promotion within the household: just as with the dream about frogs quoted above, the point is presumably that the slave is imagining taking on part of his master's normal role (4.61):

> Someone dreamt that his master sent his own wife into bed with him. And no enmity at all arose between him and his master, but the master entrusted his whole property to his management, and he supervised the entire household. It stands to reason that a man who sends his own wife to another's bed would not feel any jealousy.

Sexual relations and even marriage between slaves (or former slaves) and their owners were evidently common enough in real life (1.79.7, 3.30), and it is no surprise to find Artemidorus recording 'real-life' dreams that reflect jealousy and suspicion between mistresses and their female slaves (4.59.4, 5.53). Artemidorus treats such unions as symbolically unnatural, as reflecting a linking of the superior and inferior (1.26.9):

> I know of someone who dreamt that his eyes dropped out and fell to his feet. He did not go blind, but he married his daughters to his household servants, thus bringing about that conjunction of higher and lower.

Nonetheless, one of the most distinctive features of Artemidorus' treatment of slavery is the 'ethical neutrality' (in the words of Roger Pack) with which he approaches both slaves' dreams and their real-life experiences. Slaves are, both in reality and in the world of dream-symbols, 'lower' than their master's daughters, but only because that is how the social order happens to be arranged. Artemidorus recognizes that slaves have an inner psychological life that operates in the same way as that of free persons; he is happy with the idea that slaves might understand the rules of allegorical dream-interpretation (4.Pref.9, quoted above); slaves' dreams can exemplify important general principles just as readily as the dreams of kings (e.g. 4.24.3: dreams of Alexander the Great and of Antipater's slave Syrus).

Perhaps most significantly of all, there is no indication that Artemidorus regards slaves as in any way morally inferior to free men and women. Artemidorus never blames slaves for their condition, on either natural or ethical grounds. Indeed, the dividing line between slaves and the free poor is not a hard one: poor men and slaves can be grouped together as categories of dreamer, since both are in others' power (2.12.5), and both wish to improve their station (4.15.1).

One does wonder, finally, how Artemidorus and other practising dream-interpreters dealt with their real-life slave-clients. You are presumably on fairly safe ground in predicting manumission, or even transfer to a better household (ideally the imperial court: 2.68.3), as long as you are appropriately vague about the time-frame. But how should the dream-interpreter respond to a query from a slave who has had a dream about a cuttlefish or climbing out of a window (2.14.6, 2.68.5)? The dream predicts success in running away from one's master: it is, in Keith Hopkins's words, a 'rebellion of the mind'. Do you tell them?

Work and Leisure

One of the most distinctive and unusual features of the value-system of the *Oneirocritica* is Artemidorus' unquestioning assumption that work is a good thing, and 'leisure' (*scholē*) is bad. The term *scholē* appears nine times in the *Oneirocritica*, and invariably has strongly negative connotations, as do its near-synonyms *anergasia, apragia, apraxia*, and *argia*: it signifies not the pleasures of free time, but the affliction of unemployment. This is all the more striking in the light of the near-universal position of elite Greek and Latin literary authors that leisure (*scholē, otium*) is something to be valued, while labour is despised as unfitting for a free man or woman.

Artemidorus is virtually the only author from the entire Greco-Roman world to espouse anything remotely resembling a Protestant work-ethic.

In the first two books of the *Oneirocritica* alone, some thirty discrete dream-elements are said to signify leisure or inactivity: having food stuck in your teeth (1.31.8), artichokes (1.67.1), a calm sea (2.23.6), flying flat on your back (2.68.6). So far as I can tell, in every single case this outcome is clearly signalled as malign: 'leisure' is directly associated with illness (1.50.8, 1.66.1, 2.36.3), poverty (1.32.1, 1.76.6), harm, and loss (2.22.2, 2.55.1). It is, says Artemidorus, good for a poor man to dream of lying awake in bed at night, since the dreams indicates that he will not have 'leisure' (*scholē*) (2.1). The *universally* negative connotations of leisure in the *Oneirocritica* seem to me to be profoundly significant. Artemidorus could have chosen to distinguish between the 'good' leisure of the cultured rich and the 'bad' leisure of the working poor. He could, for instance, have said that dreams of flying while lying on one's back or sitting on a chair are bad for the poor (unemployment) but good for the rich (reclining at leisure, being carried on a litter)—but no, such dreams are bad for everyone (2.68.6–7). Indeed, when he does evoke the genuinely leisured lifestyle of the very rich, he does so in a strikingly disparaging manner (3.18):

> To dream of being harnessed to a cart like some four-footed draught-animal foretells slavery, exhausting work, and sickness, even if the dreamer is some great celebrity (*lampros*) accustomed to the life of luxury (*habrodiaitos*).

The word *habrodiaitos* has stern and moralizing connotations of effeminate and delicate living, and it is remarkable to find it here being applied to (apparently) the wealthiest classes in society. For Artemidorus, being a successful person—and, what is perhaps more startling still, 'living a life of your own choosing'—is intrinsically bound up with work and activity (2.55.1):

> To dream of going down into Hades, and seeing all that is traditionally said to be there, signifies inactivity (*apraxia*) and harm for successful people who live a life of their own choosing, because the inhabitants of Hades are inactive, cold, and static.

More explicitly still, Artemidorus identifies 'work' with life, and 'work-lessness' with death (4.40):

> Here is a dream you can store away to demonstrate that work has the same meaning as life. A woman dreamt that she had finished the web on her loom. She died on the following day. She had no more work to do, which meant no more life to live.

It is telling that the only categories of person in the *Oneirocritica* to receive unconditional moral condemnation from Artemidorus are 'parasites' who receive an income without having to work for it: beggars (3.53), tax-farmers (1.23, 4.42), hucksters, and bandits (4.57.3).

Leisure is, as we might expect, particularly inauspicious for artisans (*cheirotechnai*, literally 'hand-craftsmen'). Dreaming of being born has bad consequences for an artisan, 'as babies do not work and have their hands wrapped up' (1.13.1); likewise, having hair on one's palms is bad for both artisans and farmers, as 'when the hands are no longer being worn by work or the surface skin hardened, that is when hair is likely to appear' (1.42.6). By contrast, says Artemidorus, 'to dream of having many hands is auspicious for the artisan, since he will have no shortage of work: in a way the dream is telling him, "With all this work crowding in, you need more hands!"' (1.42.7). It is good for a craftsman to dream of having many ears, since 'he will hear from many employers giving him contracts' (1.24.1). A dream of having sex with one's mother is auspicious for artisans, because 'a man's trade is commonly called his "mother", so coupling with this "mother" can only mean keeping busy [literally, 'not having *scholē*'] and earning a living from one's trade' (1.79.3). However, a dream of entering the ephebate—an elite age-class of citizen youths in their late teens, who spent a year engaged in ethical and intellectual training—is bad for the artisan who wishes to stay active (1.54.1):

> For any artisan or orator the dream signifies a year of inactivity and unemployment, because the ephebe must keep his right hand tucked inside his cloak, and not bring it out to employ it in any manual work or speech-making throughout the whole year.

Artemidorus generally assumes that men work harder than women, because women, like children, are weaker than men (2.56.2; on women's work, see Chapter 5). Prostitutes are an honourable exception to this, and so seeing a prostitute in a dream can have positive connotations, because of their dedication to hard work: brothel-based prostitutes 'are auspicious for every undertaking, as some call them "working girls" (*ergasimoi*) and they make themselves available with nothing refused' (1.78.3). It is good for a prostitute to dream of being transformed into a man, since she will have more endurance for work and 'will be able to take no end of fucking' (1.50.4). It is noteworthy how many different dream-elements, when seen by a woman dreamer, signify falling into a state of prostitution (1.58, 3.16.2, 3.23.3, 4.66) or even being prostituted by one's husband for profit (5.2), and I think we must assume that this was a realistic fear for free women of limited financial means (1.56.9):

A dream of driving through the city in a chariot is auspicious for women and unmarried girls who are both freeborn and wealthy, as it wins them advantageous positions as priestesses. But for poor women riding through the city foretells prostitution.

The ideal state of activity, for Artemidorus, is not leisure, but the kind of work which comes easily and comfortably, without undue toil or exhaustion (*ponos, kamatos*). The best kind of flying dream is not a dream in which one has to do no work at all, but a dream where motion comes easily: 'Most auspicious of all is being able to fly at will and stop at will: this foretells much ease (*rhaistōnē*) and smoothness in the running of one's affairs' (2.68.5). Dreaming of weightlifting 'foretells temporary failure and pain, followed by success and comfort (*praxeis meta rhaistōnēs*), as this sort of exercise essentially tones one's arms for their work' (1.55). As the final clause indicates, 'comfort' (*rhaistōnē*) here signifies the comfort that comes from work that is easily within one's capabilities, not that of leisured inactivity. Most explicit of all is Artemidorus' explanation of why it is auspicious to dream of penetrating one's mother when she is straddling the dreamer in the 'rider' position (1.78.5). For people in good health, this dream signifies that they will 'live the rest of their lives entirely at their ease (*meta rhaistōnēs*) and just as they would choose—a consequence which makes perfect sense. In all other positions the exertion and heavy breathing mostly fall to the male, and the female has less work to do: but in this particular position the complete opposite is true, and the man has his pleasure without exerting himself.' Once again, the point is not that the dreamer will go on to live a life of total leisure, but a life of easy, pleasant, and comfortable work without excessive exertion.

Perhaps the most vivid praise of work in the *Oneirocritica* comes in Artemidorus' account of dreams about swallows (2.66.2). Here Artemidorus is arguing (against some of his predecessors) that dreams of swallows are not malign, despite the existence of a gloomy metamorphosis-myth involving the swallow (the myth of Procne and Philomela):

Its song is no funeral dirge, but a tune which acts as a prelude and encouragement to the work of the day. Proof of this can be seen in the fact that the swallow does not fly or utter a sound in the winter, and that is the season when there is no working of the land or sea, and men as well as all other creatures retreat inside their homes and cease all activity. But when spring approaches the swallow is the first to emerge, and draws attention to all the work which needs to be done. And when the swallow does reappear, it never sings in the evening, but only in the morning when the sun comes up, reminding any it finds not dressed for work of what they have to do.

It is worth noting Artemidorus' assumption here about the basic seasonality of work, not only for farmers and sailors, but for all possible classes of dreamer. In the late 1940s, when the British archaeologist George Bean asked some Turkish farmers of the upper Xanthos valley what they did in winter, the reply was simply 'we sit'.

12

An Invisible Empire

Greeks and Romans

Rome and the Roman empire occupy a curiously marginal position in Artemidorus' thinking. It is no accident that we find it so hard to date the *Oneirocritica* with any precision: the relative 'timelessness' of so much of Artemidorus' work reflects a near-total lack of interest in the contemporary world of high Roman politics. Only two named Roman emperors make walk-on appearances in the *Oneirocritica*, and then only in order to identify specific athletic festivals (1.26.3, 1.64.4). The upper echelons of Roman society and imperial administration—the imperial court, the senate, the senatorial and equestrian orders, provincial governors and other Roman officials, even the Roman army—are almost entirely absent. Even though Artemidorus claims to have attended great religious festivals in Italy (1.Pref.4; 5.Pref.2), he is not terribly interested in the Italian peninsula, or even in the city of Rome. His silence about Europe and the Mediterranean north and west of Italy is complete: in the world of the *Oneirocritica*, the entire western half of the Roman empire might as well not exist.

That is not to say that Artemidorus pays no attention at all to Roman culture and institutions. The Roman courts and penal system are depressingly prominent in the *Oneirocritica*, as are slavery and manumission in their specifically Roman form. Artemidorus is interested in Roman dress and Roman names, and he dedicates some lengthy chapters to characteristically Roman cultural practices, such as gladiatorial shows and public bathing. But perhaps the most striking feature of Artemidorus' Roman interests (or lack of them) is his intuitive classification of certain things, people, and practices as distinctively Roman *and therefore foreign and alien*. Here, for example, is Artemidorus in *Oneirocritica* Book 1, in the course of a discussion of dreams about learning to read and write (1.53.2):

If a Roman (*Rhōmaios*) learns to read Greek (*Hellēnika grammata*) or a Greek (*Hellēn*) learns to read Latin (*Rhōmaika grammata*), the one will come to embrace Greek culture (*Hellēnikai diatribai*) and the other Roman culture (*Rhōmaikai diatribai*). And there are many cases of Romans (*Rhōmaioi*) marrying Greek women (*Hellēnides*) and Greeks (*Hellēnes*) marrying Roman women (*Rhōmaiai*) after seeing this sort of dream. I know of someone who dreamt that he was learning to read Latin. He was condemned to slavery: such a sentence is never delivered in Greek.

As it happens, there is no sign in the *Oneirocritica* that Artemidorus could read or speak Latin himself. It is hard to say how typical this would have been for a man of his background and status. There were certainly teachers of Latin in the larger towns of Roman Lydia: we know of a Latin teacher, a *grammatikos Rhōmaikos*, at the town of Thyateira (*TAM* V 2, 1119). But that is not the main point of interest here. Artemidorus casually assumes, without comment or qualification, that there are 'Romans' (*Rhōmaioi*), and that there are 'Greeks' (*Hellēnes*), and that the two are different. Romans speak Latin, they have their own distinctive Roman culture, and you can spot a Roman woman when you see one; Greeks speak Greek, and do their own distinctive Greek things. Of course, a Greek can learn Latin (or at least dream of doing so); he can choose to adopt Roman 'behaviours' (*diatribai*), and can even marry a Roman woman. But, Artemidorus warns us, perils await the person who dreams about crossing cultures in this way. Under Roman court procedure, judgements were always delivered in Latin, even if the remainder of the trial had been conducted in Greek. Hence if you, as a Greek, dream about learning to read Latin, that may signify not that you will end up wearing a toga and marrying a nice girl from Tuscany, but that you will end up being condemned to slavery by a Roman magistrate—so watch out.

To a modern historian of the high Roman empire, the assumptions embedded in this passage are not at all what we would expect. In Artemidorus' day, very many Greeks, of both high and low social status (from civic elites to recent freedmen), possessed Roman citizenship—we do not know whether Artemidorus himself was among them. In AD 212, shortly after the completion of the *Oneirocritica*, Roman citizenship was extended to the entire free population of the empire. In legal terms, such Greeks were indubitably *Rhōmaioi*. Yet Artemidorus clearly regards 'Romanness' and 'Greekness' as distinct and essentially non-overlapping categories. These categories encompass both linguistic knowledge and cultural behaviour: learning to read Latin symbolizes an adoption of Roman cultural practices (*diatribai*), or marriage into a 'Roman' family, or subjection to Roman jurisdiction.

Crossing from one category to the other is a dangerous process in the *Oneirocritica*. In Book 4, Artemidorus reports the inauspicious outcome of a dream involving marriage of a 'Roman' to a 'Greek' (4.33.1):

> A doctor dreamt that he said to someone: 'You are a Roman (*Rhō-maios*), so do not marry a Greek woman (*Hellēnis*)': his own marriage caused him much trouble from his wife.

There is nothing bad about Greek wives per se; the problem is 'mixed' marriages. On the contrary, for a Greek dreamer (that is, for most of Artemidorus' anticipated readers), Greekness is a profoundly positive quality in a wife, as Artemidorus suggests in his discussion of dreams of swallows (2.66.3):

> To dream of swallows is auspicious for work, for business, and for music, but most of all for marriage. A swallow signifies that the dreamer's wife will be loyal and a good housekeeper, and more often than not that she will be Greek (*Hellēnis*), and musical.

Similarly, even receiving Roman citizenship—which one would have thought would be an unambiguous boost to one's status and prestige—is presented in a curiously equivocal manner in the *Oneirocritica*, in the course of a long account of dreams about decapitation (1.35.8):

> I know of someone who dreamt that he had been beheaded. He was a Greek (*Hellēn*) who had obtained Roman citizenship (*Rhōmaiōn politeia*), and so lost his former name and status.

As a way of thinking about the acquisition of Roman citizenship, this is seriously odd. When a Greek received Roman citizenship, he typically retained his original Greek name as his *cognomen*, and took on the *praenomen* and gentilician of the Roman through whom he was granted citizenship (compare 1.45.4, on manumission). He did not strictly 'lose' either his former name or his former status; so far as we know, he always retained citizenship in his native Greek city-state. But that is the verb that Artemidorus uses: *aphairethēnai*, 'to have taken away'.

It would, I think, be quite wrong to see Artemidorus as harbouring any overt or covert 'anti-Roman' sentiments. As we have seen, one of the founding principles of Artemidorus' theory of dream-interpretation is that dreams are auspicious when their content accords with the dreamer's physical nature, customs, profession, and so forth (1.3; 4.2), so it is hardly surprising that it should be inauspicious for a Greek to have a dream with a manifestly 'Roman' content. What is interesting from our perspective is his instinctive assumption that some things *are* in fact manifestly 'Roman' and others manifestly 'Greek'. Artemidorus experienced the Roman empire as a world of two separate cultures, Greek and Roman; a hyphenated 'Greco-Roman' world it most emphatically was not.

Two Cultures?

Very many of the cultural practices described by Artemidorus were uniform across the Greek- and Latin-speaking halves of the Roman empire. So far as we know, people used a downward nod to say 'yes' and an upward head-flick to say 'no' in both the Greek East and the Latin West; there is nothing distinctively Greek about Artemidorus' anthropology of nodding (5.71–72). Likewise, certain practices of Roman origin had become so widespread and naturalized in the Greek East by Artemidorus' day that they were clearly no longer felt to be distinctively 'Roman'. One thinks, for example, of gladiatorial combat, enthusiastically adopted in the Greek East in the Roman imperial period, and the subject of a long and intricately differentiated chapter in the *Oneirocritica* (2.32: see Chapter 11). Artemidorus himself emphasizes that the views of earlier dream-interpreters on dreams about public baths and bathing had become completely obsolete by his own day, due to the broad diffusion of Roman bathing culture in the Greek world (1.64).

But in fields of life where typical Greek and Roman practices differed, Artemidorus seems always to describe Greek rather than Roman cultural norms. He consistently assumes that the dead will be buried, rather than cremated (1.13.3, 1.15, 2.49, 2.59.1); cremation was normal throughout the entire western Roman empire in the first and second centuries AD. He assumes that houses will have clearly distinct 'women's quarters' (2.10.1); true of houses in the Greek world, but emphatically not true of, say, Roman Italy. He assumes that you will not beat your wife unless she is suspected of adultery (2.48.1: see Chapter 5); husbands in the Latin West were very much freer with their fists (Augustine, *Confessions* 9.9.19).

This is, of course, just as we should expect; most of Artemidorus' expected clientele were Greeks. But we should note how rarely Artemidorus bothers to indicate that the Romans did things differently. Explicit comparison and contrast are confined to spheres where his audience might expect to come across both Greek and Roman practices. Manumission of slaves, Greek-style and Roman-style, is a particularly clear example (see Chapter 11). To dream of wearing white clothes is usually inauspicious, says Artemidorus, because it indicates inactivity (one does not wear white clothes while at work). White clothes can be auspicious for a slave, since they foretell his or her manumission, but only if the slave is owned by a Greek (2.3.2):

> As for slaves owned by Romans, the dream is only auspicious for the conscientious among them: for the others it is malign, as the white clothes show up their bad conduct. Because for the most part these slaves wear the same sort of clothing as their masters, having this dream does not bring them their freedom, as it does for slaves owned by Greeks.

It seems that during Greek manumission ceremonies, white garments were worn by the newly freed slave as a symbol of his or her liberty (cf. 2.9.4); but different dress-symbolism was used in Roman manumission (typically the *pileus*, a felt cap). The distinction matters here—as it does not matter in the case of, say, wife-beating—because Artemidorus' clientele must have included both Greek slaves owned by Greeks and Greek slaves owned by Romans. Sometimes only slaves with Roman owners are concerned, as in a manumission-dream that foretells the bestowing of the owner's *praenomen* and *nomen* on a newly liberated slave (1.45.4 = 5.91):

> I know of a man, at the time a slave, who dreamt that he had three penises. He was set free, and then had three names instead of the one, taking the extra two names from the man who had freed him.

Conversely, Artemidorus' interpretation of dreams of enlisting as a soldier is only meaningful in a context of slavery and manumission *à la grecque* (2.31.2):

> For slaves the dream [of enlisting as a soldier] signifies high standing, but not yet their complete freedom: many who have been freed have still continued nonetheless in slavery and subjection. A soldier may be a free man, but he is nonetheless in service.

Artemidorus is here referring to the characteristically Greek practice of 'deferred manumission'. In the Greek world, an owner could manumit his slave on condition of *paramonē* ('remaining'), which obliged the slave to 'remain' with his or her owner for a specified period of time, usually until the owner's death; apparently the manumission did not take effect until the expiry of the *paramonē* period (cf. perhaps 1.47.3, 4.81). There is no analogy to this practice in Roman slavery.

Clothing is one of the most noticeable fields of cultural distinction between Greeks and Romans in the *Oneirocritica*. Artemidorus twice refers in passing to a distinctively Roman heavy woollen cape 'called a *paenula* in Latin' (5.29; also 2.3.7). This is the only instance of a Latin loan-word explicitly indicated as such by Artemidorus in the entire five books of the *Oneirocritica*. A longer discussion of a characteristically Roman garment comes early in Book 2, where Artemidorus is discussing dreams of wearing 'barbarian' dress (2.3.6):

> A dream of wearing barbarian clothes and being kitted out in barbarian fashion signifies, for anyone who wants to visit a country where the inhabitants wear that sort of clothing, that his time spent there will be profitable, and it often foretells that he will actually end his days there: for all others it signifies sickness or lack of success. The same holds true

of the Roman dress called the 'toga' (*tebennos*). The name comes from Temenus of Arcadia, who was the first to wrap his outer garment round him in this fashion, after he had sailed across the Ionian Gulf and been welcomed by the inhabitants of that country. The indigenous people then took up his example and adopted the same style of dress, calling it 'Temenian' after its inventor Temenus. In the passage of time the name became corrupted into *tebennos*.

The basic assumption here (that for a Greek to dream of wearing a toga signifies either a successful journey to Italy, or sickness and failure) fits perfectly with Artemidorus' belief that dreams are only auspicious when they conform to the dreamer's customary practice: it is bad for non-toga-wearers to dream of togas. But to find the Roman toga classified along with 'barbarian' forms of dress, as if it were a pair of trousers or a hat with ear-flaps, is something else altogether.

The foreignness of the toga is underlined—in a slightly paradoxical way—by a long and most un-Artemidoran ethnographic digression on the etymology of the Greek word for toga, *tebennos*. This story seems to be unique to Artemidorus, and has the air of an ad hoc concoction. The Greek hero Temenus was traditionally from Argos, not Arcadia, and no other author has him travelling across the 'Ionian Gulf' (Adriatic) to Italy. His transplantation to Arcadia probably reflects a long-standing tradition of mythological kinship between Rome and the Arcadians via the hero Evander (most famously in Vergil's *Aeneid* Book 8). Artemidorus' etymological connection between *Temenos* and *tebennos* is of course entirely spurious; the word *tebennos* is in fact probably of Etruscan origin (Dionysius of Halicarnassus rightly says that 'the word doesn't seem Greek to me', 3.61.1).

Artemidorus clearly saw 'Roman dress' as a distinctive and recognizable package. Late in Book 4, he explains that when gods appear in inappropriate clothes, anything they say should be considered as false and misleading (4.72.1):

Chrysampelus the lyre-player was involved in a law-suit about a boy being taken into slavery, and dreamt that he saw Pan sitting in the market-place wearing Roman dress and footwear: he asked Pan about the case, and was told 'You will win.' He lost the case, and this was a logical outcome of his dream, because here was the god who frequents uninhabited places, takes no part in human affairs, and possesses only a little fawnskin, a little shepherd's stick, and a little reed-pipe, sitting all day in the market-place and wearing the dress of a city-dweller.

We should presumably imagine Pan as wearing a Roman toga and ankle-boots (*calcei*), the quintessential garb of a good Roman citizen (Cicero, *Philippics* 2.76; Aulus Gellius, *Attic Nights* 13.22). I assume that the point here is that Pan's clothing was doubly incongruous: urban rather than rural, and Roman rather than Greek (toga and *calcei* rather than *pallium* with sandals). It is easy to see why the distinction between Roman and Greek might have been particularly potent in this specific dream-context. The unsuccessful plaintiff Chrysampelus was evidently a Greek, and the hostile judge in the law-suit was no doubt a Roman official, most likely a provincial governor holding his public tribunal in the market-place of some Greek city of Asia Minor.

Dreaming of the Emperor

In 1972, Brian Masters wrote an absorbing little book called *Dreams about H.M. The Queen*. On the basis of several hundred interviews, Masters came to the striking conclusion that 'up to one third of the country has dreamt about the Royal Family'. What is more, 'nearly fifty per cent of the dreams gathered for this book involve having tea with one or other member of the Family'. This is from one Kate Hutchison, of Wrington, Somerset:

> The Royal Family came to tea. It seemed I had nothing for them to eat, so having dyed an old blanket dark blue, I cut this up and made sandwiches with it, hoping they wouldn't notice it was a blanket.

One wonders what the future social historian of 1970s Britain will make of this. All those nocturnal cups of tea must mean something. But what? Countless thousands of individual tea-related childhood traumas? Half-remembered newsreel of the Queen Mother having tea in bombed-out East End terraces? Or even a vague notion that tea with the Queen is the kind of thing one is supposed to dream about? (And are Royal tea-dreams still normal in 2019? Do you dream about going to Starbucks with Meghan Markle?)

Perhaps millions of inhabitants of the Roman empire suffered from awful anxiety-dreams about eating stuffed dormice with Caracalla. But if so, there is no sign of it in the *Oneirocritica*, where the emperor is a distinctly hazy figure. As we have seen, only two emperors are mentioned by name (Hadrian and Antoninus Pius: 1.26.3, 1.64.4), and then only in order to identify specific athletic festivals ('the Eusebeian games which were first held in Italy by the emperor Antoninus in honour of his father Hadrian').

In the first two books of the *Oneirocritica*, which claim to offer a comprehensive and rationally ordered catalogue of dream-elements and their significance, the emperor is almost entirely absent. Nowhere does Artemidorus explain the significance of seeing or meeting the emperor in a dream; we can, I think, reasonably infer that this was not something that his clients usually dreamt of. (Although some members of the provincial elite certainly did: in his autobiographical *Sacred Tales*, the orator Aelius Aristides records four dreams involving Marcus Aurelius.) Only once in Books 1 and 2 does Artemidorus discuss 'ruler'-dreams in detail, at the start of a chapter on dreams about taking on high office of one kind or another (civic magistracies, priesthoods, and so forth)—and his discussion is a deeply odd one (2.30.1):

To dream of being a *basileus* foretells death for anyone who is sick: only a *basileus* is subject to no one else, and that is also true of the dead. For someone in good health the dream foretells the loss of all his relatives and dissociation from his partners—*basileia* is not shared. For a criminal it signifies imprisonment and reveals his secrets, as a *basileus* is exposed to public view and surrounded by many guards. The same is signified by the insignia of a *basileus*, by which I mean the diadem, the sceptre, and the purple robe. If a poor man dreams of being a *basileus*, he will achieve much which brings him fame but no profit. For a slave this dream predicts his freedom, because a *basileus* must always be a free man. Most auspicious of all is for philosophers or seers to dream of being a *basileus*, as we can conceive of nothing more noble or charac-teristic of a *basileus* than the possession of sound judgement.

The word that Artemidorus uses throughout this paragraph is *basileus*, a word which can signify either '(Greek) king' or '(Roman) emperor'. The natural assumption is of course that Artemidorus must have the Roman emperor in mind. But is this in fact right? He assumes that *basileia* ('kingship/imperial office') cannot be shared; but under the Antonine and Severan dynasties, under whom Artemidorus was writing, the imperial office was often held jointly (Marcus Aurelius and Lucius Verus, AD 161–169; Marcus and Commodus, AD 177–180; Septimius Severus and Caracalla, AD 198–211).

Even more striking is his list of distinctive royal/imperial insignia: diadem, sceptre, purple robe. The diadem (a flat strip of white cloth, worn high on the hair, and knotted behind with the ends hanging loose) was the universal and characteristic attribute of Hellenistic kings after Alexander the Great, but was not worn by Roman emperors as part of their official regalia until the fourth century AD. Nor was the sceptre a standard element of Roman imperial apparel. The use of these three particular objects as *synecdoche* for Hellenistic kingship is beautifully illustrated by a famous mosaic from Pompeii, which depicts a skull balanced on a wheel, hanging from a builder's level above; on the two arms of the level hang respectively a wooden staff, ragged cloak, leather food-pouch (the attributes of the Cynic beggar-philosopher), a royal sceptre, white diadem, and purple cloak or *chlamys* (the regalia of the Hellenistic king) (Fig. 12.1).

The conclusion seems inescapable. In 2.30.1, Artemidorus is in fact talking about dreams of becoming a Hellenistic king, not of becoming a Roman emperor. This is, to put it mildly, strange. We could of course assume that Artemidorus is simply reproducing the wording of an earlier, pre-imperial writer on dream-interpretation, for whom 'ruler-dreams' would naturally mean dreams about Hellenistic monarchs—and indeed, that seems to me rather more likely than the notion that ordinary Greeks around AD 200 regularly dreamed about becoming a Hellenistic king (on anachronisms in the *Oneirocritica*, see further Chapter 2, with another example of *basileus* apparently referring to a Hellenistic king). But then we would still be left with the puzzle of why Artemidorus failed to update this passage to make it fit the political context of his own day. There are few other signs of 'anachronism' in this part of the *Oneirocritica*: the rest of this chapter (2.30.2–6) is concerned with dreams about

Fig. 12.1. Mosaic from House of Tragic Poet, Pompeii. Naples National Archaeological Museum, Inv. 109982.
Photo: © Marie-Lan Nguyen/Wikimedia Commons.

civic offices, all of them perfectly characteristic of the Greek *polis* of the second century AD, and Artemidorus will shortly afterwards go on to talk about the quintessentially Roman institution of gladiatorial combat (2.32). Whatever the explanation for this baffling blind spot, a blind spot it most certainly was. To all appearances, the emperor was just not a figure who interested Artemidorus very much.

When the Roman emperor does turn up in Artemidorus' dream-world, it is usually symbols and images of the emperor that are in question rather than the person of the emperor himself: eagles, elephants, coins, statues. It is no surprise to find that dreams of eagles, the royal bird par excellence, often signify something to do with emperors (2.20.2):

To dream of riding on the back of an eagle prophesies death for emperors, the rich, and the great and good. When men of that eminence have died, it is a long-standing convention to depict them in painting or sculpture as riding on eagles, and to pay them honour with this sort of artistic monument.

Deceased emperors were indeed often depicted riding on eagles, as a symbol of their apotheosis (Herodian, *Roman History* 4.2.11). One of the best-known examples is a sculptural relief-panel on the Arch of Titus at Rome, depicting the late emperor being borne up to heaven on an eagle's back (Fig. 12.2). Similarly, says Artemidorus, if a woman dreams that she has given birth to an eagle, her son (if he is well off) will become a prize athlete, and be presented to the emperor (see Chapter 10); if he is rich, he may even become emperor himself (2.20.3).

Elephants are also a distinctively 'imperial' animal for Artemidorus. (Lions are not specifically regal in the *Oneirocritica*, instead signifying

Fig. 12.2. Apotheosis of Titus from the Arch of Titus in Rome.
Photo: DAI Rom, D-DAI-ROM-79.2393.

power and mastery more generally: 2.12.6.) Elephants, we are told, are inauspicious when seen in a dream anywhere other than in India (their place of origin) or in Italy: 'in Italy it signifies one's master, the emperor, or a man in high position' (2.12.9). Ownership of elephants in the Roman world was the exclusive prerogative of the reigning emperor (Juvenal, *Satires* 12.102–7), and elephants are often depicted on Roman coins as a symbol of imperial power; indeed, elephants would seldom have been seen outside the city of Rome, where they were regularly used in imperial processions. It is interesting to find that Artemidorus here conceives of Italy, not the city of Rome, as the distinctive 'space of the emperor'. The same idea appears late in Book 2, where we are told that dreams of flying up to heaven signify a journey to Italy: 'just as heaven is the seat of the gods, so Italy is the seat of emperors' (2.68.3). Italy would later lose its special status as the 'seat of empire'; by the end of the third century AD, it had become, in administrative and ideological terms, just a province like any other. But for Artemidorus, Italy was clearly still a privileged space associated with the emperor (who in his day still generally resided at Rome, though that would change).

The richest account of emperor-dreams in the *Oneirocritica* comes in Book 4, in the course of a longer section on 'reversible' dream-elements (a cloak can signify a house, but a house can also signify a cloak, and so forth: 4.30). The relevant chapter is made up—very unusually for the *Oneirocritica*—of five specific dreams and their outcomes, attributed to five named individuals (4.31):

The emperor, a temple, a soldier, an imperial letter, coined money, and all else in that category have reciprocal significance. Stratonicus thought that he was kicking the emperor. When he went out he found a gold coin, happening to tread on it: there was no difference between kicking or treading on the emperor himself or his image on the coin. Zeno imagined that he had become a centurion, and when he went out he found that there were a hundred letters from the emperor for him to deal with. Our Cratinus was given money in a dream, and became the revenue-collector of an imperial temple. Zoïlus imagined that he was the curator of public works, but became an accountant at the imperial mint. Whatever issues from the mouth of the emperor will benefit the recipient by means of a pronouncement. Chrysippus of Corinth dreamt that he was given two teeth from the emperor's mouth: pleading in the emperor's court he won with two verdicts in a single day.

When the emperor appears in a dream, says Artemidorus, he just signifies 'something imperial'; likewise, anything imperial in a dream can refer back to the emperor, or can refer across to any other 'imperial thing'. A dream-emperor can therefore stand in for a real-life imperial letter or imperial court-verdict, and vice versa. In his 1977 book *The Emperor in the Roman World*, Fergus Millar argued that imperial power was felt only when it was actively exercised, usually in response to an initiative from the emperor's subjects; in Millar's crisp formulation, 'the emperor was what the emperor did'. In the Artemidoran dream-world, just as for Millar, the person of the emperor is indeed conceptually identical to what the emperor says and does (rescripts, verdicts, and so forth). But Artemidorus goes a step further than Millar, claiming that the person of the emperor is also interchangeable with any other representation of imperial power: with coins, which carry the emperor's image; with imperial temples, where living or deceased emperors are worshipped; with directly appointed imperial officials, such as the curator of public works at Rome; and even with officers of the Roman army, whose rewards and promotion were owed directly to the emperor. Monarchic power as pure representation: not for the first time, Artemidorus ends up sounding really quite startlingly modern.

It is abundantly clear that 'the emperor' as a single, actually existing individual hardly impinged on the world of Artemidorus and his readers at all. There is no sign that Artemidorus knew or cared much about emperors' roles as generals or as legislators; nor did he see one emperor as differing very much from any other. (Artemidorus distinguishes many different varieties of dances, birds, and gladiators, but knows only a single flavour of emperor.) Insofar as the emperor appears as an active agent at all in the *Oneirocritica*, it is solely in his judicial function, as final arbiter of appeals from provincial law-courts (4.31.2; 4.51; 4.80.2). To judge from Artemidorus, for the inhabitants of small-town Asia Minor in the late second and early third century AD, 'the emperor' did not really connote a distinct person at all, so much as a cluster of state institutions (the imperial cult, judicial appeals) and a bundle of images and symbols (eagles and elephants, statues and coins, Italy and Rome).

The Roman State

Less elevated agents and functionaries of the Roman state are equally marginal in the *Oneirocritica*. The near-complete absence of the Roman army is particularly striking, and no doubt reflects the status of the Roman province of Asia as an *inermis provincia* ('unarmed province'), garrisoned only by small and unobtrusive auxiliary units. As Aelius Aristides says in his oration *To Rome*, 'Cohorts and cavalry units are sufficient to guard entire provinces, and only a few of them are quartered in the cities of each province; compared to the size of the population, they are thinly scattered throughout the countryside, and many provinces do not even know where their garrison is situated' (26.67). Soldiers are a very rare class of dreamer (only five times in the *Oneirocritica*), and in most cases appear so briefly that it is hard to believe that they could have been a significant part of Artemidorus' clientele (1.17; 1.26.3, generically grouped with 'anyone in the emperor's court'; 2.12.16; 2.39.5). The only more extended example of a soldier's dream comes in Book 4, as an illustration of dreams which cannot be explained until they have had their outcome (4.24.2):

A Roman legionary officer dreamt that the letters *iota, kappa, theta* were inscribed on his dagger. The Jewish War in Cyrene had broken out, and the man who had this dream distinguished himself in the war—and this exemplified my point. From the *iota* we get 'to the Jews' (*Ioudaiois*), from the *kappa* 'to the Cyreneans' (*Kurēnaiois*), and from the *theta* 'death' (*thanatos*)—'death to the Cyrenean Jews'.

This dream is tied to an event that took place before Artemidorus was born (the Jewish uprising at Cyrene in AD 115–117), and he no doubt found it in some earlier collection of dreams; it is immediately followed by another 'historic' dream, the dream of Alexander the Great during his siege of Tyre. Likewise, dreams of becoming a soldier are covered in a single rather brief and generic chapter (2.31), and I think only two dreams foretell that the dreamer will join the army (2.20.3: if a woman dreams that she gives birth to an eagle and her son is poor, he will become senior centurion in a legion; 4.30.3, a man becomes a cavalryman after dreaming of wearing horseshoes). Death at the hands of soldiers was only a very remote possibility; to dream of bees settling on your head is bad, since you will usually end up being killed by a mob or by soldiers (2.22.1).

For many communities in the Greek East, one of the most burdensome aspects of Roman rule was the arbitrary requisitioning of vehicles and draught-animals for compulsory public service. We have numerous surviving petitions and imperial edicts illustrating abuses of the system by soldiers and other Roman officials, and its impact on ordinary provincials is vividly evoked in Apuleius' novel *The Golden Ass* (9.39) and, most famously, in the Gospel of Matthew (5:41)—'whosoever shall compel thee to go a mile, go with him twain'.

Only a single dream in the *Oneirocritica* alludes to this much-resented system, albeit in such a manner as to make it clear that the scenario was thoroughly familiar to Artemidorus and his audience (5.16):

> A shipowner dreamt that he was in the Isles of the Blest and detained there by the heroes, but then Agamemnon came on the scene and released him. He had his ship requisitioned for public service by the emperor's procurators: but then he appealed to the emperor himself, and was granted immunity from this conscription.

Apparently the shipowner's vessel was requisitioned by state officials for the transport of grain or other staple goods (the *annona*); he successfully petitioned the emperor for the obligation to be lifted (an entirely standard form of petition, well paralleled in Roman legal sources). The emperor and his agents are rather nicely symbolized by King Agamemnon and the lesser Achaean heroes under his command. Remarkably, this is Artemidorus' only reference to procurators (Roman financial officials in the provinces), reflecting a wider lack of interest in Roman taxation and fiscal administration in the *Oneirocritica*. Tax-farmers appear in passing only a handful of times, usually as figures of proverbial shamelessness and wickedness (bracketed at 4.57.3 with 'innkeepers, bandits, short-changers, and other frauds'; also 1.23, 4.42, 5.31), although a longer chapter on dreams about toll-collectors (3.58) does say that they are auspicious because of their loyalty and trustworthiness. The role of local civic elites in tax-collection is evoked only once: a dunghill is good for a rich man, for just as everyone contributes to a dung-hill, so everyone contributes part of their tax-payments to civic magistrates (3.52). The imperial treasury also turns up only once, in the case of a woman whose husband had apparently died intestate, and whose estate was thus claimed by the imperial treasury; the woman took the case to court, but was unsuccessful (4.59.4).

This is not a very impressive haul from five long books of dreams and their meanings, and due weight should be placed on the complete absence of the provincial governor and his court, the Roman senate and senatorial order (nowhere mentioned, aside from a single Greek dreamer 'of senatorial rank', 1.73.2), and the empire's vast apparatus of financial and civil administrators. Only a single passage of the *Oneirocritica* shows or requires any knowledge of the internal structure of the Roman administrative *cursus*, and this is a very idiosyncratic dream indeed, brought in to illustrate the necessity of paying attention to all the constituent elements of a dream (4.28.2):

A man of the equestrian order who was petitioning the emperor for a military command dreamt that someone had summoned him, and that he went out of the house where he was staying, descended two flights of steps, and was given by the man who summoned him an olive-wreath of the sort worn by Roman equestrians in their parades. He was very happy at this dream, and his circle of friends were cheered on his behalf: but he failed in his petition. He had been given the wreath after going down the steps rather than up, and we speak of promotion as a step up, and its opposite as a step down. In fact the effect of this wreath was to have him marry a virgin, because a wreath is something woven together, and the olive, sacred to a virgin goddess, is symbolic of a virgin. I have recorded this dream for you to have you understand that one should not concentrate on the first images in a dream, but rather take equal account of the whole sequence of what the dreamer has seen. All those who interpreted this dream solely on the basis of the wreath failed by not taking account of the steps down.

This young man had petitioned the emperor for appointment to the prefecture of an auxiliary cohort, the first of the three military officer commands (the *tres militiae*) open to members of the equestrian order. Men who met the equestrian census-qualification (400,000 *sesterces*) were two a penny in the high Roman empire; but only a few, it seems, had full equestrian rank conferred on them, marked (apparently) by the grant of a public horse and the right to participate in the annual cavalry parade of the *equites* (the *transvectio equitum*), held on 15 July each year in the city of Rome. The man dreamed that he had an olive-wreath conferred on him; having interpreted this (wrongly) as a dream-allusion to the olive-wreaths worn by young *equites* in the *transvectio equitum* (Dionysius of Halicarnassus, *Roman Antiquities* 6.13.4), he jumped to the conclusion that he would shortly be promoted to equestrian military office.

In its casual assumption of a detailed understanding of Roman institutions, the dream is unique in the *Oneirocritica*. But as the final sentence of the passage shows ('all those who interpreted this dream . . .'), this was not a dream that Artemidorus was called on to interpret himself in his professional capacity, and he presumably only heard of it at second- or third-hand. Nothing else in the *Oneirocritica* suggests that he was regularly consulted by aspirant members of the Roman political or military élite. One wonders whether the young equestrian's dream might have been a famous textbook 'dream-riddle' (like the dream of the Roman officer at Cyrene, discussed above), originating in a very different, far more 'Roman' social milieu than the ordinary provincial world of the *Oneirocritica*.

The Roman Penal System

To all I have said about the marginality of Rome and Romans in the *Oneirocritica* there is one huge and depressing exception. The Roman courts and penal system loom appallingly large in the subconscious of Artemidorus and his clientele. This was not a personal idiosyncrasy of Artemidorus. As Brent Shaw wrote in an illuminating essay on 'judicial nightmares' in early Christian texts, 'for the subjects of the Roman empire, the experience of witnessing and participating in a trial was arguably *the* quintessential civic experience of the state'. Trials and punishments are central to the plots of many extant Greek and Latin novels (notably Apuleius' *The Golden Ass*), and it is clear that the Roman state was concerned to make the judicial process—particularly the regular public tribunals held by the provincial governor in major cities of his province—as theatrical and hair-raising as possible, for the edification and terror of the general populace.

The different kinds of punishment imposed by the Roman state on convicted criminals are evoked in bleak and repetitive detail. As we saw earlier, Artemidorus knew a man who dreamed of learning Latin; he was put on trial and condemned to slavery, since judgement in such cases was always delivered in Latin (1.53.2). Two men dreamed of having sex with a lump of iron: one was condemned to slavery, and the other was castrated (4.65.2). Loss of civil rights, often accompanied by exile, is evoked several times (1.35.6, 2.9.6). A man dreamt that he lost his name; he was convicted of crimes against the state, lost his property and civil rights, and was exiled (1.4.4). Another man dreamt that he lost his nose: he was convicted of forgery, lost his civil rights and was sent into exile (4.27.3). A third man dreamt of sailing over the ocean in the bowl of a tripod, and ended up suffering banishment to an island (5.21). An alarming range of dreams signify that the dreamer will end up in prison and bondage: having hair on your hands (1.42.6), having many hands (1.42.7), having many feet (1.48.2), singing in a bath-house (1.76.6), wearing an ivy- or vine-wreath (1.77.8), wearing purple clothing (2.3.4), braiding your hair (2.6), having a snake coiled around you (2.13.1), seeing Cronus and the Titans (2.39.7), being buried alive (2.49.5), having lice (3.7.1), wearing clogs (3.15), anything involving hemp (3.59.2).

Condemnation to hard labour was a present and realistic fear. If someone without a clear conscience dreams he is bald on either side of the head, 'he will find himself convicted and sentenced to hard labour for the state, as that is the nature and the place of the mark used to identify convicts' (1.21.3). This kind of half-shaving of the head was a standard marker of convicts condemned to hard labour, as seen in Apuleius' horrific description of slaves or convicts working in a mill ('letters branded on their foreheads, half-shaved heads, and irons on their legs', *The Golden Ass* 9.12). Artemidorus knew a man 'who dreamt that he was disqualified at the Olympic games', probably as being too old for the age-class he entered for: he was condemned to the mines (1.59). He also knew a man 'who dreamt that only his feet were walking while the rest of his body remained stationary, and for all their movement his feet made not the slightest advance' (1.48.3). He too was condemned to hard labour working a mechanical treadmill for bailing water, probably also in a mine.

A large part of Artemidorus' long analysis of dreams about death and dying (2.49–66) is dedicated to dreams about different kinds of capital punishment: being hanged, decapitated, burned alive, crucified, or thrown to wild beasts (2.50–4). The impact of such dreams is intensified if the dream also explicitly includes a judicial death-sentence (2.49.5). Execution by wild beasts was the most extreme form of capital punishment in the Roman world, and at least one of Artemidorus' clients ended up being executed in this way (5.49):

> A man dreamt that he had been transformed and had a bear's paws instead of hands. He was condemned to death in a wild-beast show, tied to a stake, and eaten by a bear. When a bear hibernates, it puts a paw in its mouth as if it was eating it, and sucks on it for nourishment.

Decapitation is also prominent in the *Oneirocritica*, both as something one is expected to dream about (the long chapter 1.35), and as a dream-outcome. If you dream of horns sprouting from your head, you will be decapitated, since that is the characteristic fate of sacrificial horned animals like oxen and sheep (1.39). A Pergamene baker dreamt that he defecated lumps of bread; he was decapitated (4.33.4). A man dreamt that he drank mustard which had been separated in a sieve; he was convicted on a charge of murder by a judge (one who 'sieves' the evidence) and decapitated (5.5).

But the form of execution to which Artemidorus dedicates the most space and interpretative zeal is crucifixion (2.53). This, it seems, was the punishment that most haunted the dreams of Artemidorus' clients. Many different dreams foretell crucifixion, particularly if the dreamer is criminally inclined. If a criminal imagines flying with the birds, he will be crucified (2.68.3). If he dreams of carrying one of the gods of the underworld, he will be crucified, because 'a man about to be nailed to a cross must first carry it' (2.56.1). If he dreams of dancing on an elevated surface, he will be crucified, 'because of the height he is at and his outstretched arms' (1.76.4). Artemidorus cites the real-life example of a man who dreamed of lighting his lamps from celestial fire rather than his own hearth: he too ended up being crucified (5.34).

In Book 4 of the *Oneirocritica*, Artemidorus gives two further real-life crucifixion-dreams, in both cases dreams which were seen by members of the provincial elite (who would not normally be in danger of crucifixion, typically reserved for low-status individuals). The philosopher Alexander of Aphrodisias 'dreamt that he had been condemned on a capital charge, and had only just managed to beg himself off a death on the cross'; in fact, the following day, 'in the course of an argument with a Cynic, he was hit over the head with a wooden club' (4.33.3—he survived). Artemidorus also cites the example of a certain Menander from his own native town of Daldis, who 'dreamt that he was crucified in front of the temple of Zeus of the City, and he was appointed the priest of that same god, to his greater distinction and wealth' (4.49). That crucifixion-dreams can have positive connotations may seem counter-intuitive to us; the point is that the elevation of the body to so prominent and visible a position might be desirable to an aspiring civic magnate (2.53.2).

The *Oneirocritica* is littered with dreams concerning litigation on a wide range of day-to-day matters, usually landed property (1.35.4, 1.67.2, 2.9.6, 2.49.4), sums of money (1.35.6, 2.9.6), or inheritance (4.51, 4.59.4, 5.38). More serious criminal cases are occasionally evoked, concerning forgery (4.27.3), murder (5.5), and even high treason (*maiestas*: 5.10). Countless different dream-elements can connote success or failure in law-suits: babies (1.13.4), multiple ears (1.24.1), wrestling-holds (1.60.1), carrots (1.67.2), garlands of helichrysum (1.77.3), new clothes (2.3.1), wild boars (2.12.15), Hecate and other chthonic deities (2.39.4), eggs (2.43)—I could go on. Evidently low-level litigation was part of the normal experience of Artemidorus and his clientele, whether before Roman officials or in local civic courts; local courts are in fact never explicitly mentioned, and capital crimes at any rate would always have been tried before the provincial governor. The figure of the judge, as we should expect, is an unambiguously negative one in the *Oneirocritica*: 'dreams of law courts, judges, lawyers, or teachers of law prophesy troubles, discouragement, and inordinate expenses for all' (2.29). Judges are like rivers, 'because they do just what they want at their own discretion without answering to anyone' (2.27.1, 4.66); they are like the sea, because they too arbitrarily treat some people well, and others badly (3.16.1).

Conclusion

The *Oneirocritica* offers us a deeply unusual perspective on the cultural politics of the high Roman empire. Artemidorus draws a very hard line between Greek and Roman culture: he instinctively assumes that Greeks and Romans are different from one another, in behaviour, practices, dress, and language. As we saw in Chapter 9, the gods of the *Oneirocritica* are the old gods of Greece: no imperial cult, no personified Roma. Even so standard a thing as the Roman month July has to be explained to his readers ('the month that is called July', not 'July': 5.70). The emperor is a remote and generic figure; the Roman administrative system is a hazy blur; the western Roman empire and the frontiers are *terra incognita*.

Whether this is in any way representative of attitudes towards Roman rule and Roman culture among the 'middling' social classes of the eastern Roman provinces is very difficult to judge. Let us assume for a moment that the three bronze coins of Daldis illustrated in Chapter 2 were indeed struck by our Artemidorus during his tenure of the chief civic magistracy at Daldis. These coins carry portraits of the three chief living members of the imperial house, complete with names and titles. One of the coins carries a full-length image of the Roman emperor in military dress, holding a globe, being crowned by a winged Victory; a second bears the images of two local Lydian deities (Apollo Mystes and Cybele); the third carries an image of a Graeco-Egyptian deity (Serapis) whose cult was widespread throughout the Greek East. (By the by, the iconography of this last coin precisely fits a pair of Serapis-dreams in Book 5 of the *Oneirocritica*: 5.92–3.) These three objects are, on the face of it, beautiful symbols of harmonious cultural and political integration: Daldis is presented as part of a single world-culture under Rome, in which the emperor's victories are 'our' victories just as much as Apollo Mystes is 'our' local patron deity.

My point is, of course, hardly a novel one: different kinds of evidence give us different pictures of Greek attitudes towards Rome in the high imperial period. Official public documents and monuments—coins, inscriptions, public buildings—will naturally tend to leave a strong impression of loyalty, ideological engagement and cultural assimilation. The *Oneirocritica* is not necessarily a 'better' source for Greek attitudes towards Rome. But I think we have to assume that Artemidorus understood his clientele and their interests. For the ordinary craftsmen, slaves, and merchant shippers of Daldis and Ephesus, it was a long way from the agora to the forum.

Epilogue

Artemidorus after Antiquity

We have no idea how and why the *Oneirocritica* survived the end of antiquity. The main dream-book traditions of both Byzantium and the medieval West stem from a much shorter work, the *Somniale Danielis* (attributed to the Hebrew prophet Daniel), compiled some time between the fourth and seventh century AD; the author of the *Somniale* seems not to have known or used Artemidorus' book. Indeed, for some 650 years after the book's completion (around AD 210), we cannot securely identify a single reader of the *Oneirocritica*. The dream-interpreter 'Artemidorus of Ephesus' is mentioned in passing by the anonymous author of the *Philopatris*, a curious Greek dialogue on paganism and Christianity attributed to the satirist Lucian; unfortunately, the date of the *Philopatris* is completely uncertain (proposed dates stretch from the mid-fourth to the twelfth century AD). Macrobius' Latin *Commentary on the Dream of Scipio*, composed around AD 400, includes a typology of dreams (*oneiros, horama, chrematismos, enhypnion, phantasma*: 1.3.2) which superficially resembles that of Artemidorus (1.1–2, especially 1.2.4), but it requires the eye of faith to suppose that Macrobius was drawing directly on the *Oneirocritica*.

Not until the mid-ninth century AD does the *Oneirocritica* resurface in, of all places, 'Abbasid Baghdad. A single manuscript, now in Istanbul, preserves an Arabic translation of the *Oneirocritica*, undertaken by the prolific Nestorian Christian physician and translator Ḥunayn b. Isḥâq (died AD 877). The surviving copy of Ḥunayn's translation is incomplete (it omits the opening of Book 1, and the whole of Books 4–5), but the use made of his work by later Muslim dream-interpreters makes it clear that Ḥunayn did indeed translate the whole thing. Ḥunayn's translation sticks very closely to the Greek, although he does make a few quiet alterations in order to make Artemidorus conform to contemporary religious norms. For example, Artemidorus claims in Book 2 that 'to dream of Asclepius set up as a statue in his temple and standing on his plinth, and to do him worship, is auspicious for all' (2.37.4). Ḥunayn converts Asclepius into an angel (a standard strategy for dealing with pagan deities) and excises the reference to worship (only appropriate for God): 'as for the angel called Asclepius, when someone saw him as if he was in a temple or standing on a pedestal, howsoever he saw him—this is a good sign in all things and all actions'.

This ninth-century translation is, in fact, our earliest (indirect) witness to the text of the *Oneirocritica*, and here and there, where our later Greek manuscripts have errors or omissions, Ḥunayn's translation seems to preserve Artemidorus' original wording. Perhaps the most spectacular example comes towards the end of Artemidorus' account of dreams about the gods in Book 2, where our extant Greek manuscripts tell us that 'the so-called Mother of the Gods' has the same significance as the chthonic Hecate and the Erinyes (2.39.4). The Arabic translation, instead of 'Mother of the Gods', reads *d.n.dūmī*, which can only be a transliteration of the Greek *Dindymie* or *Dindymene*, a rare local epithet for the Mother of the Gods in Artemidorus' native Asia Minor (e.g. Herodotus, *Histories* 1.80.1).

Ḥunayn's translation of Artemidorus exercised an enormous influence on later Muslim divinatory literature. Large chunks of it were incorporated piecemeal into later compilations of dream-wisdom like those of Dīnawarī (AD 1008) and Kharkūshī (before AD 1015). But the most sustained and powerful engagement with Ḥunayn's Arabic *Oneirocritica* is to be found in the dream-manual composed by the great Persian scholar Avicenna (Ibn Sīnā, AD 980–1037). Avicenna explicitly rejects the standard 'Arabic' structure of dream-manuals (which tend to begin with dreams of God, the prophets, angels, and so forth) in favour of the 'Greek' (i.e. Artemidoran) approach which begins with the human body. His own dream-book opens with a long philosophic discussion of sleep and dreams, much of which summarizes and expands on the theoretical treatises that open Books 1 and 4 of the *Oneirocritica*; his main catalogue of dream-elements and their significations follows the structure and content of the *Oneirocritica* with remarkable fidelity.

Artemidorus' profound influence on early traditions of Muslim dream-interpretation was not paralleled in the medieval Greek-speaking world. The earliest evidence for the rediscovery of the *Oneirocritica* in

Byzantium comes from the tenth and eleventh centuries AD. The vast tenth-century Byzantine encyclopaedia known as the Suda includes a short biographical entry for Artemidorus (see Chapter 2), as well as a large number of unattributed quotations from the *Oneirocritica*; our earliest surviving Greek manuscript of the *Oneirocritica* (L, *Codex Laurentianus 87.8*) dates to the eleventh century AD. However, Artemidorus seems never to have been widely read in Byzantium. It was long believed that the longest and richest surviving Byzantine dream-book, the *Oneirocriticon* of Achmet (probably tenth century AD), was directly influenced by Artemidorus; in fact, we now know that Achmet's work was wholly based on Arabic sources, and these apparent links result from Artemidorus' spectral presence (via Ḥunayn) in ninth- and tenth-century Arabic dream-books. The only other individual in the Byzantine world known to have so much as cast his eyes over a Greek text of the *Oneirocritica* is a certain Pascalis Romanus, author of a short Latin work on dream-interpretation called the *Liber thesauri occulti* (AD 1165); large parts of this book consist of verbatim translations of miscellaneous bits of the *Oneirocritica*.

At any event, what matters most for us is that two complete Greek manuscripts of the *Oneirocritica* survived the fall of Constantinople in 1453, both of them apparently shipped out to Crete by a notable Greek scholar and scribe by the name of Michael Apostolis. Artemidorus arrived for the first time in western Europe at the end of the fifteenth century: one of Apostolis' two manuscripts (L) ended up in Florence, and a copy of the other (V), in Apostolis' own hand, is now in Venice. The first printed edition of the *Oneirocritica* was produced by the Aldine press in 1518. Two decades later, Artemidorus was translated into Latin by Janus Cornarius (1539), and this was quickly followed by a rush of vernacular translations: into German, by Walter Hermann Ryff (1540); into Italian, by Pietro Lauro of Modena (1542); into French, by Charles Fontaine (1546).

In England, the earliest (partial) vernacular translation seems to have been Thomas Hill's *A pleasaunt treatise of the interpretation of dreames, gathered part of out of Ponzettus, and part out of the Greek Author Artemidorus* (1559). This book no longer survives, but its contents must have been more or less identical to Hill's extant *The most pleasuante arte of the interpretacion of dreames* (1576). In the long central chapter of this book ('Of those Dreames whiche were reported to have bene proved'), Hill translates a large number of dreams cherry-picked from all five books of the *Oneirocritica*, including—perhaps surprisingly— some of the more hair-raising sex-dreams from Book 1, which are silently omitted in most other early modern translations of the *Oneirocritica* (1.78.6–7):

> To be moved therto of a richer or older man signifyeth good, for that the manner is to take of suche. And to be moved of a yonger and needy person, is evil for to suche the manner is to give. And the same signifycation also if the elder shall be the mover or procurer, and a begger. And a certayne person beyng a servaunt dreamed that he thought he handled his maysters privitye: who after was made schole mayster, and bringer up of his children, for he had then in his hands the masters privityes, being signified of the proper children of his master.

In the seventeenth and eighteenth centuries, Artemidorus reached a wider English readership through the drastically abridged translation by 'R.W.' (probably Robert Wood, a prolific translator of Latin and French texts), first published in 1606. Originally entitled *The iudgement, or exposition of dreames, written by Artimodorus [sic], an auncient and famous author*, this frankly execrable little book went through twenty-six cheap editions between 1606 and 1786 (fourteen of which survive today). Wood, unlike Hill, followed the original sequence of topics in the *Oneirocritica*, but he hacked down the contents to around a tenth of their original length. The long Prefaces to Books 1 and 4 are omitted altogether, and Book 5 is reduced from ninety-five to seventeen dreams, padded out with a few dream-anecdotes from Valerius Maximus' *Memorable Deeds and Sayings*. Other vernacular translations and abridgements of Artemidorus continued to appear throughout the seventeenth and eighteenth centuries, including—remarkably—a Welsh-language epitome, *Gwir ddeongliad breuddwydion*, published at Shrewsbury in 1698. (No complete English translation of the *Oneirocritica* would appear until 1975.)

Today, Artemidorus' *Oneirocritica* remains a fairly niche interest, though a few imaginative historians of the Roman world—most memorably Michel Foucault (Chapter 5)—have amply demonstrated quite how much there is still to be got out of this extraordinary book. It is,

I suppose, unlikely that anyone will again read Artemidorus as a practical guide to interpreting dreams. Curiously, one of the very last people to take Artemidorus seriously as a 'living' source of dream-wisdom was Sigmund Freud, with whom this book may appropriately draw to a close. In the first edition of *Die Traumdeutung* (published in 1899), Freud referred only twice to Artemidorus, once to castigate an earlier German translator for omitting Artemidorus' account of sex-dreams, and once as an illustration of the 'popular method of dream-interpretation' as a sort of cryptography, that involves 'decoding' the various elements of a dream by means of a fixed key:

> An interesting variant of this decoding procedure, which to some extent corrects its character as a purely mechanical transposition, appears in the treatise on dream-interpretation by Artemidorus of Daldis. Here not only the content of the dream but also the personality and the circumstances of the dreamer are taken into account so that the same element in the dream has a different meaning for the rich man, the married man, or the orator from the meaning it has for the poor man, the unmarried man, or, say, a merchant. The essential thing about this procedure is that the work of interpretation is not directed towards the dream as a whole, but at each piece of the dream-content by itself, as if the dream were a conglomerate in which each little fragment of rock required a separate definition. (Translation by Joyce Crick.)

In later editions of *Die Traumdeutung*, Freud added several further references to Artemidorus, highlighting the continuities between Artemidorus' method and his own. He quotes Alexander the Great's dream of a dancing satyr (4.24.3) both as 'the most beautiful example of a dream-interpretation handed down to us from antiquity', and as an exemplary case of why a dream cannot be translated into another language (because the interpretation depends on a wordplay that only works in Greek: see Chapter 3). He praises Artemidorus' focus on 'the principle of association', and goes so far as to declare that his own technique of dream-interpretation differs only in one essential respect from 'the ancient method', namely that 'it imposes the task of interpretation on the dreamer himself', rather than the interpreter.

Freud's emphasis on the similarities between the new science of psychoanalysis and Artemidorus' techniques in the *Oneirocritica* is, as Simon Price rightly emphasized in a classic essay on Freud and Artemidorus, deeply misleading. Freud was increasingly concerned to place his work in an intellectual lineage stretching back to antiquity, and this naturally led him to downplay the profound differences between Artemidorus' approach and his own. As we saw in Chapter 3, Artemidorus has no particular interest in the origins of dreams; he does not believe that the meaning of a dream depends on a dreamer's individual personality, let alone his suppressed desires; he assumes that dreams are precognitive, offering insight into future events. The only real connection between Artemidorus and the Freudian tradition is the use of the allegorical or 'decoding' method for interpreting individual dream-elements, and this method is employed to very different ends. If Artemidorus' *Oneirocritica* still commands our attention today—as it most certainly should—it is because of the remarkably sharp and unexpected light that it sheds on the norms and assumptions of people in the past, not for any practical value that it might be thought to possess for the modern psychoanalyst.

Further Reading

Chapter 1. The Snake and the Whale

The dream-swapping scene at the start of Aristophanes' *Wasps* (lines 1–53) is discussed in the commentaries on *Wasps* by Alan Sommerstein (1983), 152–6, and by Zachary P. Biles and S. Douglas Olson (2015), 75–100. For the symbolism of the eagle and the snake in Greek literature and art, see Diana Rodríguez Pérez, 'Contextualizing symbols: the eagle and the snake in the ancient Greek world', *Boreas* 33 (2011), 1–21; the epitaph of Cleobulus the seer is edited by Peter A. Hansen, *Carmina Epigraphica Graeca* 2 (1989), no. 519. The most comprehensive study of Greek and Roman dreaming is William V. Harris's invaluable *Dreams and Experience in Classical Antiquity* (2009); particularly useful is Harris's collection of 'Greek and Roman opinions about the truthfulness of dreams' (123–228). For the 'objectification' of dreams in the ancient Greek world, see E.R. Dodds, *The Greeks and the Irrational* (1951), 102–34. Wider perspectives on ancient Greek divination are offered by Matthew Dillon, *Omens and Oracles: Divination in Ancient Greece* (2017); Peter T. Struck's *Divination and Human Nature* (2016) is a brilliant and provocative reading of ancient divination as a form of intuition (see further Chapter 3).

Chapter 2. Artemidorus and the *Oneirocritica*

The standard edition of the Greek text of the *Oneirocritica* is Roger Pack's Teubner edition (1963); the best translation of the *Oneirocritica* is now that of Martin Hammond in the Oxford World's Classics series (2019). Among earlier translations, the most helpful are those by André J. Festugière, *Artémidore d'Éphèse: La clef des songes* (1975), and Robert J. White, *The Interpretation of Dreams: The Oneirocritica of Artemidorus* (second edition, 1990). There are useful notes in the recent edition by Daniel E. Harris-McCoy, *Artemidorus' Oneirocritica: Text, Translation, & Commentary* (2012), but the translation is not to be relied upon. Christophe Chandezon and Julien du Bouchet are currently preparing a major new Budé edition of Artemidorus, and I have benefited from advance sight of their superb translation and notes on Books 1 and 2.1–45.

The best short biographical sketch of Artemidorus is that of Christophe Chandezon, 'Artémidore: le cadre historique, géographique et social d'une vie', in *Études sur Artémidore et l'interprétation des rêves*, ed. J. du Bouchet and Chr. Chandezon (2012), 11–26. A Severan date for the later books of the *Oneirocritica* was convincingly proposed by Glen Bowersock, 'Artemidorus and the Second Sophistic', in

Paideia: The World of the Second Sophistic, ed. B. Borg (2004), 55–6, on the basis of the three identifications of people in *Oneirocritica* Book 4 mentioned in the text. On the 'private' character of *Oneirocritica* Books 4 and 5, see D. Harris-McCoy, 'Writing and reading Books IV and V of Artemidorus' *Oneirocritica*', in *Artemidor von Daldis und die antike Traumdeutung*, ed. G. Weber (2015), 17–37.

The surviving fragments of earlier Greek writers on dream-interpretation were collected by Darius del Corno, *Graecorum de re onirocritica scriptorum reliquiae* (1969); for the surviving scrap of a Greek dream-book from Roman Egypt (third century AD), see Luigi Prada, '*P.Oxy.* XXXI 2607 re-edited: A Greek *Oneirocriticon* from Roman Egypt', in *Proceedings of the 27th International Congress of Papyrology* (2016), 623–46. The evidence for amateur and professional dream-interpreters at all social levels is collected by Gil H. Renberg, 'The role of dream-interpreters in Greek and Roman Religion', in *Artemidor von Daldis und die antike Traumdeutung*, ed. G. Weber (2015), 233–62. For Antiphon the dream-interpreter, see Michael Gagarin, *Antiphon the Athenian: Oratory, Law, and Justice in the Age of the Sophists* (2010), 99–101, and for Aristander of Telmessus, see Alex Nice, 'The reputation of the *mantis* Aristander', *Acta Classica* 48 (2005), 87–102. Aristotle's short but pungent *On Divination in Sleep* is translated in the Oxford World's Classics series by Fred D. Miller, Jr., *Aristotle on the Soul and Other Psychological Works* (2018), 122–5; there is a detailed critical study, with Greek text and translation, by David Gallop, *Aristotle on Sleep and Dreams* (1996). For an attempt to show that substantial parts of Artemidorus' system of dream-classification can be traced back to Panyasis of Halicarnassus, see Miguel A. Vinagre, 'Les sources d'Artémidore: Panyasis d'Halicarnasse', in *Artémidore de Daldis et l'interprétation des rêves: Quatorze études*, ed. Chr. Chandezon and J. du Bouchet (2014), 33–52 (not, in my view, convincing). For long hair as characteristic of Hellenistic kings, see R.R.R. Smith, *Hellenistic Royal Portraits* (1988), 47–8, 79–81. An optimistic view of the likely breadth of Artemidorus' original readership is taken by Gregor Weber, 'Artemidor von Daldis und sein "Publikum"', *Gymnasium* 106 (1999), 209–29.

Chapter 3. How to Interpret a Dream

The most lucid and convincing account of Artemidoran dream-theory (and its relationship to the psychoanalytic tradition) is provided by Simon Price, 'The future of dreams: from Freud to Artemidorus', originally published in *Past & Present* 113 (1986), 3–37, updated and revised in *Studies in Ancient Greek and Roman Society*, ed. R. Osborne (2004), 226–59. On the distinction between *enhypnion* and *oneiros*, see Vered Lev Kanaan, 'Artemidorus at the dream gates', *American Journal of Philology* 137 (2016), 189–218. Artemidorus' six *stoicheia* are discussed by Jean-Marie Flamand, 'Recherches sur la causalité dans les *Oneirokritika* d'Artémidore', in *Artémidore de Daldis et l'interprétation des rêves: quatorze études*, ed. Chr. Chandezon and J. du Bouchet (2014), 107–37. On the relationship between ancient theories of divination and the modern concept of intuition, see Peter T. Struck, *Divination and Human Nature: A Cognitive History of Intuition in Classical Antiquity* (2016).

Chapter 4.   The Body

On right and left in Greek thought, see Geoffrey E.R. Lloyd, 'Right and left in Greek philosophy', *Journal of Hellenic Studies* 82 (1962), 56–66. The most important parallel for the Artemidoran nexus of body-symbolism is Polemo's *Physiognomy*, which survives in Arabic translation: see Simon Swain (ed.), *Seeing the Face, Seeing the Soul* (2007), especially 185–90 and 392–5, on masculinity and femininity (and effeminacy). On the gendered body in second-century Greek thought, see also Maud Gleason, *Making Men: Sophists and Self-Presentation in Ancient Rome* (1995), 58–81. For beards, see Paul Zanker, *The Mask of Socrates* (1995), 198–266. The spatial placement of the future 'behind' the dreaming observer is discussed by M. Bettini, *Anthropology and Roman Culture* (1991), 151–7 (the quotation in the text is from p. 153).

On ancient attitudes towards physical disability, see Martha Rose, *The Staff of Oedipus: Transforming Disability in Ancient Greece* (2003), and Christian Laes, *Disability and the Disabled in the Roman World* (2018). For mental illness in antiquity, see William V. Harris (ed.), *Mental Disorders in the Classical World* (2013), and Chiara Thumiger, *A History of the Mind and Mental Health in Classical Greek Medical Thought* (2017). Blindness and eye-diseases are discussed by Lisa Trentin, 'Exploring visual impairment in ancient Rome', in *Disabilities in Roman Antiquity*, ed. C. Laes, C.F. Goodey, and M. Lynn Rose (2013), 89–114.

Chapter 5.   Sexuality and Gender

Michel Foucault's classic analysis of Artemidorus on sex-dreams can be found in *The History of Sexuality, Volume 3: The Care of the Self* (1986: French original, 1984), 3–36. The most important subsequent treatment is that of John J. Winkler, *The Constraints of Desire* (1990), 17–44. I do not find Winkler's interpretation of sex-dreams 'contrary to nature' (38–40) convincing: he sees the category as made up of acts that 'do not involve any representation of human social hierarchy', which seems to me arbitrary. For a strong challenge to the Foucauldian decentring of gender and biological sex in favour of social status, see James Davidson, 'Dover, Foucault, and Greek homosexuality: penetration and the truth of sex', *Past & Present* 170 (2001), 3–51 (focused on Classical Greece), and for an extreme version of the 'structuralist' position (in which penetration and relative status trump all other considerations), see Holt Parker, 'The teratogenic grid', in *Roman Sexualities*, ed. J.P. Hallett and M.B. Skinner (1997), 47–65. Against the assumption that Artemidorus represents a 'standard ancient view' on sexuality, see Glen W. Bowersock, *Fiction as History* (1994), 82–6. For a clear statement of the view (in my opinion mistaken) that Artemidorus saw all sexual acts between females as unnatural, see Craig A. Williams, *Roman Homosexuality* (second edition, 2010), 417–18, with further references.

On gender in the *Oneirocritica*, see Suzanne MacAlister, 'Gender as sign and symbolism in Artemidoros' *Oneirokritika*', *Helios* 19 (1992), 140–60. For the Classical Athenian social conventions about naming free women, see David Schaps, 'The woman least mentioned', *Classical Quarterly* 27 (1977), 323–30. Mothers' dreams of animal-births are discussed by Gregor Weber, *Kaiser, Träume und Visionen in Prinzipat und Spätantike* (2000), 134–73. For the 'personification' of grammatical gender in ancient thought, see Anthony Corbeill, *Sexing the World: Grammatical Gender and Biological Sex in Ancient Rome* (2015). Wife-beating in antiquity is the subject of an outstanding study by Leslie Dossey, 'Wife beating and manliness in Late Antiquity', *Past & Present* 199 (2008), 3–40.

Chapter 6. The Natural World

On 'bird's-eye' views of the world in Severan art, see Alexia Petsalis-Diomidis, 'Landscape, transformation, and divine epiphany', in *Severan Culture*, ed. S. Swain et al. (2007), 250–89. Cultivated landscapes in the *Oneirocritica* are explored by Christophe Chandezon, 'La terre et les campagnes chez Artémidore', in *Artemidor von Daldis und die antike Traumdeutung*, ed. G. Weber (2015), 67–99. I discuss the exploitation of mountain-resources in western Asia Minor in *The Maeander Valley* (2011), 279–83.

Ancient Greek metamorphosis-myths, and the underlying assumptions about relations between humans and the natural world, are discussed by P.M.C. Forbes Irving, *Metamorphosis in Greek Myths* (1990), especially chapters 4 and 5 on birds and plants, and by Richard Buxton, *Forms of Astonishment: Greek Myths of Metamorphosis* (2009). For Polemo's classification of animal characteristics and human personality-types, see Simon Swain (ed.), *Seeing the Face, Seeing the Soul* (2007), 384–91. On ancient ideas about animal communication, and the privileged status of birds as coming closest to human speech, see Thorsten Fögen, 'Animal communication', in *The Oxford Handbook of Animals in Classical Thought and Life*, ed. G.L. Campbell (2014), 216–32. The first port of call for ancient bird-lore is now Jeremy Mynott's *Birds in the Ancient World* (2018). Stork- and crane-migrations over the Aegean are vividly evoked by Patrick Leigh Fermor, *Mani* (1958), 136–7, 266–7, and in *The Broken Road* (2013), 54–8. On the term *lykabas*, see most recently Martin L. West, *Glotta* 89 (2013), 253–64.

On Greco-Roman plant-lore, the best short introductions are Helmut Baumann's *The Greek Plant World in Myth, Art and Literature* (2003) and Annette Giesecke, *The Mythology of Plants: Botanical Lore from Ancient Greece and Rome* (2014). Ancient classifications of plants are discussed by Gavin Hardy and Laurence Totelin, *Ancient Botany* (2016), 63–92. On arable farming in the ancient world, see Paul Halstead, *Two Oxen Ahead: Pre-Mechanized Farming in the Mediterranean* (2014), and for the challenges of farming in Roman Asia Minor, Johannes Nollé, 'Boars, bears, and bugs: farming in Asia Minor and the protection of men, animals, and crops', in *Patterns in the Economy of Roman Asia Minor*, ed. S. Mitchell and C. Katsari (2005), 53–82.

Chapter 7. Cities of Dreams

The obsessive interest in the Greek *polis* of the Classical period among Greek civic elites of the Antonine and Severan periods is brilliantly evoked by Simon Swain,

Hellenism and Empire (1996), 65–100. The near-total absence of Artemidorus from Swain's book, and from other recent work on the so-called 'Second Sophistic' (the classicizing Greek elite culture of the second and third centuries AD), tells its own story. The most vivid short sketch of urban life in Roman Asia Minor is that of Stephen Mitchell, *Anatolia: Land, Men, and Gods in Asia Minor* (1993), I.198–226; for a thorough study of Greek civic institutions in western Asia Minor during the Hellenistic and Roman periods, see Sviatoslav Dmitriev, *City Government in Hellenistic and Roman Asia Minor* (2004). For Greek magistrates' retinues during the Roman imperial period, see Christopher J. Fuhrmann, *Policing the Roman Empire* (2012), 61–75. On the radiate crown, see Jonathan Bardill, *Constantine, Divine Emperor of the Christian Golden Age* (2012), 28–57. For riotous civic assemblies, see C.P. Jones, *The Roman World of Dio Chrysostom* (1978), 19–25. On the *gynaikonomos*, see Daniel Ogden, *Greek Bastardy* (1996), 364–75.

Artemidorus' knowledge of local Ephesian customs is discussed by Hans Schwabl, 'Ephesiaka', in *Religio Graeco-Romana*, ed. J. Dalfen et al. (1993), 131–43, and by François Kirbihler, 'Artémidore, témoin des sociétés ephésienne et romaine du IIe siècle', in *Artémidore de Daldis et l'interprétation des rêves: quatorze études*, ed. Chr. Chandezon and J. du Bouchet (2014), 53–103. For 'local' elements in the *Oneirocritica* more generally, see Louis Robert, *Documents d'Asie Mineure* (1987), 234–9. On the fishermen of Ephesus, see Ephraim Lytle, 'A customs house of our own', in *Tout vendre, tout acheter*, ed. V. Chankowski and P. Karvonis (2012), 213–24. On trade associations and burial-clubs in Roman Asia Minor, see Onno van Nijf, *The Civic World of Professional Associations in the Roman East* (1997), 31–69. On 'fosterage' in Roman north-east Lydia, see Marijana Ricl, 'Legal and social status of *threptoi*', in *From Hellenism to Islam*, ed. H.M. Cotton et al. (2009), 93–114; I am currently preparing an extended study of the phenomenon. The modern literature on the Lydian 'confession-inscriptions' is vast: see e.g. Angelos Chaniotis, 'Ritual performances of divine justice', in *From Hellenism to Islam*, ed. H.M. Cotton et al. (2009), 115–53; Richard Gordon, 'Negotiating the temple-script', *Religions of the Roman Empire* 2/2 (2016), 227–55; the text quoted here is no.1 in the corpus of Georg Petzl, *Die Beichtinschriften Westkleinasiens* (1994). For the civic ephebe in the Roman imperial period, see Saskia Hin, 'Class and society in the Greek East', *Ancient Society* 37 (2007), 141–66.

Chapter 8. Books and Literary Culture

On Artemidorus' literary quotations, see Dimitri Kasprzyk, 'Belles-Lettres et science des rêves: les citations dans l'*Oneirocriticon* d'Artémidore', *L'antiquité classique* 79 (2010), 17–52; for his knowledge of Greek tragic and comic drama, Danièle Auger, 'Artémidore et le théâtre', in *Études sur Artémidore et l'interprétation des rêves*, ed. J. du Bouchet and C. Chandezon (2012), 99–170. The use of Homer, Hesiod, Euripides, and Menander as school-texts in the Greek East is discussed by Raffaella Cribiore, *Gymnastics of the Mind: Greek Education in Hellenistic and Roman Egypt* (2001), and for the ubiquity of Homer in the Greek literary and popular imagination, see Richard Hunter, *The Measure of Homer: The Ancient Reception of the Iliad and the Odyssey* (2018). For ancient prose summaries of Euripides, see Monique van Rossum-Steenbeck, *Greek Readers' Digests? Studies on a Selection of Subliterary Papyri* (1998). On Evenus of Paros, see Ewen Bowie, 'An early chapter in the history of the *Theognidea*', in *Approaches to Archaic Greek Poetry*, ed. X. Riu and J. Pòrtulas (2012), 121–48. Artemidorus' linguistic register is briefly discussed by Glen Bowersock, 'Artemidorus and the Second Sophistic', in *Paideia: The World of the Second Sophistic*, ed. B. Borg (2004), 60–2; for symbolic correspondences in the *Oneirocritica* as indirect evidence for pronunciation, see I. Avotins, 'Artemidorus of Daldis on the pronunciation of Greek', *Glotta* 55 (1977), 222–5.

Chapter 9. The Gods

Perpetua's habit of 'nattering' with God is recorded in ch. 4 of the remarkable *Passion of Perpetua and Felicity*, for which see Jan N. Bremmer and Marco Formisano (eds), *Perpetua's Passions* (2012). Artemidorus' relatively 'secular' outlook on dreams is rightly highlighted by William V. Harris, *Dreams and Experience in Classical Antiquity* (2009), 273–7; for the idea of a personal *daimon* in the *Oneirocritica*, see J. Puiggali, 'Remarques sur *daimonion* et *daimon* chez Artémidore', *Prudentia* 15 (1983), 117–21. On the complex question of the 'standard' Greek pantheon, see Robert Parker, *On Greek Religion* (2011), 64–102. Artemidorus' classification of the gods, and its echoes in contemporary Middle Platonism, is discussed by Brigitte Pérez-Jean, 'Artémidore et la philosophie de son temps', in *Études sur Artémidore et l'interprétation des rêves*, ed. J. du Bouchet and Chr. Chandezon (2012), 53–77. The standard work on the Roman imperial cult is still Simon Price, *Rituals and Power: The Roman Imperial Cult in Asia Minor* (1984); the quotation in the text here comes from p. 5. For the rich and diverse cultic landscape of inland Asia Minor in the Roman imperial period, the best starting point is Stephen Mitchell, *Anatolia: Land, Men, and Gods in Asia Minor* (1993), II 11–31.

A characteristic group of epiphany-dreams in Artemidorus where the meaning is determined by the god's characteristic spheres of influence is discussed by Jovan Bilbija and Jaap-Jan Flinterman, 'Dreaming of deities: Athena and Dionysus in the *Oneirocritica*', in *Artemidor von Daldis und die antike Traumdeutung*, ed. G. Weber (2015), 161–87. On the complex relationship between dream-visions of the gods and their cult statues, see Verity Platt, *Facing the Gods: Epiphany and Representation in Graeco-Roman Art, Literature and Religion* (2011), 275–87. A good short introduction to Aphrodite in her various cultic and non-cultic manifestations is Monica S. Cyrino, *Aphrodite* (2010). Artemidorus' position on 'solicited dreams' is clearly laid out by Gerard Boter and Jaap-Jan Flinterman, 'Are petitionary dreams non-predictive?' *Mnemosyne* 60/4 (2007), 589–607. The definitive study of incubation sanctuaries in the Greco-Roman world is now Gil H. Renberg, *Where Dreams May Come* (2016). On Geminus of Tyre's three-book collection of incubation-dreams, see John J. Winkler, 'Geminus of Tyre and the patron of Artemidorus', *Classical Philology* 77 (1982), 245–8.

Chapter 10. Festivals and Games

There is an excellent extended study of all aspects of theatre-performance and imagery in the *Oneirocritica* by Danièle Auger, 'Artémidore et le théâtre', in *Études sur Artémidore et l'interprétation des rêves*, ed. J. du Bouchet and C. Chandezon (2012), 99–170. For the athletic culture of the Greek East in the Roman imperial period, the key primary text is Philostratus' *Gymnasticus*, translated in the Loeb series by Jason König (2014); see further Zahra Newby, *Greek Athletics in the Roman World: Victory and Virtue* (2005), and Jason König, *Athletics and Literature in the Roman Empire* (2005). On the various categories of athletic festivals ('sacred' or 'eiselastic' games with wreaths as prizes; 'thematic' games with cash-prizes), see William Slater, 'The victor's return, and the categories of games', in *Epigraphical Approaches to the Post-Classical Polis*, ed. P. Martzavou and N. Papazarkadas (2013), 139–63. For the technical and linguistic precision with which Artemidorus describes Greek athletic contests, see Louis Robert, *Hellenica XI–XII* (1960), 330–42, and for monumental prize-crowns, Katherine Dunbabin, 'The prize table: crowns, wreaths, and moneybags in Roman art', in *L'argent dans les concours du monde grec*, ed. B. Le Guen (2010), 301–45. On age-categories and the *enkrisis*, see Mark Golden, *Sport and Society in the Ancient Greek World* (1998), 104–16. For draws in Greek athletics, see Onno van Nijf, 'Local heroes: athletics, festivals and elite self-fashioning in the Roman East', in *Being Greek Under Rome*, ed. S. Goldhill (2001), 326–7. On gladiators, see Christian Mann, 'Gladiators in the Greek East: A case-study in Romanization', in *Sport in the Cultures of the Ancient World*, ed. Z. Papakonstantinou (2009), 124–49; the *arbelas* is discussed by Michael Carter, *ZPE* 134 (2001), 109–15.

Chapter 11. Status and Values

The centrality of social status to Artemidoran dream-interpretation was emphasized by Simon Price, 'The future of dreams: from Freud to Artemidorus', in *Studies in Ancient Greek and Roman Society*, ed. R. Osborne (2004), 226–59, and by Istvan Hahn, *Traumdeutung und gesellschaftliche Wirklichkeit* (1992). Social mobility in the Roman army is discussed by Géza Alföldy, 'Kaiser, Heer und soziale Mobilität im Römischen Reich', in *Army and Power in the Ancient World*, ed. A. Chaniotis and P. Ducrey (2002), 123–50 (referring to Artemidorus 2.20.3). The different diets of rich and poor in Roman Asia Minor are brilliantly evoked by Stephen Mitchell, *Anatolia: Land, Men, and Gods in Asia Minor* (1993), I.167–70; there is an extended account of different types of bread and their social distribution in the first book of Galen's *On the Powers of Foods*, translated by Mark Grant, *Galen on Food and Diet* (2000), 78–96. There is an extensive modern literature on slavery in the *Oneirocritica*: most helpful are Jacques Annequin, 'Les esclaves rêvent aussi', *Dialogues d'histoire ancienne* 13 (1987), 71–113; Fridolf Kudlien, *Sklaven-Mentalität im Spiegel antiker Wahrsagerei* (1991), 68–81; and Edith Hall, 'Playing ball with Zeus', in *Reading Ancient Slavery*, ed. R. Alston et al. (2011), 204–27. For Artemidorus' 'ethical neutrality' (except when it comes to tax-farmers), see Roger Pack, 'Artemidorus and his waking world', *Transactions and Proceedings of the American Philological Association* 86 (1955), 280–90 (quotation from p. 288). 'Rebellion of the mind': see Keith Hopkins, 'Novel evidence for Roman slavery', in *Sociological Studies in Roman History* (2018), 422. On the positive connotations of work in the *Oneirocritica*, see Jacques Annequin, 'Travail et discours symbolique: *La Clé des songes* d'Artémidore', in *Le travail: recherches historiques*, ed. J. Annequin et al. (1999), 43–54.

Chapter 12. An Invisible Empire

The most detailed study of the Roman imperial state in the *Oneirocritica* is Christine Hamdoune, 'Servir l'empereur dans le traité d'Artémidore', in *Artémidore de Daldis et l'interprétation des rêves: quatorze études*, ed. Chr. Chandezon and J. du Bouchet (2014), 209–53. On Artemidorus' attitude to Roman society and culture, see the excellent short discussion by Glen Bowersock, 'Artemidorus and the Second Sophistic', in *Paideia: The World of the Second Sophistic*, ed. B. Borg (2004), 57–9. For cultural variation between the 'Greek' and 'Latin' parts of the Roman empire, see e.g. Ian Morris, *Death-ritual and Social Structures in Classical Antiquity* (1992), 52–68 (cremation vs inhumation); Lesley Dossey, 'Wife-beating and manliness in late antiquity', *Past & Present* 199 (2008), 3–40 (wife-beating being rare in the Greek East). On 'deferred manumission', see Joshua D. Sosin, 'Manumission with *paramone*: conditional freedom?' *TAPA* 145 (2015), 325–81.

For Aelius Aristides' emperor-dreams, see Jaap-Jan Flinterman, 'Sophists and emperors', in *Paideia: The World of the Second Sophistic*, ed. B. Borg (2004), 369–73. On Hellenistic royal regalia, see R.R.R. Smith, *Hellenistic Royal Portraits* (1988), 34–8, and for the Pompeii mosaic, Katherine Dunbabin, 'Sic erimus cuncti', *Jahrbuch des Deutschen Archäologischen Instituts* 101 (1986), 213–14. On eagle-ascent, see Mary Beard and John Henderson, 'The emperor's new body', in *Parchments of Gender*, ed. M. Wyke (1998), 191–219. On the presence (or absence) of the Roman army in the province of Asia, see my *The Maeander Valley* (2011), 151–7; for compulsory public service, Fergus Millar, 'The world of the *Golden Ass*', *JRS* 71 (1981), 67–8. The nature of the 'equestrian order' in the Roman imperial period remains controversial: see e.g. Greg Rowe, *Princes and Political Cultures* (2002), 67–84. Judicial material in the *Oneirocritica* is collected by Hélène Ménard, 'Pratiques et representations de la justice dans l'oeuvre d'Artémidore de Daldis', in *Artemidor von Daldis und die antike Traumdeutung*, ed. G. Weber (2015), 101–25; for the prominence of courts and punishment in the Roman provincial imagination, Brent Shaw, 'Judicial nightmares and Christian memory', *Journal of Early Christian Studies* 11 (2003), 533–63.

Epilogue. Artemidorus after Antiquity

There is no comprehensive study of the medieval and modern reception of Artemidorus. On the dream-book of pseudo-Daniel, see Lawrence T. Martin, *Somniale*

Danielis (1981), and Steven M. Oberhelman, *Dreambooks in Byzantium* (2008). Ḥunayn b. Isḥâq's Arabic translation of Artemidorus was first published by Toufic Fahd, *Artémidore d'Éphèse: Le livre des songes* (1964); see further John C. Lamoreaux, *The Early Muslim Tradition of Dream Interpretation* (2002), 45–77. For the Byzantine *Oneirocriticon* of Achmet, see Maria Mavroudi, *A Byzantine Book on Dream Interpretation* (2002), who convincingly argues against any direct link with Artemidorus; she discusses Ḥunayn's translation and its influence on the Arabic tradition at 135–42. For Pascalis Romanus' *Liber thesauri occulti*, see Roger A. Pack, 'Pascalis Romanus and the text of Artemidorus', *Transactions of the American Philological Association* 96 (1965), 291–5. Artemidorus' fortunes in early modern England are traced by Janine Rivière, *Dreams in Early Modern England* (2017), 50–88. For Freud's use of Artemidorus, see Fabio Stok, 'Psychology', in *A Companion to the Classical Tradition*, ed. C.W. Kallendorf (2010), 355–70, and, above all, Andreas Mayer, 'Conflicting interpretations of Artemidorus's *Oneirocritica*', *Psychoanalysis and History* 20/1 (2018), 89–112. For the danger of reading Artemidorus through a Freudian lens, see Simon Price, 'The future of dreams: from Freud to Artemidorus', in *Studies in Ancient Greek and Roman Society*, ed. R. Osborne (2004), 226–59.

Index of Passages Cited

Artemidorus' *The Interpretation of Dreams* (all references are to Martin Hammond's Oxford World's Classics translation):

Other ancient authors:

Subject Index